Skyhorse Publishing books may be purchased in bulk at special discounts for sales promotion, corporate gifts, fund-raising, or educational purposes. Special editions can also be created to specifications. For details, contact the Special Sales Department, Skyhorse Publishing, 307 West 36th Street, 11th Floor, New York, NY 10018 or info@skyhorsepublishing.com.

Skyhorse® and Skyhorse Publishing® are registered trademarks of Skyhorse Publishing, Inc.®, a Delaware corporation.

Visit our website at www.skyhorsepublishing.com.

10 9 8 7 6 5 4 3 2 1

Library of Congress Cataloging-in-Publication Data is available on file.

Cover design by Rain Saukas
Cover photo: Thinkstock

Print ISBN: 978-1-62914-457-3
Ebook ISBN: 978-1-63220-136-2

Printed in China

STRANGE

True Stories of the Mysterious and Bizarre

Colin Wilson and Damon Wilson

Skyhorse Publishing

Contents

The Unexplained

The pages of human history abound with unexplained phenomena, shadowy figures, and elusive monsters. Often dismissed as irrelevant fiction, distracting superstition, or outright hoaxes, these mysteries have dogged our footsteps from the most ancient past straight through to the present. Some of them hover at the edge of our will to investigate: who among us truly wishes to come face-to-face with a werewolf or a possessing demon or the wild yeti? We have lost our grip on other mysteries, time and rumors ripping them from the cold light of historical documentation and forcing us to acknowledge that we may never know the truth of some things. The true identity of Jack the Ripper and the facts surrounding the death of Alexander I, tsar of Russia, now rest forever beyond our grasp.

This book probes some of humanity's most lasting and most fascinating mysteries, from controversies surrounding Stone Age travelers to modern monsters, such as the goat-devouring *chupacabra* and alien visitors. Answers are hard to come by in the wilderness of strange occurrences, but the questions continue to provoke our interest. Did the lost continent of Atlantis exist, and have we already found evidence of its destruction? Did vampires really roam the wolf-haunted nights of the Carpathian Mountains? What beast, if beast it was, left a 40-mile trail over the snow-covered English countryside in 1855? Can we discover a scientific explanation for the disappearances inside the Bermuda Triangle, or must we continue to pay a tithe of lives, ships, and aircraft to the vexatious region?

Some of the mysteries covered here have plagued us since antiquity; the Greek philosopher Plato brought Atlantis to light as a vanished continent, drowned by the wrath of a vengeful god. Now we know that the story may hold at least a grain of truth, with evidence of a massive volcanic eruption and the resulting destruction of an early Mediterranean civilization providing a tantalizing backdrop to the ancient mystery. Similarly the discovery of giant sea squids and the knowledge that we have yet to fully explore the depths of the ancient ocean lend credence to tales of vast sea monsters, which have for centuries terrorized sailors around the world. Other mysteries, such as the ape-like Bigfoot of the North American wilderness, are new on the scene, but have already provoked much speculation and controversy.

If the human experience—all of its history and knowledge—can be envisioned as a map, then the questions covered here sail us into uncharted territory. Eerie tales of the afterlife, monsters of lake, forest, and mountain, and more human mysteries confound and delight those who brave the edges of the map. Delving these dark waters have cost some their reputations, and some their lives, and should indeed be approached with caution; for here, in truth, be dragons.

Colin Wilson
2009

Ancient Mysteries

The Puzzle of the Hobbit People

(100,000 to 10,000 BCE)

Homo floresiensis

Flores is part of a chain of Indonesian islands that includes Sumatra and Java. It was there, in Ling Bua cave, in 2004, that a team of archaeologists discovered a female skeleton that they labeled "the Hobbit." Like J. R. R. Tolkien's invention, this creature was tiny: when she died about 18,000 years ago at about 30 years old, she had stood only a little higher than 3 feet and weighed about 55 pounds—about the size of a 3-year-old modern human. These tiny creatures, named *Homo floresiensis*, likely evolved from another early species of human, *Homo erectus*, which arrived on Flores about 850,000 years ago.

Soon archaeologists had unearthed additional Hobbit bones in Ling Bua cave. These bones confirmed that this early human had a skull the size of a grapefruit. It looked as though its kind might even be the origin of our legends of "little people"—fairies, dwarfs, elves, leprechauns, and the rest.

Ling Bua cave on the Indonesian island of Flores. This limestone cave has yielded numerous specimens of *Homo floresiensis*, also known as the Hobbit people.

The Little People

The dates do seem to leave open the possibility that the Hobbit people gave rise to little people folklore. The Hobbit people came to Flores about 100,000 years ago and were around until about 13,000 years ago. Our species, *Homo sapiens*, has been in Asia and Europe about 40,000 years.

Indonesian folklore describes a creature called *Ebu Gogo,* which means "meat-eating grandmother." This race of little, hairy people had potbellies and ears that stuck out. Were the Ebu Gogo really *Homo floresiensis?*

The people of Flores believe that these creatures existed as recently as 400 years ago—when the first Portuguese traders arrived on the island in their quest for spices. Others contend that the Ebu Gogo were still around a mere 100 years ago. The local population evidently regarded these little people as scavenging nuisances.

Was It Genocide?

Did the Flores locals find the Ebu Gogo so annoying that they eventually exterminated them? An October 30, 2004, article in *New Scientist* magazine included this account of the Ebu Gogo.

> *The Nage people of central Flores tell how, some 300 years ago, villagers disposed of the Ebu Gogo by tricking them into accepting gifts of palm fiber to make clothes. When the Ebu Gogo took the fiber into their cave, the villagers threw in a firebrand to set it alight. The story goes that all the occupants were killed, except perhaps for one pair, who fled into the deepest forest, and whose descendants may be living there still.*

The article also tells us that such tales are common in Indonesia, according to anthropologist Gregory Forth. Folktale abound about the Ebu Gogo kidnapping human children, hoping to learn from them how to cook. The children always easily outwit them.

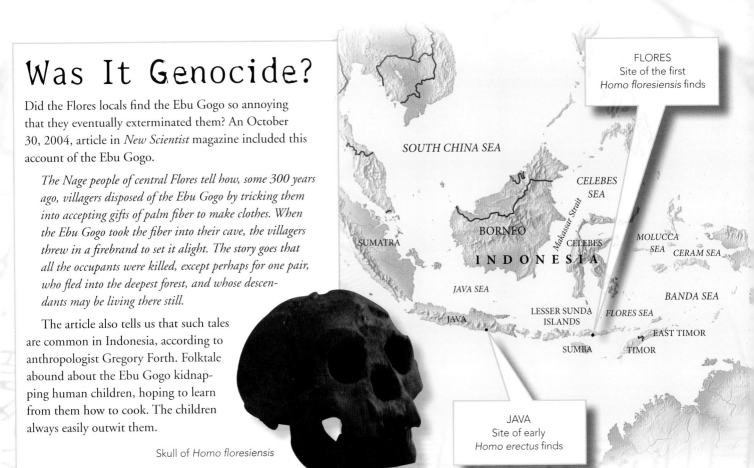

Skull of *Homo floresiensis*

FLORES
Site of the first
Homo floresiensis finds

SOUTH CHINA SEA

CELEBES
SEA

Makassar Strait

BORNEO

CELEBES

SUMATRA

I N D O N E S I A

MOLUCCA
SEA

CERAM SEA

JAVA SEA

BANDA SEA

JAVA

LESSER SUNDA
ISLANDS

FLORES SEA

EAST TIMOR

SUMBA

TIMOR

JAVA
Site of early
Homo erectus finds

Speech and Intelligence

All this raises an interesting question about our human ancestry. How did we humans begin to develop intelligence? The probable answer: when we learned to speak.

In 1997, while exploring an ancient lake bed at Mata Menge, on the island of Flores, a group of paleoanthropologists from the University of New England in New South Wales, Australia, found stone tools. Mike Morwood and his colleagues found the tools in a bed of volcanic ash dated from more than 800,000 years ago, the time of *Homo erectus*. Animal bones from nearby gave the same date. What was unusual is that Flores is a relatively small island and was not known to be a site of ancient humans. The nearest such site is the far larger island of Java, the home of Java Man, who also belongs to the species *Homo erectus*.

To reach Flores, these primitive humans would have had to sail from island to island, making crossings of around a dozen miles. This sounds a modest distance, but members of the species *Homo erectus* are regarded as little more than "glorified chimps," as

Morwood puts it. But if they were able to sail the seas, they must have been rather more than that. Moreover, Morwood argues, the organizing ability required by a fairly large group to cross the sea suggests that *Homo erectus* possessed some kind of linguistic ability. In other words, ancestors of nearly a million years ago were intelligent enough to collaborate on the building of rafts.

But if the Ebu Gogo of Flores were actually Hobbit people, descendants of those island-hopping *Homo erectus*, then they have helped us to solve this interesting scientific puzzle, and we can say with confidence that *Homo erectus* could speak. The description of Ebu Gogo earlier, after mentioning that Ebu Gogo walked awkwardly and had prominent ears, adds: "They . . . often murmured in their own language and could repeat what is said to them in parrot-like fashion." And if, as the above story tells us, two of them escaped the fire that destroyed their kind, then it is possible that we may yet have a chance to study them and discover whether they had language or could merely parrot responses.

A Clovis spearhead

Did the Stone Age French Discover America?

(15,000 to 19,000 BCE)

In 1933 a flint spearhead was discovered in a dried-up riverbed near the town of Clovis, New Mexico. The find was remarkable in a number of ways. First, it lay among the bones of a mammoth, having presumably been used to kill the animal. Second, it was beautifully made: double-bladed and double-faced, light and aerodynamic, and intricately flint-knapped—chipped out using sophisticated bone tools. It was also 11,500 years old.

Clovis People

The Clovis spearhead was the first discovered artifact from the oldest known settlers of the Americas, who are now commonly referred to as the Clovis people. But soon Clovis spearheads—all dating to about 11,500 years ago—were cropping up all over North America.

Based on the geographical spread of the unearthed spearheads and other evidence, scientists concluded that the Clovis people crossed the Bering Strait into northwest North America from Siberia during the last ice age. And it became scientific dogma that the Clovis people were the first human inhabitants of the Americas and the sole ancestors of all modern American Indians.

But were they really the first?

European Settlers?

There is no evidence of Clovis technology in Siberia at the time of the Bering Strait migration, which leads us to ask, where did the skill develop to create such spearheads? The obvious answer is in the Americas, *after* the migration.

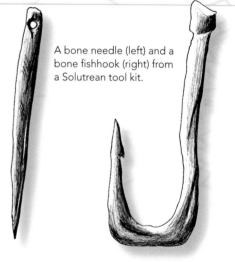
A bone needle (left) and a bone fishhook (right) from a Solutrean tool kit.

But another people had acquired flint-knapping skills identical to those of the Clovis during the last ice age. These were the Solutrean hunter-gatherers of what is now western France. One of the most highly creative early cultures, the Solutreans invented the eyed needle, made carvings and cave paintings, and used flint-knapping techniques intricate enough to construct stone fishhooks and barbed arrowheads. They also made spearheads almost identical to the Clovis spearheads found in the Americas. But the Solutreans were making their spearheads between 17,000 and 21,000 years ago—at least 5,500 years before the Clovis people. Despite this, there was apparently no intermediate link between the two cultures, until very recently.

During the last 30 years, an archaeological dig at Meadowcroft, Pennsylvania, has started to provide clear evidence of human activity between 16,000 and 19,000 years ago—before the Clovis people migrated to North America. And at another dig in Cactus Hill, Virginia, researchers discovered Clovis/Solutrean–style spearheads dating from about 15,000 to 17,000 years ago.

NORTH AMERICA

SIBERIA

EUROPE

PACIFIC OCEAN

• Meadowcroft, Pennsylvania
• Cactus Hill, Virginia
• Clovis, New Mexico

ATLANTIC OCEAN

HUMAN MIGRATION IN THE ICE AGE

Solutrean migration
Clovis migration
Solutrean origin
Maximum ice coverage

Gone Fishing

Perhaps it was the European Solutreans who were the first to arrive in North America. The theory is controversial because it controverts more than 70 years of scientific orthodoxy: that the Clovis people from Siberia were the first to reach the New World around 12,000 years ago.

How, opponents of the "Solutrean-first" theory ask, did Stone Age hunter-gatherers manage to cross the 3,000, storm-wracked miles of the Atlantic Ocean during an ice age?

During the last ice age the northern hemisphere was covered by solid ice sheets as far south as northern France in Europe and the Great Lakes in North America. But far from being an impediment to the traveling Solutreans, the resulting ice packs in the North Atlantic would have formed easy stepping-stones for canoe-based travel. In fact Inuit tribes living on the modern northern ice sheets regularly traveled in this way up to a few decades ago, camping on ice floes and living on trapped fish and seals.

The Solutrean invention of the eyed needle shows that they were the first people able to make such a journey; sewn leather clothes and boat hulls would have been essential to keep out the freezing water of the Atlantic.

Solutrean First

The "Solutrean-first" theory has met with opposition from American Indians as well as conservative archaeologists. Given what the second wave of post-Columbus European settlers did to American Indians, it is not surprising that many dislike the thought that some of their remotest ancestors might have been European colonizers.

Genetic Footprints

Mitochondrial DNA (mtDNA) is part of the human genome, one that mutates at an exact, regular pace. Studying mtDNA mutation markers and comparing differences among population groups allows scientists to reconstruct early human migration. That's because every human shares mtDNA markers from the early African period of human history, but groups that migrated west and those that migrated east after leaving Africa have different subsequent mtDNA markers. This shows that this is where the human population branched at that time.

Initial studies of mtDNA seemed to back the Solutrean-first theory, indicating a typically European strain in certain groups of northeastern American Indians dating back to between 15,000 to 30,000 years ago. But a subsequent genome study has shown the same strain in modern native Siberians as well. This, opponents of the Solutrean-first theory claim, shows that all American Indians descend from the Siberian/Clovis stock.

In fact, nothing could be further from the case. It is a grim fact that East Coast American Indian tribes were those that came closest to obliteration at the hands of post-Columbus European colonists. If there had been a Solutrean DNA strain in American Indians, it might well have been wiped from the slate of history.

The Cactus Hill and Meadowcroft archaeological sites prove that humans inhabited North America millennia *before* the influx of the Clovis people from Siberia. The only questions left to be answered are: who were the pre-Clovis Americans and where did they come from?

The Dogon and the Ancient Astronauts: Evidence of Visitors from Outer Space?

(3200 BCE)

A Dogon wearing a traditional tribal mask

The theory that Earth has been visited, perhaps even colonized, by beings from outer space has been a part of popular folklore since the 1968 release of Stanley Kubrick's cult movie *2001: A Space Odyssey* (written by Arthur C. Clarke). But it had already been in the air for many years—in fact, since 1947. That's when a businessman named Kenneth Arnold was flying his private plane near Mount Rainier in Washington State and reported seeing nine shining disks traveling at an estimated speed of 1,000 miles per hour. Arnold called them "flying saucers." Soon, sightings of unidentified flying objects (UFOs) were occurring all over the world.

Flying Saucers Everywhere

In 1960 a book appeared in France: *The Morning of the Magicians (Le matin des magiciens)* by Louis Pauwels and Jacques Bergier. It became an instant best-seller. It also may claim the dubious credit of having initiated the occult boom of the 1960s. The book included speculations about the Great Pyramid, the statues of Easter Island, Hans Hoerbiger's theory that the moon is covered with ice (soon to be disproved by the moon landings), and the reality of alchemical transformation. There was also the obligatory section on the famous Piri Reis map (see pages 24–25), in which the authors succeed in confusing the sixteenth-century pirate Piri Reis with a Turkish naval officer who presented a copy of the map to the Library of Congress in 1959. They conclude the discussion of this map with: "Were these copies of still earlier maps? Had they been traced from observations made on board a flying machine or space vessel of some kind? Notes taken by visitors from Beyond?"

After an American pilot described the mysterious objects he saw speeding through the sky as "flying saucers," reports of similar sightings began pouring in from observers around the world.

The Swiss writer Erich von Daniken developed the "ancient astronaut" theme in a book called *Chariots of the Gods?* (1963), but an almost willful carelessness about facts finally destroyed his creditability as a serious scholar.

These speculations caused excitement because the world was in the grip of flying-saucer mania. Books by people who claimed to be "contactees" became best-sellers. And though many "sightings" could be dismissed as hysteria—or as what Carl Jung called "projections" (meaning religious delusions)—a few were too well authenticated to fit that simplistic theory.

The Dogon of Mali

The "ancient astronaut" theorists have at least one extremely powerful piece of evidence on their side. Members of an African tribe called the Dogon, who live some 300 miles south of Timbuktu in the Republic of Mali, possess knowledge of astronomy that some claim was transmitted to them by "spacemen" from the star Sirius A, which lies 8.7 light-years away from Earth. Dogon mythology insists that the "Dog Star" Sirius A (so-called because it is in the constellation Canis) has a dark companion that is dense, very heavy, and invisible to the naked eye. This is correct: Sirius A does indeed have a dark companion, which is known as Sirius B. Changes in Sirius A's motion led a German astronomer to predict the existence of Sirius B in 1844, and in 1862 an American telescope maker finally observed it—although it was not described in detail until the 1920s. Astronomers concluded that it was a white dwarf star.

An artist's impression shows the binary star system of Sirius A and its diminutive blue companion, Sirius B. Sirius A, the large, bluish white star at left, appears to overwhelm Sirius B, the small but very hot and blue white-dwarf star on the right.

The Dog Star

Two French anthropologists, Marcel Griaule and Germaine Dieterlen, first revealed the "secret of the Dogon" in an obscure paper in 1950; it was entitled "A Sudanese Sirius System" and was published in the *Journal de la Societe des Africainistes.*

The two anthropologists had lived among the Dogon since 1931, and in 1946 Griaule was initiated into the religious secrets of the tribe. He was told that fishlike creatures called the Nommo had come to Earth from Sirius A to civilize its people. The Dogon called Sirius B *po tolo* (naming it after the seed that forms the staple part of their diet, and whose botanical name is *Digitaria*).

Sirius B is made of matter heavier than any on Earth and moves in an elliptical orbit, taking 50 years to do so. It was not until 1928 that Sir Arthur Eddington postulated the theory of white dwarfs—stars whose atoms have collapsed inward, so that a piece the size of a pea could weigh half a ton.

Griaule and Dieterlen went to live among the Dogon three years later. Is it likely that some traveler carried a new and complex astronomical theory to a remote African tribe—one that had never possessed telescopes—in the three years between 1928 and 1931?

A ground-based image of the constellation Canis Major shows how bright Sirius A, at center, appears in the night sky. Sirius B, however, is invisible to the naked eye.

Temple in Paris

In the mid-1960s an American scholar named Robert Temple traveled to Paris to study the Dogon with Germaine Dieterlen. He soon concluded that the knowledge shown by the Dogon could not be explained away as coincidence.

The Dogon appeared to have an extraordinarily detailed knowledge of our solar system. They said that the moon was "dry and dead " and drew Saturn with a ring around it (Saturn's rings are visible only with the aid of a telescope). The Dogon knew that the planets revolved around the sun. They knew about the moons of Jupiter (first seen through a telescope by Galileo). They had recorded the movements of Venus in their temples. They knew that the earth rotates and that the number of stars is infinite. And when they drew the elliptical orbit of Sirius, they showed the star off center, not in the middle of the orbit—as someone without knowledge of astronomy would naturally conclude.

Saturn, photographed by the *Cassini* orbiter. Although the Dogon people did not have telescopes when European researchers studied their culture in the 1930s, they knew that Saturn had its distinctive rings.

A Dogon village in Mali. The remote, arid land inhabited by the Dogon people seems a surprising place to inspire myths about amphibious creatures like the Nommo.

The Nommo

The Dogon insist the amphibious Nommo brought their knowledge to them from a "star," which, like Sirius B, rotates around Sirius A and whose weight is only a quarter of Sirius B's.

The Dogon worshipped the Nommo as gods. They drew diagrams to portray the spinning of the craft in which these creatures landed and were precise about the landing location.

Our telescopes have not revealed the "planet" of the Nommo, but that is hardly surprising. Astronomers discovered Sirius B only because its weight caused perturbations in the orbit of Sirius A. The Dog Star is 35.5 times as bright (and hot) as our sun, so any planet capable of supporting life would have to be in the far reaches of its solar system and would almost certainly be invisible to telescopes. Temple surmises that the planet of the Nommo would be hot and steamy and that this probably explains why intelligent life evolved in its seas, which would be cooler. These fish-people would spend much of their time on land but close to the water; they would need a layer of water on their skins to be comfortable, and if their skins dried, it would be as agonizing as severe sunburn. Temple sees them as a kind of dolphin.

Ancient Civilizations

But what were such creatures as the Nommo doing in the middle of the desert, near Timbuktu? In fact, the idea seemed obviously absurd to Temple. For many reasons, he is inclined to believe that the landing of the Nommo took place in Egypt, not Mali.

Temple also points out that a Babylonian historian named Berossus—a contemporary and apparently an acquaintance of Aristotle (fourth century BCE)—claims in his history, of which only fragments survive, that Babylonian civilization was founded by alien amphibians, the chief of whom is called Oannes—the Philistines knew him as Dagon. The Greek grammarian Apollodorus (about 140 BCE) had apparently read more of Berossus, for he criticizes another Greek writer, Abydenus, for failing to mention that Oannes was only one of the "fish-people"; he calls these aliens "Annedoti" ("repulsive ones") and says they are "semi-demons" from the sea.

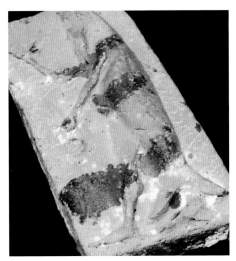

An ancient plaque depicts the Babylonian god Oannes. Greek texts recount how Oannes came out of the sea to teach the Babylonians the arts of civilization. Oannes appeared as half human and half fish, and he spoke in a human voice.

Stars in the Sky

Why should the Dogon pay any particular attention to Sirius A, even though it was one of the brightest stars in the sky? After all, it was merely one among thousands of stars. There, at least, the skeptics can produce a persuasive answer. Presumably the Dogon learned from the Egyptians, and for the ancient Egyptians, Sothis (as they called Sirius A) was the most important star in the heavens—at least, after 3200 BCE, when it began to rise just before the dawn, at the beginning of the Egyptian New Year, and signaled that the Nile was about to rise.

A nineteenth-century illustration of a Siren. Were these mythological water spirits inspired by creatures from Sirius?

Temple suggests that the ancients may have looked toward the Canis Major constellation for Sirius B and mistaken it for Al Wazn, another star in the constellation. He also suggests that Homer's Sirens—part mermaidlike, part birdlike creatures who are all-knowing and who try to lure men to their deaths—are actually "Sirians," amphibious goddesses. He furthermore points out that the famous boat of Greek mythology, Jason's *Argo*, is associated with the goddess Isis and that it has 50 rowers—50 being the number of years it takes Sirius B to circle Sirius A. There are many fish-bodied aliens in Greek mythology, including the Telchines of Rhodes, who were supposed to have come from the sea and to have introduced humans to various arts, including metalwork. Significantly, the Telchines had dogs' heads.

Evidence in Africa

Temple published his theories about the Dogon's source of knowledge in the book *The Sirius Mystery* in 1976. *The Sirius Mystery* is full of "evidence" based on his reading of mythology. Critics have attacked his theories as examples of stretching interpretation too far. Yet what remains when all the arguments have been considered is the curious fact that members of a remote African tribe had some precise knowledge of an entire star system not visible to the human eye alone and that they attribute this knowledge to aliens from that star system. That single fact suggests that in spite of von Daniken's absurdities, we should remain open-minded about the possibility that alien visitors once landed on our planet.

Tutankhamun's mask

The Curse of the Pharaohs

(1922)

On November 26, 1922, the English archaeologist Howard Carter made a fabulous discovery in the Valley of the Kings, near ancient Thebes (modern Luxor). He peered through a small opening above the door of an ancient pharaoh's tomb, holding a candle in front of him. What he saw dazzled him: "everywhere the glint of gold." He and Lord Carnarvon had made the greatest find in the history of archaeology. Thrilled, they pressed on with their excavation, undeterred by a clay tablet with the hieroglyphic inscription, DEATH WILL SLAY WITH HIS WINGS WHOEVER DISTURBS THE PEACE OF THE PHARAOH.

Disturbing the Peace

By 1929, 22 people who had been involved in opening the tomb had died prematurely. Other archaeologists dismissed talk about "'the curse of the pharaohs" as journalistic sensationalism. Yet it is difficult to imagine that this long series of deaths was merely a frightening coincidence.

Relief of Akhenaten and his wife, Nefertiti, with two of their children. Prominent in the background is the sun. Tutankhamun may have been one of the royal couple's children.

King Tut

The tomb Carter discovered belonged to Tutankhamun, heir of the "great heretic" Akhenaten. Ruling from about 1353 to 1336 BCE, Akhenaten was the first monotheistic king in history.

Akhenaten abandoned the capital at Thebes, with all its temples to Egypt's numerous gods, and built himself a new capital, also called Akhenaten (Horizon of Aten), at a place now called Amarna, or Tel el-Amarna. He worshipped only one god, the sun god Aten. His people disliked this new religion and were relieved when Akhenaten died young. (So were the priests.) Tutankhamun, either Akhenaten's son or son-in-law, was a mere child when he came to the throne, and died from a blow to the head at the age of 18. No one knows the circumstances surrounding his death, only that his skull was cracked. Historically speaking, Tutankhamun is virtually a nonentity, whose short reign deserves little attention. His only achievement was to restore the old religion and move his capital back to Thebes.

The Odd Behavior of Horemheb

At the time of Tutankhamun's death, Egypt's high priest was a man called Ay. Ay quickly seized power and married Tutankhamun's 15-year-old widow, Ankhesenamun. He had reigned for fewer than four years when once again a usurper seized the throne, this time a general named Horemheb. As soon as Horemheb became pharaoh, he set out to erase the memory of Akhenaten and Tutankhamun from history; he had their names chiseled off all hieroglyphic inscriptions and used the stones of the great temple of the sun at Amarna to build three pyramids in Thebes.

Yet he neglected to do the most obvious thing of all: destroy the tomb of Tutankhamun. Why? Horemheb must have had some very persuasive reason for deciding to leave the tomb of his enemy inviolate.

The Valley of the Kings is a valley in Luxor, Egypt, where, for nearly 500 years, from the sixteenth to eleventh century BCE, kings, queens, and other nobles had their tombs constructed. It was here that Carter found the tomb of Tutankhamun in 1922. Although there are at least 63 tombs and chambers in the valley, Tut's may be the most famous.

The Play's the Thing

The first signs of trouble relating to Akhenaten and his progeny—known to the modern world at least—occurred even before Carter opened Tutankhamun's tomb in 1922. In 1909 Joe Linden Smith worked on excavations in the Valley of the Kings. He was married to an attractive 28-year-old woman named Corinna. Among their closest friends were Arthur and Hortense Weigel. One day when they were descending the slope into the Valley of the Queens, Joe Smith and Arthur Weigel came upon a natural amphitheater. They decided to present their own play and invite most of the archaeological community from Luxor. Their aim was not pure entertainment; they intended nothing less than to intercede with the ancient gods to lift an ancient curse that had consigned Akhenaten's spirit to wander for all eternity.

Smith and Weigel decided to present their play on January 26, 1909, the presumed anniversary of Akhenaten's death. On January 23 they held their dress rehearsal. In the play, the god Horus appeared and conversed with the wandering spirit of Akhenaten, offering to grant him a wish. Akhenaten asked to see his mother, Queen Tiy. The queen, played by Corinna, was summoned by a magical ceremony. Akhenaten told her that even in his misery he still drew comfort from the thought of the god Aten and asked his mother to recite his hymn to the sun god.

As Corinna began to recite the hymn, the rising wind drowned out her words. Suddenly a violent storm, blowing sand and hailstones, was upon them, forcing a dramatic end to the rehearsal.

Later that evening Corinna complained of a pain in her eyes, and Hortense of cramps in her stomach. That night both had similar dreams; they were in the nearby temple of Amen, standing before the statue of the god. This came to life and struck them with its flail—Corinna in the eyes, Hortense in the stomach. The next day Corinna had to be rushed to a specialist in Cairo, who diagnosed one of the worst cases of trachoma—a debilitating eye disease often resulting in blindness—that he had ever seen. Twenty-four hours later, Hortense joined Corinna in the same nursing home; during the stomach operation that followed, she nearly died. The play had to be abandoned.

Carter's Career

Howard Carter, the man who finally discovered Tutankhamun's tomb, was born in 1873 and had moved to Egypt as a teenager. Carter became Chief Inspector of Monuments for Upper Egypt and Nubia while still in his 20s. Later Carter advised Theodore Davis, a wealthy American, to finance the excavation of the Valley of the Kings, which he agreed to do in 1902. This now-famous valley houses the remains of kings, queens, and nobles from Egypt's New Kingdom (c. 1550 to 1100 BCE). Carter himself, however, landed in some trouble surrounding a dispute between site guards and unruly tourists; he lost his job in 1905.

Carter, kneeling at center above, opens Tutankhamun's tomb. The opening was the culmination of years of dedicated effort. Carter, who had become somewhat obsessed with finding the burial place of an obscure young pharaoh, saw his efforts pay off. It would take 10 years just to catalog all of the artifacts from this one magnificent tomb, which are currently in the Egyptian Antiquities Museum in Cairo.

The Second Door

By 1914 Theodore Davis had abandoned his excavations, and Lord Carnarvon, an English aristocrat, snapped up the concession. Interested in financing digs in the Valley of the Kings, he and Carter made a perfect pair.

World War I made it impossible to begin work until 1917. Then Carter began to dig, moving hundreds of tons of rubble left from earlier digs, but to no avail: the pharaohs held their secrets close. By 1922 Carnarvon felt he had poured enough money into the Valley of the Kings. Carter begged for one more chance.

On November 4, 1922, Carter began new excavations, digging a ditch southward from the tomb of Rameses IV. Just days later, on November 7, the workmen uncovered a step, below the foundations of some huts Carter had discovered in an earlier dig. By the evening 12 steps had been revealed, leading to a sealed stone gate. Carter sent a telegram to Carnarvon in England, and Carnarvon arrived just over two weeks later. Together Carnarvon and Carter broke their way through the sealed gate, now in a state of increasing excitement as they realized that this tomb had gone unnoticed (and thus unplundered) by grave robbers. Thirty feet below the gate, they came upon a second door.

At left, Carter and a helper work beside Tut's coffin, removing the consecration oils, which covered the third, or innermost coffin.

Death Will Slay

With trembling hands, Carter scraped a hole in the debris in the doorway's upper corner and peered through; the candlelight showed him an antechamber with strange animal statues and objects of gold. It was here that they found the tablet with the inscription: DEATH WILL SLAY WITH HIS WINGS WHOEVER DISTURBS THE PEACE OF THE PHARAOH. Carter recorded the discovery, but the pair, afraid rumors of the inscription would terrify the workmen, removed it. A statue of the god Horus also carried an inscription, stating that it was the protector of the grave. On February 17, 1923, it took two hours to chisel a hole into the burial chamber. Though only two sets of folding doors separated them from the magnificent gold sarcophagus—soon to become world-famous—they decided to leave it until later.

Carnarvon's Strange Death

Lord Carnarvon was never to see the golden resting place of Tutankhamun's body, for that April he fell ill, possibly due to a mosquito bite. At breakfast one morning in late March he had a 104° temperature, and it continued for 12 days. Howard Carter was sent for. Carnarvon died just before 2:00 AM on April 5, 1923. As the family came to his bedside, summoned by a nurse, all the lights suddenly went out, and they were forced to light candles. Later they discovered that the power failure had affected all of Cairo.

According to Carnarvon's son, another peculiar event took place that night; back in England, Carnarvon's favorite fox terrier began to howl, then died.

Lord Carnarvon

The Curse of the Pharaohs

Lady Carnarvon

The newspapers quickly began printing stories about the "curse of the pharaohs." Arthur Mace, the American archaeologist who had helped unseal the tomb, began to complain of exhaustion soon after Carnarvon's death; he fell into a coma and died not long after Carnarvon. George Jay Gould, son of the famous American financier, came to Egypt when he heard of Carnarvon's death, and Carter took him to see the tomb. The next day Gould had a fever; by evening he was dead. Joel Wool, a British industrialist who visited the grave site, died of fever on his way back to England. Archibald Douglas Reid, a radiologist who x-rayed Tutankhamun's mummy, suffered attacks of feebleness and died on his return to England in 1924.

George Jay Gould

Over the next few years 13 people who had helped open the grave also died, and by 1929 the figure had risen to 22. In 1929 Lady Carnarvon died of an "insect bite," and Carter's secretary Richard Bethell was found dead of a circulatory collapse. Professor Douglas Derry, one of two scientists who performed the autopsy on Tutankhamun's mummy, had died of circulatory collapse in 1925; the other scientist, Alfred Lucas, died of a heart attack at about the same time.

Was the curse of the pharaohs a reality? Given the number of unexpected deaths, it is hard not to consider the possibility.

The one man who seemed to have escaped the curse of the pharaohs: Harold Carter

History's Mysteries

The Piri Reis Map and the Ancient Sea Kings

(7000 BCE)

Detail from the Piri Reis map

On August 26, 1956, American professor Charles Hapgood happened to hear a panel from Georgetown University arguing about the so-called Piri Reis map, found in the Topkapi Palace in Istanbul in 1929. Piri Reis was a Turkish admiral and one-time pirate, who in 1513 had set out to construct a map of the Atlantic Ocean, showing Europe and the New World. This was difficult because the Americas had been discovered so recently. Piri Reis said he had consulted many old maps to draw his, including one used by Christopher Columbus.

The Hidden Coast

Amazingly Piri Reis's map not only showed the whole coast of South America—in impressive detail—but also a fragment of Antarctica in the extreme south. The map also depicted certain bays on Antarctica's coast, bays that could no longer be seen because they were buried under about a mile of ice. It wasn't until 1949 that an expedition took ice core samples and used radar to penetrate the ice and reveal the land beneath. The coast of Antarctica had undoubtedly been covered in ice in 1513—and for thousands of years before that. And yet the 1513 Piri Reis map showed that coast.

The ice core samples taken by the 1949 expedition were 6,000 years old, from 4000 BCE. And although civilization existed in 4000 BCE, writing had not yet been invented, and so the map could not have been produced that early.

A composite image of the continent of Antarctica, derived from satellite photos

Hapgood Explores

Hapgood wrote to the Library of Congress in Washington, D.C., which owned a copy of the document, to inquire whether it had any other ancient maps. The reply was that it owned hundreds. Such maps were called *portolans*, which means "from port to port." *Portolans* were used by mariners to find and sail the shortest routes.

The library invited Hapgood to look at its collection. What he saw took away his breath. Among the dozens of maps laid out on trestle tables, there were some that showed the whole of Antarctica. Yet Antarctica was not officially discovered until 1818. The existence of these maps meant that ancient mariners must have sailed around it. But they must also have explored it from end to end, for other maps showed Antarctica without the ice, including rivers and mountains in the interior. In fact the maps were so detailed that it seemed fairly clear that they must have been made by inhabitants of the continent, because sailors, no matter how hardworking and conscientious, could never have managed it.

Other maps, including those of Russia and China, made it clear that these mysterious explorers must have traveled to every corner of the globe. But who were they?

Hapgood summarized his conclusions in *Maps of the Ancient Sea Kings: Evidence of Advanced Civilization in the Ice Age,* which he published in 1966. He argued that the old maps proved the existence of a worldwide maritime civilization around 7000 BCE. He took care not to mention the word *Atlantis.* He wanted to give his fellow academics no chance to dismiss him as a member of the lunatic fringe.

The surviving fragment of the Piri Reis map

The Argument Dismissed

Unfortunately an appalling piece of bad luck meant that Hapgood was labeled a kook anyway. By the time Hapgood published, the Piri Reis map was already regarded as the happy hunting ground of cranks. In 1960 a book called *The Morning of the Magicians* by Louis Pauwels and Jacques Bergier became a worldwide best-seller. It argued that the Piri Reis map showed such detailed knowledge of the coast of South America that it could only have been observed from the air by a spaceship. So Hapgood already had a hostile academic audience prepared to dismiss his book as fantasy.

The Mystery Lingers On

Worse was to follow. In 1967, the year after its publication, Hapgood's work was mentioned with approval in the book *Memories of the Future,* written by Erich von Daniken, a Swiss hotelier. Translated into English as *Chariots of the Gods?,* it went on to sell millions of copies. Daniken argued that all of the earth's greatest monuments—from the pyramids to the statues on Easter Island—were built by visitors from outer space.

The book was full of absurdities and inaccuracies, such as the argument that the Nazca lines in Peru were built as runways for spaceships. Worse, von Daniken cited Hapgood as asserting that the Piri Reis map must have been based on an aerial photograph taken by these space visitors. With that Hapgood's last chance of being taken seriously evaporated. And the mystery of the Piri Reis map remains unsolved.

A statue of Robin Hood

Did Robin Hood Really Exist?

(1100s)

Those who believe Robin Hood was a real person assume that he was an outlaw who lived in Sherwood Forest, becoming so popular in his lifetime that, like Billy the Kid of America's Old West, he soon became the subject of tales and ballads.

Early ballads call Robin a yeoman—a farmer who owns his own land—and that is partly why he became such a hero: not because he was a nobleman, but because he represented the people. Certain place-names in what may once have been his territory indicate his long-lasting popularity; a small fishing town in Yorkshire, not far from Whitby, is called Robin Hood's Bay, while nearby stand two hillocks called Robin Hood's Butts.

Robin Identified

Although medieval records list a number of Robert Hoods and Robin Hoods, in 1852 historian Joseph Hunter claimed that he had stumbled upon a man who might be the source of the legend. The candidate's name was Robert (Robin was then a common diminutive of Robert), and he was the son of Adam Hood, a forester in the service of John de Warenne, earl of Surrey. Robert was born about 1280, and on January 25, 1316, he and his wife, Matilda, paid two shillings for permission to take a piece of the earl's waste ground in Bickhill (or Bitch-hill) in Wakefield. It was merely the size of a kitchen garden—30 feet (9 m) long by 16 feet (4.9 m) wide—with a rent of sixpence a year.

The King's Problems

The year 1316 landed midway through the reign of Edward II, the foppish king who was finally murdered in September 1327. After his coronation in 1307, Edward dismissed his father's ministers and judges and made his male lover, Piers Gaveston, earl of Cornwall—to the fury of his nobles.

The most powerful of these, Thomas, earl of Lancaster, finally executed Piers Gaveston in 1312. Edward's lack of attention to affairs of state allowed the Scots to throw off their English masters when they defeated Edward II at Bannockburn in 1314.

Five years later the earl of Lancaster raised an army to fight against the king and Edward's new favorites, a father-and-son team called the Despensers. Lancaster's army was defeated at Boroughbridge and its leader beheaded.

EDWARD II.

Son of the ruthless Edward I, Edward II in no way matched his father in ambition or ability. England suffered during the reign of this ineffectual monarch.

The ancient Major Oak in Sherwood Forest. Legend claims that Robin Hood and his band used the tree as a hideout and sleeping place.

Robin Takes to the Forest

Lancaster's supporters were declared outlaws, and one document states that confiscated property included a "building of five rooms" in Bickhill. One historian believes that this was Hood's home and that the outlaw took refuge in the nearby forests of Barnsdale (at the time this Yorkshire forest ran into Sherwood Forest in Nottinghamshire), where he soon became a highly successful robber.

Hood did not remain an outlaw for long, though. In 1323 the king spent three days hunting at Plumpton Park in Knaresborough Forest. Noting that deer seemed scarce, the king learned that this was due to the depredations of Robin Hood. A forester suggested that the king disguise himself as an abbot, riding with a band of monks. Robin and his men stopped the party, but Robin recognized the king. Finding Robin likable and gentlemanly, the king pardoned him and invited the outlaw to join the royal household as a valet, a gentleman of the royal bed-chamber. The king returned to Westminster in February 1324. The royal household accounts for April record a payment of the past month's wages to "Robyn Hod" and 28 others.

A ballad tells us that after serving the king for somewhat more than a year, Robin received permission to return to Barnsdale for seven days. But he never returned to court; instead he regrouped his Merry Men and lived on in the forest for another 22 years. If this is true, then he died about 1346, in his mid-60s.

The End of Edward

The king's fortunes took a downward turn after Robin's departure from his court. Edward had recalled the banished Despensers, and the younger of the two had become his favorite—to the disgust of his queen, Isabella, who had already had to contend with Piers Gaveston. She took a romantic interest in Roger de Mortimer, an unpleasant and ambitious young baron who had been thrown into the tower for opposition to the Despensers. Queen Isabella became his mistress and probably plotted Mortimer's escape. Mortimer fled to Paris, where Isabella (on a mission for the hapless king) joined him. They landed at Orwell, in Suffolk, with an army of almost 3,000 men. The king fled, but he was captured, imprisoned in Berkeley Castle, and forced to abdicate. His 15-year-old son was crowned Edward III.

Mortimer and Isabella ruled England as regents for four years before the young king asserted himself. Edward III had Mortimer seized and executed at Tyburn as a traitor. The loss of her lover almost drove the queen mad. But, restored to favor, Isabella lived on for another 28 years.

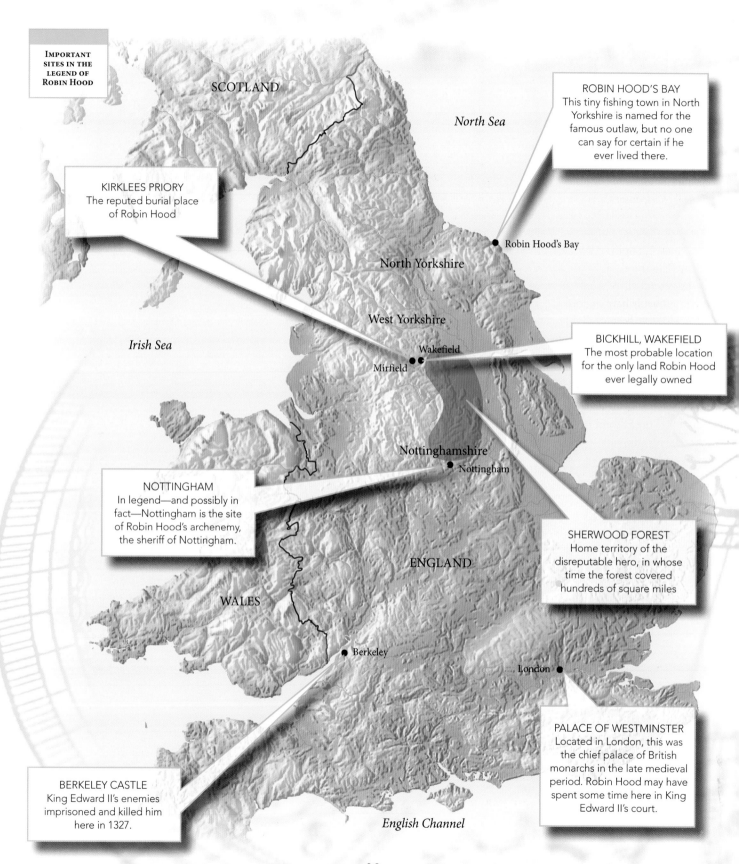

SCOTLAND

North Sea

ROBIN HOOD'S BAY
This tiny fishing town in North Yorkshire is named for the famous outlaw, but no one can say for certain if he ever lived there.

Robin Hood's Bay

North Yorkshire

KIRKLEES PRIORY
The reputed burial place of Robin Hood

West Yorkshire

Irish Sea

Wakefield
Mirfield

BICKHILL, WAKEFIELD
The most probable location for the only land Robin Hood ever legally owned

Nottinghamshire

Nottingham

NOTTINGHAM
In legend—and possibly in fact—Nottingham is the site of Robin Hood's archenemy, the sheriff of Nottingham.

ENGLAND

SHERWOOD FOREST
Home territory of the disreputable hero, in whose time the forest covered hundreds of square miles

WALES

Berkeley

London

PALACE OF WESTMINSTER
Located in London, this was the chief palace of British monarchs in the late medieval period. Robin Hood may have spent some time here in King Edward II's court.

BERKELEY CASTLE
King Edward II's enemies imprisoned and killed him here in 1327.

English Channel

28

Robin the Legend

If Robin became an outlaw in 1322, as a result of Lancaster's unsuccessful rebellion, then he spent only one year in Sherwood Forest before the king pardoned him. The story of his pardon by the king certainly rings true—as does his appointment as a gentleman of the bedchamber. It is natural to speculate that he may have found that his duties in the bedchamber involved more than he had bargained for, although at this time the king's favorite was the younger Hugh le Despenser (later executed by Mortimer and Isabella in 1326). So he returned to the woods and became a hero of legend.

We do not know whether he became the archenemy of the sheriff of Nottingham, but the sheriff would have been responsible for law and order in Nottinghamshire and south Yorkshire and would certainly have resented a band of outlaws who lived off the king's deer. A concerted attempt to flush him out would probably have succeeded, though most of the peasants and tenant farmers would have been on Robin's side. There had been a time when the forests of England were common land, and the half-starved peasantry must have resented that thousands of square miles of forest should now be reserved for the king's hunting, when the king could not make use of even a fraction of that area.

There could be another reason that Robin operated without too much opposition. When at court he must surely have met the 14-year-old boy who would become Edward III, and Edward would have been exactly the right age to look with admiration on a famous outlaw. This is only speculation, but it could explain why Robin was allowed to become the legendary bane of authority in the last decades of his life.

The weapon with which Robin Hood, above left, often appears in legend is the English longbow, shown below. The longbow could even punch through plate armor, and it leveled the playing field, to some extent, between the armored nobility and bow-wielding peasants.

How He Died

Authority has its own ways of striking back. According to the Sloane manuscripts at the British Museum, Robin fell ill and went to his cousin, the prioress of Kirklees, to be bled—the standard procedure for treating illness in those days. The prioress decided to avenge the many churchmen he had robbed and allowed him to bleed to death.

Robin was buried on nunnery grounds, within bow shot of its walls. *Grafton's Chronicle* (1562) says he was buried under an inscribed stone, and a later chronicle reported that his tomb, with a plain cross on a flat stone, could be seen in the cemetery. In 1665 Dr. Nathaniel Johnstone made a drawing of it; Gough's *Sepulchral Monuments* (1786) also has an engraving of the tombstone. In the early 1800s engineers employed to build a railway broke up the stone—it is said that its chips cured toothaches. So the last trace of the real existence of Robin Hood disappeared. Meanwhile the prioress's grave had been discovered among the nunnery ruins, and it bore some resemblance to the tomb of Robin Hood. It also mentioned the prioress's name—Elizabeth Stainton.

The real significance of Robin Hood is that he lived in a century when the peasants were beginning to feel an increasing resentment about their condition—a resentment that expressed itself in the revolutionary doctrines of John Ball and which exploded in the Peasants' Revolt of 1381, only a short time after Robin is first mentioned in print in *Piers Plowman* by the poet William Langland. The Peasants' Revolt is generally considered to mark the end of the Middle Ages, but in the ballads of Robin Hood we can see the state of mind known as the Middle Ages coming to an end.

Did Joan of Arc Return from the Dead?

(1436)

Joan of Arc at the siege of Orléans

On May 30, 1431 Joan of Arc, who had been born a peasant girl in eastern France, but regarded herself as a messenger from Heaven, sent to save the French from their enemies, died at the stake, burned as a heretic by the English. Known as the Maid of Orléans, 19-year-old Joan's military career was brief but spectacular: in a year she headed the armies that liberated many parts of France and won several remarkable victories, and she saw Charles VII crowned at Rheims, before her capture, trial, and execution.

But burning at the stake, oddly enough, was not quite the end of the Maid of Orléans. In May 1436 a 25-year-old woman arrived in Lorraine, calling herself *Jeanne la Pucelle*, or, in English, Joan the Maid.

Joan, Recognized

Joan's miraculous return was greeted with much skepticism, but Joan's two younger brothers, Petit-Jean and Pierre, both recognized their sister—much to their own astonishment. The returned Joan went straight to Metz, where she was surrounded by various people who had known her during her spectacular year fighting the English, including Nicole Lowe, the king's chamberlain. In fact Metz would have been an absurd place for an imposter to go. Former acquaintances also recognized her at Vancoleurs, where she spent a week while Petit-Jean brought word to the king. We do not know the king's reaction, but he ordered his treasurer to give Petit-Jean 100 francs.

On June 24, 1437, Joan's miraculous powers (credited with her victories over the English in 1429) returned to her. By then she had become something of a protégée of Count Ulrich of Württemberg, who took her to Cologne. The inquisitor general of Cologne became curious about the count's guest, and was apparently shocked to learn that Joan practiced magic and that she danced with men and ate and drank more than she ought. The inquisitor excommunicated her, but Joan apparently shrugged this off and married a nobleman named Robert des Armoires (although the original Joan had sworn a vow of chastity).

The city of Metz in 1900, left, looked very much as it did in Joan's day

La Dame des Armoires

In 1440, Joan, now the dame des Armoires, finally went to Paris and met the king. And for the first time she received a setback; after the meeting the king declared her an impostor. It is odd, however, that the king did not denounce her immediately, but waited until after the interview. And now, according to the *Journal of a Bourgeois of Paris*, Joan was arrested, tried, and publicly exhibited as a malefactor. She was forced to confess publicly that she was an impostor.

And yet Joan then returned to Metz, where people continued to accept her as *Jeanne la Pucelle*. Fourteen years later she appeared in the town of Saumur, and was again accepted by the town's officials as the Maid. After that she vanished from history, presumably living out the rest of her life quietly with her husband in their house in Metz.

Slipping into a Quiet Life

What then are we to make of the story of the king's declaration and her public confession? First of all, its only source is the *Journal of a Bourgeois of Paris*. This in itself is odd, if she was involved in such a public scandal. The aristocracy, however, had always been hostile to Joan, resenting her power over the king in her heyday. The priesthood, too, especially at the University of Paris, had accepted her condemnation as a heretic.

So as far as the clerks and magistrates of Paris were concerned, then, the return of Joan would have been nothing but an embarrassment. Even Joan's supporters in the Church would have found her return inconvenient, as a patriotic martyr carried more weight than a contentious noblewoman. Did the king find a solution? If he rejected her, she could drop out of the limelight, live her life, and let everyone get on with it. And that, it seems, is precisely what happened.

Joan of Arc proved to be an inconvenient woman, but one who could make people see things her way. Although she was tried and convicted for heresy, it is possible that she did not die at the stake.

Charles VII owed much to Joan, who had inspired his sagging armies to defeat the English, finally ending the Hundred Years' War.

Saint Joan of Arc

This still leaves one question: how had Joan escaped the flames in 1431? In fact the notion of a rescue is not so far-fetched. We know that Joan was an extraordinarily persuasive young lady, persuading even many skeptics that she truly heard the voices of saints and angels. Even some Englishmen must have been susceptible, and it is assuredly odd that at her execution, 800 English soldiers kept the crowd at such a distance that no one who knew her could come close enough to recognize the Maid.

If the dame des Armoires were genuine, she must have felt there was a certain irony in the situation. She had been an embarrassment to everyone during her first career as the saintly virgin warrior; now she was just as much an embarrassment as the heroine returned from the dead. Indeed, it was not until 1456 that the pope reversed her conviction of heresy, and not until 1920 that the Catholic Church canonized her as a saint.

Who Was Shakespeare?

(1564–1616)

William Shakespeare

In the 1770s a clergyman named James Wilmot retired to his native Warwickshire and devoted his declining years to the study of his two favorite writers, Francis Bacon and William Shakespeare. The village of which he was now the rector—Barton-on-the-Heath—lay only a half dozen miles from Stratford, so he began making inquiries to find out whether any stories and traditions of the great actor-playwright Shakespeare now survived in his native town. Apparently no one knew of any. But from his study of Shakespeare's plays, Wilmot had concluded that the playwright must have been a man of wide learning and must therefore have possessed a considerable library. Over the course of many years he made diligent inquiries in the area, investigating small private libraries for 50 miles around. He found nothing—not a single volume that might have belonged to Shakespeare. And finally he was struck by an astonishing conviction: the man called Shakespeare was not the author of the plays attributed to him. In fact, the man who possessed all the qualifications for writing them was Wilmot's other favorite author, Francis Bacon.

Shakespeare Onstage

So who was this actor to whom about 40 plays are attributed?

We know that a child called William was born to Mary and John Shakespeare in Stratford-upon-Avon in 1564. At the age of 6 or 7 William began attending school in Stratford, leaving at the age of 12 because his father, a glove maker, went bankrupt. William may have then worked as a butcher and as a schoolmaster. When William was 18, he seduced a girl named Anne Hathaway, who was 27. Hathaway became pregnant, the pair married, and Shakespeare became the father of three children, including one set of twins. It was at this point that Shakespeare went to London and somehow succeeded in securing a job as an actor. He wrote a play called *Titus Andronicus*, full of blood and horror, which became an instant success.

Soon after the English defeat of the Spanish Armada in 1588, Shakespeare wrote a series of immensely successful (and patriotic) history plays, and finally became part owner of the theater in which they were performed. In his 40s he bought himself a large house in Stratford-upon-Avon and retired there, dying at age 52, possibly of venereal disease. During his lifetime no one had the least doubt that he wrote his own plays.

Shakespeare was born in this half-timbered house in Stratford-upon-Avon in 1564. It now serves as a museum.

How About Marlowe?

Christopher Marlowe, born about 1564, is a popular contender for an alternate author of the Shakespeare plays.

In 1593 Shakespeare's friend and rival playwright Christopher Marlowe was murdered in a tavern brawl at the age of 29. Marlowe worked as a government spy and mixed with many dubious characters. Two weeks earlier officers looking for "treasonable materials" had arrested Marlowe's friend Thomas Kyd, author of the play *The Spanish Tragedy*, but among Kyd's papers were certain "atheistical writings" denying the divinity of Christ. Under torture Kyd confessed they belonged to Marlowe. So at the time of his death, Marlowe was in serious trouble with the law. Moreover he made no secret of his homosexuality, another hanging offense in those days. It has therefore been suggested that Marlowe had good reason to die.

An American scholar, Calvin Hoffman, has suggested in a book *The Murder of the Man Who Was Shakespeare*, that with the help of friends in the nobility, someone else was murdered in Marlowe's place, that Marlowe escaped abroad, and that Marlowe wrote the plays attributed to the actor Shakespeare.

Then whose was the body examined at the coroner's inquest? Possibly someone else who had died in a brawl—Elizabethan London was a violent place . . .

The Elizabethan scholar A. L. Rowse has one objection to this theory. He points out that Shakespeare's works are full of bawdy jokes, whereas Marlowe tended to be slightly prudish about sex and that there are no bawdy jokes in his plays. So it is unlikely, after all, that Marlowe was Shakespeare.

So How About Bacon?

In 1888 there appeared the most influential of all the works of the Shakespeare heretics, Ignatius Donnelly's *The Great Cryptogram: Francis Bacon's Cipher in the So-called Shakespeare Plays*. In a vast two-volume work on Bacon, Donnelly, an American congressman, tried to prove that Bacon had hidden ciphers about himself in the plays of Shakespeare, to prove his own authorship. (Bacon was in reality fascinated by ciphers.) After years of studying the plays and trying out every possible key to the ciphers, he finally began to perceive such obscure messages as: "Seas ill said that More low or Shak'st spur never writ a word of them," meaning, according to Donnelly: "Cecil [the queen's chief minister] said that Marlowe or Shakespeare never writ a word of them." The book inspired thousands of cranks to seek ciphers in Shakespeare and other famous authors.

In fact anyone who takes the trouble to read a biography of Francis Bacon will see why it is impossible that he could have written Shakespeare's plays. The two men's characters are utterly different. The author of *A Midsummer Night's Dream* and *As You Like It* is obviously a kindly and good-natured human being; it is easy to understand why Ben Jonson referred to him as "gentle Shakespeare." No one would have called Bacon gentle. He was a man of immense intelligence who was permanently dissatisfied with himself and with his lot in life. He was driven by the most superficial kind of ambition: "political power is what I want, power over men and affairs." He was a calculating, rather heartless man who believed that successful men should learn how to "work" their friends by discovering their weaknesses.

One of the more frivolous scenes from *A Midsummer Night's Dream*, in which the besotted fairy queen dotes upon the enchanted Bottom—hardly likely to be a product of the humorless Bacon.

The Trouble with Bacon

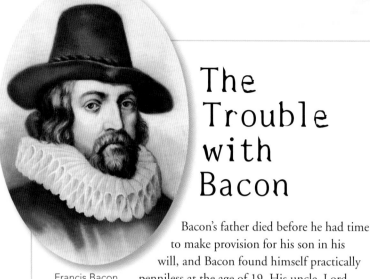

Francis Bacon

Bacon's father died before he had time to make provision for his son in his will, and Bacon found himself practically penniless at the age of 19. His uncle, Lord Burghley (William Cecil), was lord treasurer, and could easily have procured his nephew advancement, but he preferred to help his own son, Robert. Bacon became a lawyer. He then decided to pay court to the queen's favorite, the accomplished and dashing earl of Essex; with charm and flattery Bacon had soon gained the earl's friendship. Essex frequently gave him money—Bacon was a spendthrift—and tried hard to persuade the queen to grant him various offices. When she passed over Bacon in favor of another candidate for master of the Rolls, Essex soothed his protégé's disappointment by presenting him with a large estate. In 1596 Essex captured Cadiz, Spain, and became one of the most popular men in England. But, to Bacon's alarm, he began to overreach himself. After an unsuccessful expedition against the Irish, Essex was politically ruined. He tried to foment a rebellion and was arrested and put on trial. Everyone recognized that he was guilty of hot temper rather than a desire to overthrow the queen, and it seemed likely that his punishment would be light. At this point Bacon betrayed his friend: he delivered a brilliant speech in which he accused Essex of treason, declaring that "as a friend" he knew that Essex meant to seize the throne. As a result Essex was sentenced to death and executed.

It is impossible to exonerate Bacon. He did what he did to gain favor with the queen and further his own career. In return for sending Essex to his death he received 1,200 pounds—but not the advancement he'd hoped for. Elizabeth distrusted him.

When Elizabeth died Bacon set out to flatter James I and succeeded. He was knighted and became attorney general in 1613. Five years later he finally reached the climax of his ambition; he was ennobled and became lord chancellor. Three years later he was impeached for accepting bribes. He admitted his guilt and died in 1626, a bitter and disappointed man.

The Earl of Oxford?

Sometime around 1914 an elementary schoolmaster named John Thomas Looney (pronounced "low-nee") became convinced that the Stratford actor could not have written the plays and, like so many others, began a systematic search for an Elizabethan who possessed the right qualifications. He deduced the character of the author from his work, then made a list of the basic requirements of such a person: he ended with a list of 17 candidates. By 1920 he had decided that only one man fit the picture: Edward de Vere, the 17th earl of Oxford. His book *Shakespeare Identified* is generally agreed to be as absorbing as a detective story, but his "unfortunate" name prevented the general public from taking the book seriously. (Other writers on the Shakespeare problem included S. E. Silliman, who supported Marlowe's case, and George Battey, who believed Daniel Defoe was Shakespeare.)

Although Looney's book was soon forgotten, another American scholar, Charlton Ogburn, took up the theory. His huge tome *The Mysterious William Shakespeare* (1984) is, in spite of its size, immensely readable. But although Ogburn argues convincingly that Oxford was a fine lyric poet who might well have written "Hark, hark the lark" and "Full fathom five," he has an almost impossible task persuading the reader that the late plays, including *King Lear*, *A Winter's Tale*, and *The Tempest*, were written before 1604, the year Oxford died. Looney overcame that problem by suggesting that other authors wrote these plays, suggesting Raleigh as the author of *The Tempest* and John Fletcher as author of *Henry VIII*. Ogburn argues vigorously that they were all written much earlier than supposed, but his arguments will leave most people as unconvinced as Looney's did.

Edward de Vere sponsored numerous artistic pursuits, including several authors and a couple of theater companies.

Bardolatry

A better line of Shakespeare inquiry might be to ask why so many people believe someone other than Shakespeare wrote these plays.

This brief romp through the exotic underworld of Shakespeare scholarship makes us aware that the real key to its dottiness is something that began to happen about a century after his death. Before that there had been a far more sensible and balanced attitude: Samuel Pepys thought *Twelfth Night* "but a silly play" and *A Midsummer Night's Dream* "the most insipid, ridiculous play that I ever saw in my life." By the mid-nineteenth century, Shakespeare was seen as a godlike genius whose feeblest lines were regarded as beyond criticism. Ralph Waldo Emerson compared him to a mountain, too big to grasp. Matthew Arnold expressed this attitude of mindless worship (Shaw called it "Bardolatry") in a sonnet that began:

Others abide our question. Thou art free.
We ask and ask: Thou smilest and art still,
Out-topping knowledge. For the loftiest hill
That to the stars uncrowns his majesty . . .

An Amusing Delusion

It was this kind of uncritical veneration that lay at the root of the various theories. If Shakespeare were really too huge to grasp, how come his friends and neighbors never noticed it? Did he possess a kind of dual personality, like Superman or Batman? Such a view inevitably suggests some kind of secret identity, a man who looked like a normal person until he slipped on his special uniform and revealed that he could fly or scale skyscrapers. When that happened he revealed he was really Francis Bacon or the earl of Oxford—or even Queen Elizabeth.

Once we face the fact that Shakespeare was a perfectly normal person, known to dozens of friends and drinking companions, unusual only in his extraordinary genius with language, we shall begin to see the whole controversy about his "true identity" as an amusing delusion.

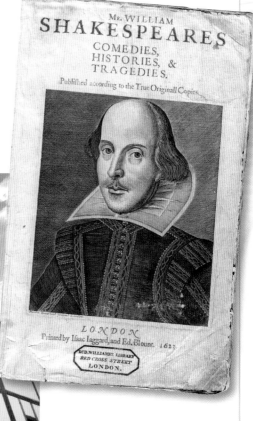

At right, the title page from a volume known as Shakespeare's First Folio. The First Folio was the earliest appearances in print of some of Shakespeare's plays and poems. It was produced just a few years after the playwright's death.

The Globe Theater, shown at left, was once home to Shakespeare's theater company and now reconstructed, is one of London's most popular tourist attractions.

Feodor Kuzmich

Alexander I and the Hermit of Nerchinsk

(1825–1864)

In 1836, nearly 11 years after the reported death of Tsar Alexander I of Russia, police arrested a 60-year-old beggar named Feodor Kuzmich near the town of Krasnoufinsk, in the Russian province of Perm. Convicted of vagrancy, Kuzmich was sentenced to 20 blows of the *knout* (whip). He was then sent to Siberia—Russia's penal colony. There, at Nerchinsk, near the city of Tomsk, he became a hermit and soon acquired a reputation for saintliness.

Kuzmich the hermit impressed all who saw him. He was a tall, broad-shouldered man, of majestic appearance, producing in everyone a sense of awe and veneration. His speech seems to have been that of an educated man, his voice gentle and deliberate. Despite his gentleness, however, there were times when he turned impatient and imperious, and the peasants who approached Kuzmich felt the urge to fall to their knees.

The Great Healer

Kuzmich always turned aside inquiries about his early life. Occasionally though, he made remarks that implied that he had fought in the Russian army against Napoleon; he spoke of the campaign of 1812 and of the victorious entry into Paris on March 31, 1814. The meticulous tidiness of his cell suggested army training.

Kuzmich had remarkable powers as a healer, and people from all over Siberia came to see him. According to one of Alexander I's biographers, General N. K. Schilder (author of a pamphlet that became immensely popular in the 1890s), two former servants from the tsar's palace were among these visitors. The two men had been exiled to Siberia, and when one of them fell ill, his companion decided to visit the healer to ask for help. According to Schilder the man entered the cell alone, leaving a guide—probably a monk—outside. When he saw the hermit, he felt obliged, like so many others, to fall to his knees. The old man raised him to his feet and began to speak; with astonishment, the man recognized the voice of Tsar Alexander I. And as he stared at the white-bearded features, he recognized the face of his former master. He fell down in a swoon.

A memorial to Feodor Kuzmich, erected in Tomsk

The guide outside heard his cry and burst into the cell. Kuzmich told him gently, "Take him back home. And when he regains his senses, warn him not to tell anybody what he saw. Tell him that his friend will recover." Kuzmich proved to be right.

Alexander I

The Rumor Spreads

The story of the sighting of Alexander I, who had ruled Russia from 1801 to 1825, soon spread all over the empire. Alexander's biographer, Maurice Paléologue, described in his 1938 book *The Enigmatic Tsar* how an old soldier who had been sent to the prison of Nerchinsk saw the hermit and instantly stiffened to attention, saying, "It's our beloved Tsar Alexander Pavlovich!"

Feodor Kuzmich died in 1864 at the age of 87—precisely the age Alexander I would have been if he had lived.

Death of a Mad Tsar

Alexander I was the first tsar who could be described as "enlightened." Even rulers we like to think of as more liberal—Peter the Great, Catherine the Great—ordered mass executions and torture. Peter the Great's niece earned herself the title of Anna the Bloody, while Catherine's son Paul—most likely the child of her first lover, Sergei Saltykov—was a madman who, after he inherited the Russian throne, oppressed the peasantry in a way reminiscent of Ivan the Terrible.

By 1801 this paranoid

Alexander I's father, Tsar Paul I

maniac, now Paul I and Alexander's father, was living in seclusion in a newly built palace that was surrounded by canals. Alexander had suffered greatly from his father's arbitrary despotism and had imbibed liberal ideas from Europe; he agreed with his father's chief adviser, Count Pahlen, that Paul had to be deposed. A group of assassins entered the palace after dark and proceeded to the tsar's bedroom. There he was ordered to abdicate, but he resisted. The assassins then struck him with a sword, strangled him with a scarf, and trampled him to death.

A New Russia?

The people of Russia were joyous when Alexander ascended to the throne; they felt that a nightmare was over. It certainly looked like it. Alexander quickly made peace with the English—to the disgust of Napoleon Bonaparte of France, who was just beginning his takeover of the European continent.

The handsome, charming young tsar met every day with a group of liberal friends to discuss over coffee the way to regenerate his country through freedom of the individual. Alexander had no doubt that the first major step was the abolition of serfdom,

but that was easier said than done. Alexander's minister Mikhail Speransky, the son of a village priest, drafted a constitution for a democratic Russia, but even he advised against freeing the serfs at one blow. Alexander had to be content with a decree that allowed anyone to own land, a right that had previously been restricted to the nobility. Alexander also made a determined effort to increase the number of schools and universities. He allowed students to travel abroad, lifted the ban on the import of foreign books, and closed down the secret police department.

The Effect of War

The liberation of the serfs was left in suspension while Russia went to war with Persia over Russia's annexation of Georgia—a war Russia eventually won. But Alexander's chief problem, of course, was Napoleon, with whom his father, Paul, had been on friendly terms. In 1805 Alexander joined Austria, England, and Sweden in an alliance against Napoleon. Britain defeated Napoleon's fleet at Trafalgar, but Napoleon defeated the Russians and Austrians at Austerlitz. A series of treaties with Napoleon followed, and Alexander became Napoleon's ally under the Treaty of Tilsit (1807). Alexander went on to fight successful wars against Turkey and Sweden, acquiring Bessarabia and Finland. The starry-eyed liberal was becoming a conquering hero.

An equestrian portrait of Alexander I, painted in 1812, depicts the tsar as the consummate Napoleonic-era warrior. The long years of the Napoleonic Wars transformed the egalitarian-minded optimist, bent on reform, to a hardened autocrat. Some historians think that his early reforms were inspired by the guilt he felt for inheriting the throne from a murdered father. Feelings of remorse and guilt may also account for the increased religiosity of his later years.

The Emperors Fall Out

By 1812 it was obvious that Napoleon and Alexander disliked each other too much to remain allies. In June Napoleon's Grand Army, strengthened by the Dutch, Germans, Italians, Poles, and Swiss, invaded Russia. It looked like the end for Alexander. Smolensk fell, the Russians were defeated at Borodino, and in mid-September the French entered Moscow. The next day the city burst into flames. Alexander declined to make terms with the French dictator, and a month later Napoleon began his disastrous retreat. Besieged by the Russian army and by the merciless cold of a Russian winter, the French troops died in droves; Napoleon fled to Paris, leaving behind half a million corpses. The Prussians now deserted Napoleon and joined the Russians. And although Napoleon raised another army and enjoyed some remarkable victories, he could not prevent the allies from entering Paris in March 1814. In April Napoleon abdicated and was exiled to Elba.

Alexander, above, stands between Napoleon, left, and the queen of Prussia. At the start of the Napoleonic Wars, Alexander had been Napoleon's staunch supporter. By the time the French dictator set his sights on Russia, Alexander had become a fierce enemy.

The Reactionary

Alexander had defeated the "Corsican monster"; he was adored by all his subjects. Unfortunately Alexander's 10 years of war had turned him into a realist and made him repent of the liberal delusions of his youth. At first he continued to live up to his liberal pledges, conferring a constitution on Poland and emancipating the serfs in the Baltic provinces. But in Russia itself, he took care to maintain the status quo. He began to tighten the screws on education, placing conservatives in charge of universities. They introduced censorship and purged liberal professors.

Yet, oddly enough, Alexander encouraged the flowering of literature that was taking place. Under Alexander Russian literature began to rank among the world's best.

Dreaming of Escape

For many years Alexander's marriage to the beautiful Elizabeth Alexeievna had been a loveless one; the couple's only children, two daughters, had both died as infants, and Alexander took a succession of mistresses. Life seemed curiously empty. When told of the proliferation of secret societies he said wearily, "I myself have shared and encouraged these errors and delusions. . . I have no right to punish them." He began to speak longingly of abdicating, of becoming a private citizen in Switzerland or a botanist on the Rhine.

Alexander began to travel feverishly all over Russia, covering 3,000 miles in four months—an achievement in those days of bumpy carriages and potholed roads.

Tsarina Elizabeth Alexeievna was born Princess Louise of Baden. Elizabeth was beautiful, charming, and intellectual, but she was also shy. She would have been happier living a simple life away from the opulent pomp of Russian court life.

Holiday by the Sea

Alexander felt that his life was falling apart. After falling ill, Elizabeth decided to try to recuperate in Taganrog, on the Sea of Azov. The tsar announced that he would go with her. People were puzzled about the choice of Taganrog, which was not a health resort but a small fortress town in wild and swampy country.

For a month Alexander and Elizabeth lived together simply and peacefully in Taganrog; it seemed that their love had achieved an Indian summer. Then Alexander was again seized by his wanderlust and set out on a tour of the Crimea. When he returned to Taganrog on November 16, he was feverish.

A Crimean waterfall. The tsar fell ill after a tour through the area.

Sudden Death?

According to the history books, Tsar Alexander I died in Taganrog on December 1, 1825.

Why should we not accept this as the truth?

First, because the diaries and letters of various witnesses contradict one another. One, for example, says he is steadily worsening, while another states that he is feeling much better and is gay and smiling. One thing is certain: the tsar consistently refused all medicines during his last illness.

November 23, 1825, seems to have been the crucial day. In the morning, after sleeping well, the tsar sent for his wife and remained in conversation with her for about six hours. They were evidently discussing something of considerable import. Could it be that this was when he told her of his plan to abdicate?

Then there is a sudden gap in the tsarina's diary. If her husband had told her that he intended to disappear, this makes sense—it is surely unlikely that she would have continued to keep her diary, with incriminating evidence.

The Russian court shown gathering at the bedside of the ill tsar

Nicholas I, above, inherited the tsardom after the death of Alexander and the abdication of his older brother, the Grand Duke Constantine.

Changing Dates

Another curious incident concerning a changed date also raises doubts. Prince Volkonsky, a member of the tsar's court, recorded in his diary that Alexander had suggested that his illness be revealed to his younger brother, the Grand Duke Constantine, who was heir to the throne. (In fact, Constantine declined it and allowed the youngest brother, Nicholas, to take over.) Volkonsky gave the date for this request as November 21 —then amended it to November 23, the day of the tsar's long talk with his wife. It may have been a genuine error. Or it may have reflected a desire to support the story that the tsar began to deteriorate on November 23. That Alexander was not in an enfeebled state is proved by the fact that after his six-hour talk with his wife, the tsar wrote a long letter to his mother, the Dowager Tsarina Maria Feodorovna. (That letter has since disappeared.) Nicholas I later destroyed the diary of the tsar's mother, as well as all papers relating to Alexander's last years. The evidence is purely circumstantial, but it certainly fits the hypothesis that November 23 was the day on which Alexander told Elizabeth that he intended to abdicate and the day on which he relayed this news to his mother, his aide-de-camp, and his physicians—with instructions to falsify their diaries.

"He Has Changed."

Ten doctors signed the autopsy report on the day after the tsar's death. This report provides the most evidence that the corpse was not that of the tsar—that another corpse had been found during the 32 hours that had elapsed since his "death." Alexander is reported to have died of typhus, which causes the spleen to hypertrophy. But the spleen of the corpse was quite normal. Examination of the brain revealed that the man had suffered from syphilis. But Alexander, says biographer Paléologue, was known to be immune to syphilis.

The back and loins of the corpse were brownish purple and red; this might be expected of a peasant who took no care of his skin—or who had been recently flogged—but hardly of a pampered tsar.

It would have been easy to obtain an "imposter" corpse. Taganrog was a garrison town full of soldiers. Paléologue reports that in Taganrog's military hospital was the body of a soldier who was roughly the same height and size as the tsar. This could explain why the skin of the loins and back was purple; soldiers were often beaten.

Oddly enough Dr. Tarassov, the imperial surgeon, later declared that he had not signed the autopsy report. Yet his signature appears on the report. Why did the doctor claim not to have signed it? Was it because he did not wish to put his name to a document he knew to be false?

It is also known that the tsar's remains were placed on public view in the church at Taganrog. Those who saw his body remarked, "Is that the tsar? How he has changed."

Filled Coffins

Yet another curious event occurred when Alexander's coffin was on its way back to Saint Petersburg the following March. When the coffin reached Babino, 50 miles from its destination, the Dowager Tsarina Maria Feodorovna came to see it. She ordered the coffin opened, took a long look at the body, and then left. It seems odd that she should have made the journey to Babino when she could just as easily have seen the body in Saint Petersburg. If the corpse were not that of the tsar, it would certainly explain her visit in midwinter. If we assume that the letter of November 23 had simply told her that Alexander had decided to abdicate, and the next news she received was of his death, then it becomes understandable that she was eager to find out as quickly as possible whether it was true that her son was still alive.

The tsar's mother, Maria Feodorovna, seemed to act oddly at the news of her son's announced death.

Empty Tombs

"Alexander" was taken to the summer palace in Tsarskoe Selo. Only the royal family filed past the coffin in the chapel. The body was then taken to the Peter and Paul Fortress in Saint Petersburg and placed in a tomb.

Forty years later the new tsar, Alexander II, heard the rumors that the hermit Feodor Kuzmich, who had died in the previous year, was actually Tsar Alexander I. He ordered the tomb to be opened; the coffin was empty. The tomb was then resealed without the coffin.

In his introduction to Leo Tolstoy's *Death of Ivan Ilich* (which contains his story "Feodor Kuzmich"), Tolstoy's translator, Aylmer Maude, states that in 1927 the Soviet government had the imperial tombs opened. They found that Alexander I's tomb contained only a bar of lead.

Doubts about the disappearance theory must be balanced against the evidence of the empty tomb and against the whole strange story of Alexander's final illness and death. It now seems unlikely that anyone will ever prove that Alexander I arranged his own disappearance. But it should be noted that the proof remains elusive because all of the relevant diaries and letters have mysteriously vanished.

The Catherine Palace at Tsarskoe Selo, Alexander's summer home. A body was brought here after the tsar's reported "death."

The Mystery of the *Mary Celeste*

(1872)

Dei Gratia's crew sights the Mary Celeste.

On the calm afternoon of December 5, 1872, helmsman John Johnson of the British merchant ship *Dei Gratia* sighted a two-masted brigantine in the North Atlantic, midway between the Azores and the coast of Portugal. Alarmed by the brig's erratic course, he alerted his second officer, John Wright, who then informed the ship's captain, David Reed Morehouse, that something was badly amiss. As the brig approached, they saw that she was sailing with only her jib and foretop mast staysail set; moreover, the jib was set to port, while the vessel was on a starboard tack—a sure sign to any sailor that the ship was out of control.

The sea was running high after recent squalls, and fully two hours passed before Morehouse could get close enough to read the name of the vessel. It was the *Mary Celeste.* Morehouse knew this American ship and its master, Captain Benjamin Spooner Briggs. The *Mary Celeste* had set sail for Genoa, Italy, with a cargo of crude alcohol on November 5, 10 days before the *Dei Gratia* had sailed for Gibraltar. So why, a month later, was she drifting in mid-Atlantic with no distress signals and no signs of life?

Deserted

Captain Benjamin Briggs

Morehouse sent his first mate, Oliver Deveau, to investigate. Deveau and his party found the ship's decks deserted; a search below revealed not a soul on board. But the ship's single lifeboat was missing, indicating that Captain Briggs had decided to abandon ship.

There was a great deal of water below decks, and two sails had blown away. But the ship seemed perfectly seaworthy. Why had the crew abandoned her? Two cargo hatches had been ripped off, and one of the casks of crude alcohol was empty. Both forward and aft storage lockers contained a plentiful supply of food and water.

A search of the captain's cabin revealed that the navigation instruments and navigation log were missing. The last entry in the ship's general log was dated November 25; it meant that the *Mary Celeste* had sailed without crew for at least nine days, and that she was now some 700 miles northeast of her last recorded position.

On to Gibraltar

Although there were no signs of a mutiny, pirate raid, or any signs of violence at all, something had compelled the crew and passengers to abruptly abandon ship.

Along with Captain Briggs and a crew of seven, the *Mary Celeste* had also sailed with Briggs's wife, Sarah, and his two-year-old daughter, Sophia Matilda. Faced with the mystery of why they had abandoned ship, Morehouse experienced a superstitious alarm when Deveau suggested that two of the *Dei Gratia's* crew should sail the *Mary Celeste* to Gibraltar; it was the prospect of £5,000 salvage money that finally made him agree.

Both ships arrived in British-controlled Gibraltar Harbor eight days later. But instead of the welcome he expected, Deveau was greeted by an English bureaucrat who nailed an order of immediate arrest to the *Mary Celeste's* mainmast. The date was Friday the 13th.

Sarah Briggs

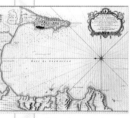

Gibraltar Harbor

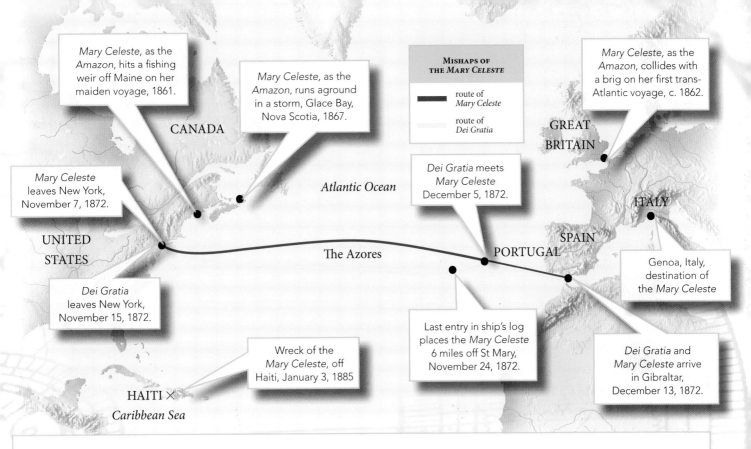

Mary Celeste, as the Amazon, hits a fishing weir off Maine on her maiden voyage, 1861.

Mary Celeste, as the Amazon, runs aground in a storm, Glace Bay, Nova Scotia, 1867.

CANADA

Mary Celeste, as the Amazon, collides with a brig on her first trans-Atlantic voyage, c. 1862.

GREAT BRITAIN

MISHAPS OF THE MARY CELESTE
— route of Mary Celeste
— route of Dei Gratia

Mary Celeste leaves New York, November 7, 1872.

Atlantic Ocean

Dei Gratia meets Mary Celeste December 5, 1872.

ITALY

UNITED STATES

The Azores

SPAIN

PORTUGAL

Genoa, Italy, destination of the Mary Celeste

Dei Gratia leaves New York, November 15, 1872.

Last entry in ship's log places the Mary Celeste 6 miles off St Mary, November 24, 1872.

Dei Gratia and Mary Celeste arrive in Gibraltar, December 13, 1872.

Wreck of the Mary Celeste, off Haiti, January 3, 1885

HAITI ✕

Caribbean Sea

Bad Luck All Around

From the beginning the *Mary Celeste* had been an unlucky ship. She was registered originally as the *Amazon*. Her first captain had died suddenly. On her maiden voyage she hit a fishing weir off the coast of Maine and damaged her hull. While this was being repaired a fire broke out amidships. Later, while sailing through the Straits of Dover, she hit another brig, which sank. This accident occurred under her third captain; her fourth accidentally ran the ship aground on Cape Breton Island and wrecked her.

The *Amazon* was salvaged, and passed through the hands of three more owners before J. H. Winchester, founder of a successful shipping line in New York, bought her. Winchester discovered that the brig—which had now been renamed *Mary Celeste*—had dry rot in her timbers. He had the bottom rebuilt with copper lining and the deck cabin lengthened. These repairs ensured that the ship would be in excellent condition before she had sailed for Genoa under the experienced Captain Briggs, and this helped to explain why she had survived so long in the wintry Atlantic after the crew had taken to the lifeboat.

The *Mary Celeste*, painted in 1861, when she was still known as the *Amazon*

Mutiny Aboard the *Mary Celeste*

British officials at Gibraltar seemed to suspect either mutiny or some Yankee plot, the latter theory based on the fact that captains Morehouse and Briggs had been friends and had apparently dined together the day the *Mary Celeste* sailed from New York. But at the inquiry mutiny was the theory that gained favor. As evidence, the Court of Inquiry was shown an ax mark on one of the ship's rails, scoring on her hull that was described as a crude attempt to make the ship look as if she had hit rocks, and a stained sword that was found beneath the captain's bunk. All this, mutiny theorists claimed, pointed to the crew getting drunk, killing the master and his family, and escaping in the ship's lifeboat.

The Americans were insulted by what they felt was a slur on the honor of the merchant navy, and indignantly denied the story. They pointed out that Briggs was not only known to be a fair man who was not likely to provoke his crew to mutiny, but also that he ran a dry ship; the only alcohol on the *Mary Celeste* was the cargo. And even a thirsty sailor would not drink more than a mouthful of crude alcohol—it would cause severe stomach pains and eventual blindness. Besides, if the crew had mutinied, why leave behind their sea chests and such items as family photographs, razors, and seaboots?

The British Admiralty remained unconvinced, but had to admit that if the theory was correct and Briggs and Morehouse had decided to claim for salvage, Briggs would actually have lost by the deal—being part owner of the ship—and his share of any salvage would have come to a fraction of what he could have made by selling his share. In March 1873 the court finally admitted that it was unable to decide why the *Mary Celeste* had been abandoned, the first time in its history that it had failed to come to a definite conclusion. The *Dei Gratia*'s owners were awarded one-fifth of the value of the *Mary Celeste* and her cargo. The brig herself was returned to her owner, who lost no time in selling her the moment she got back to New York.

Rough seas toss the *Mary Celeste*, above. Although bad weather had plagued the Atlantic the month before the brigantine set sail from Staten Island, New York, on its way to Genoa, Italy, the *Dei Gratia*, which left just days later, experienced fine weather. But had a sudden storm risen up to drive the crew and passengers of the *Mary Celeste* to abandon ship? Oliver Deveau, first mate of the *Dei Gratia*, reported that "the whole ship was a thoroughly wet mess" after he was assigned the duty of searching the empty *Mary Celeste*. Other theories about the ship's fate included a pirate raid, as the newspaper account, shown right, describes. Many believed that pirates had murdered the entire crew and Briggs's wife and child.

A Brig's Officers Believed to Have Been Murdered at Sea.

From the Boston Post. Feb. 24.

It is now believed that the fine brig Mary Celeste, of about 236 tons, commanded by Capt. Benjamin Briggs, of Marion, Mass., was seized by pirates in the latter part of November, and that, after murdering the Captain, his wife, child, and officers, the vessel was abandoned near the Western Islands, where the miscreants are supposed to have landed. The brig left New-York on the 17th of November for Genoa, with a cargo of alcohol, and is said to have had a crew consisting mostly of foreigners. The theory now is, that some of the men probably obtained access to the cargo, and were thus stimulated to the desperate deed.

The Mary Celeste was fallen in with by the British brig Dei Gratia, Capt. Morehouse, who left New-York about the middle of November. The hull of the Celeste was found in good condition, and safely towed into Gibraltar, where she has since remained. The confusion in which many things were found on board, (including ladies' apparel, &c.,) led, with other circumstances, to suspicion of wrong and outrage, which has by no means died out. One of the latest letters from Gibraltar received in Boston says: The Vice-Admiralty Court sat yesterday, and will sit again to-morrow. The cargo of the brig has been claimed, and to-morrow the vessel will be claimed.

The general opinion is that there has been foul play on board, as spots of blood on the blade of a sword, in the cabin, and on the rails, with a sharp cut on the wood, indicate force or violence having been used, but how or by whom is the question. Soon after the vessel was picked up, it was considered possible that a collision might have taken place. Had this been the case, and the brig's officers and crew saved, they would have been landed long ere this. We trust that if any of New-England's shipmasters can give any information or hint of strange boats or seamen landing at any of the islands during the past ninety days, that they will see the importance thereof.

A Mystery Worthy of Sherlock Holmes

In the year 1882 a 23-year-old newly qualified doctor named Arthur Doyle moved to Southsea, a suburb of Portsmouth. During the long weeks waiting for patients he whiled away the time writing short stories. It was in autumn 1882 that he began a story: "In the month of December 1873, the British ship *Dei Gratia* steered into Gibraltar, having in tow a derelict brigantine *Marie Celeste*, which had been picked up in the latitude 38°40′, longitude 70°15′ west."

This short sentence contains a remarkable number of inaccuracies. The year the brigantine turned up abandoned was 1872, the *Dei Gratia* did not tow the *Mary Celeste*, the latitude and longitude are incorrect, and the ship was the *Mary Celeste*, not the *Marie Celeste*. All the same, when "J. Habakuk Jephson's Statement" was published in the *Cornhill* magazine in 1884 it caused a sensation, launching Arthur Doyle's career as a writer. Soon afterward he adopted the pen name A. Conan Doyle. Most people took his tale for the truth, and from then on it was widely accepted that the *Mary Celeste*, like the *Marie Celeste* of fiction, had been taken over by a kind of Black Power leader with a hatred of white people.

Over the next few years a number of accounts surfaced of the last days of the *Mary Celeste*. They ranged from tales about straightforward mutinies to sudden, gigantic waterspouts to bizarre mass accidents; one story was that everyone fell into the sea when a platform made to watch a swimming race gave way.

Sir Arthur Conan Doyle. His fictionalized version of the *Mary Celeste* incident obscures the facts of the very real mystery of the abandoned ship.

A Cursed Ship

During the next 11 years the *Mary Celeste* had many owners, but brought little profit to any of them. Sailors were convinced that she was unlucky. Her last owner, Captain Gilman C. Parker, ran her aground on a reef in the West Indies. The insurers became suspicious, and Parker and his associates were brought to trial. But the judge, mindful of the *Mary Celeste*'s previous bad luck, allowed the men to be released on a technicality. The *Mary Celeste* herself had been left to break up on the reef.

Tragedy at Sea

In fact a careful study of the facts reveals that the solution of this particular mystery is obvious—once we take into account that the lifeboat was missing. For we know that the crew abandoned ship; the wheel was not lashed, though, which indicates that they abandoned it suddenly, in great haste. The question then presents itself: what could have caused everyone on board to leave the ship in such a hurry? And why, if the crew left the *Mary Celeste* in the lifeboat, did they make no attempt to reboard when they saw that the ship was in no danger of sinking?

The night of storms would have caused vapor to form inside the casks of alcohol that the ship was carrying, slowly building pressure until the lids of two or three blew off. Convinced that the whole ship was about to explode, Briggs ordered everyone into the lifeboat. In his rush, he failed to take the one simple precaution: to secure the lifeboat to the *Mary Celeste* by a cable.

The sea was fairly calm when the boat was lowered, but the evidence of the torn sails indicates that the ship then encountered severe gales. We may conjecture that the rising wind blew the *Mary Celeste* into the distance, while the crew in the lifeboat rowed frantically in a futile effort to catch up. The remainder of the story is tragically clear.

A typical page from the Voynich manuscript

The Mystery of the Voynich Manuscript

(1912)

In 1912 Wilfred Voynich, an American dealer in rare books, heard of a mysterious work that had been discovered in an old chest in the Jesuit school of Mondragone, in Frascati, Italy. Voynich purchased the manuscript for an undisclosed sum. It is an octavo volume, 6 by 9 inches, with 204 pages; 28 pages have been lost from the original. It is written in cipher, and the pages are covered with intriguing little drawings of female nudes, intricate astronomical diagrams, and all kinds of strange plants in many colors.

The Voynich manuscript is baffling partly because it looks so straightforward. With its plant illustrations, it seems to be an ordinary medieval herbal, a book describing how to extract healing drugs from plants. So why was it written in code?

Enter John Dee

It is likely that the famous Elizabethan "magician," Dr. John Dee, took the manuscript to Prague from England in 1584. One writer speculates that Dee may have obtained it from the duke of Northumberland, who had pillaged monasteries at the behest of Henry VIII. Joannes Marcus Marci, the rector of Prague University, believed the author of the mysterious book to be the thirteenth-century monk and scientist Roger Bacon.

An Accompanying Letter

Voynich found a letter with the manuscript. It was dated August 19, 1666, and written by Joannes Marcus Marci. Marci addressed the missive to the famous Jesuit scholar Athanasius Kircher and stated that the Holy Roman emperor Rudolf II of Prague bought the book for 600 ducats.

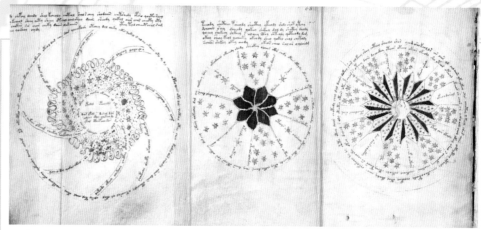

Swirling astronomical diagrams fill pages of the Voynich manuscript.

Scholars Weigh In

Voynich was fairly certain that the manuscript would not remain a mystery once modern scholars had a chance to study it. So he distributed copies to anyone who took an interest.

Most of the plants depicted on the pages proved to be imagi-nary. As for the "text," cryptanalysts tried to decode it by using the familiar method of looking for the most frequent symbols and equating them with the most commonly used letters of the alphabet. They had no difficulty recognizing 29 individual letters or symbols, but every attempt to translate these into a known language failed.

Newbold's Solution

In 1921 William Romaine Newbold, a professor of philosophy at the University of Pennsylvania, announced that he had solved the code. His method was to begin by translating the symbols into Roman letters, reducing them in the process from 29 to 17. Using the Latin *conmuto* "to change" as a key word, he went on to produce no fewer than four more versions of the text, the last of which was (according to Newbold) a straight-forward Latin text mixed up into anagrams that merely had to be unscrambled. Newbold claimed that the unscrambled manuscript was a scientific treatise written by Roger Bacon.

The Achievements of Roger Bacon

If Newbold was correct, the manuscript proved Bacon to be one of the greatest scientists before Isaac Newton. He made a microscope and examined biological cells and spermatozoa—these were the tadpole drawings in the margin of the manuscript—and had produced a telescope long before Galileo. He had even recognized the Andromeda nebula as a spiral galaxy.

Roger Bacon (c. 1214–1294) taught at Oxford University and the University at Paris before becoming a Franciscan friar.

New Questions Emerge

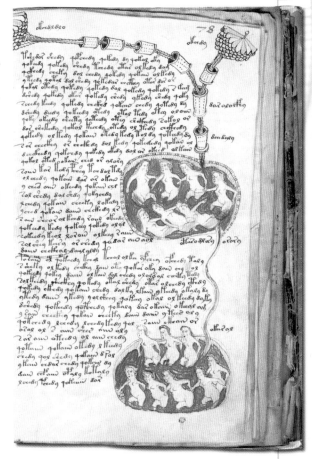

Newbold died in 1926, at only 60 years old. Two years later his friend Roland G. Kent published the results of Newbold's labors in *The Cipher of Roger Bacon*. It was widely accepted by such eminent historians of philosophy as Étienne Gilson.

But one scholar who had been studying Newbold's system was far from convinced. This was Dr. John M. Manly, a philologist who headed the department of English at Chicago University, and who had become an assistant to the great Herbert Osborne Yardley—described as the greatest code breaker in history.

Manly studied Newbold's *Cipher* and concluded that in spite of his integrity, Newbold had been deceiving himself. Newbold had also made certain shorthand signs a basic part of his system of interpretation. When Manly examined these through a powerful magnifying glass he found out that they were not shorthand at all but simply spots where the ink had peeled off the vellum. By the time he had pointed out dozens of cases in which Newbold had allowed his interpretation to be influenced by his own twentieth-century assumptions, Manly had demolished Newbold's claim that he had solved the cipher of Roger Bacon.

When Voynich's wife, Ethel, died at the age of 96 in 1960, the antiquarian bookseller Hans Kraus purchased the manuscript from her executors and put it up for sale at $160,000. Kraus explained that he thought if it could be deciphered it might be worth a million dollars. There were no takers, and Kraus finally gave it to Yale University in 1969, where it now lies, awaiting the inspiration of some master cryptographer.

The Voynich manuscript has tantalized and eluded scholars since its discovery in 1912.

Strange People

The Man in the Iron Mask

(1698–1703)

The mysterious Man in the Iron Mask

On Thursday, September 18, 1698, Lieutenant Étienne du Junca, an official of the Bastille in Paris, noted in his journal the arrival of the prison's new governor, Bénigne d'Auvergne de Saint-Mars. Du Junca also noted that with Saint-Mars was a longtime prisoner from his previous post. Du Junca wrote that Saint-Mars "brought with him, in a litter, [a man] whom he had in custody in Pinerolo, and whom he kept always masked, and whose name has not been given to me, nor recorded." Knowing that Saint-Mars had served at Pinerolo, a French-held fortress-prison near Turin, Italy, from 1665 to 1681, du Junca calculated that the masked man had been in prison for at least 18 years and possibly as long as 33.

Name Unknown

During his years in the Bastille, his jailers allowed the prisoner to attend Mass, but he always kept his face covered. When, five years after his arrival, on November 19, 1703, the prisoner died in the Bastille, du Junca, still Louis XIV's chief jailer, still did not know the identity of the mysterious masked prisoner. He merely noted in his journal that the "unknown prisoner, who has worn a black velvet mask since his arrival here in 1698," was dead and buried.

Mask of Velvet

Despite the popular misconception, the prisoner wore a mask made not of iron, but of black velvet. Alexandre Dumas was mainly responsible for propagating the inaccuracy with his 1847 novel *The Man in the Iron Mask*. According to the novel the prisoner was the twin brother of Louis XIV, born several hours later than the future king of France. That version

of the story first appeared in *Memoirs of the Duc de Richelieu*, which is known to be a forgery by the duke of Richelieu's secretary, the Abbé Soulavie, so the tale is probably an invention.

The masked prisoner aroused the public's curiosity almost immediately. The first published account of the man in the mask was by Voltaire, who included it in his 1751 historical work *The Century of Louis the Fourteenth*. Voltaire recounts that in 1661, when the king was 23, a tall, aristocratic young man was incarcerated. He wore a riveted mask with a chin composed of steel springs, so that he could raise it to eat. But the king kept two musketeers posted to the prisoner's side, ready to shoot him if he even made a move to remove the mask.

King Louis's own sister-in-law, the Princess Palatine, shown left, was intrigued by the prisoner, writing to her aunt in 1711 that the prisoner had "two musketeers at his side to kill him if he removed his mask." She had never met the prisoner before his death eight years earlier, but court rumors led her to believe that he was a refined man, who'd been treated well.

The First Suspect: Mattioli

So who was the masked prisoner? Obviously he had to be someone against whom the king held a deep grudge and someone who would be recognized without the mask. In the nineteenth century one favorite theory proposed that he was Antonio Ercole Mattioli, an Italian courtier who had indiscreetly

"leaked" the fact that the king was hoping to increase his Italian possessions. Louis concealed his rage at this piece of treachery and had Mattioli lured to Pinerolo. There he was seized and imprisoned for the rest of his life. That theory has to be abandoned, though. When Saint-Mars, the prison governor of Pinerolo, transferred to the Bastille, he took the mysterious prisoner with him. Records clearly show that Mattioli remained behind, locked in Pinerolo.

Above: Antonio Ercole Mattioli. Left: Although the famous prisoner wore a mask of velvet, every year the Italian town of Pinerolo hosts a festival celebrating the mystery of the Man in the Iron Mask. The festival includes reenactments inside the cell where the man spent his imprisonment in the Pinerolo fortress.

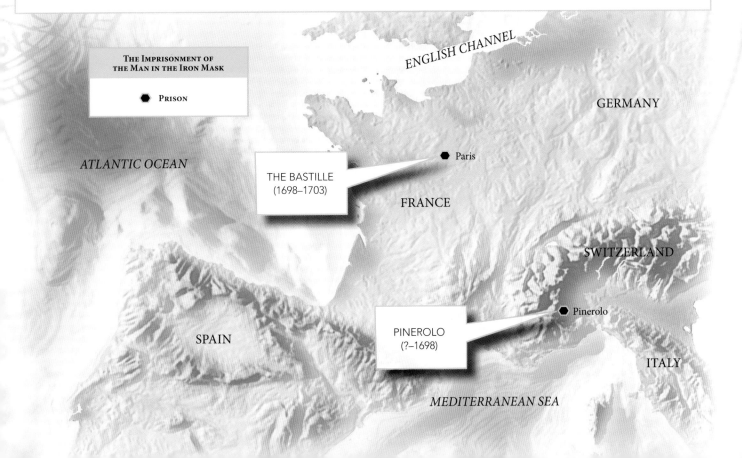

THE IMPRISONMENT OF
THE MAN IN THE IRON MASK

⬡ PRISON

ENGLISH CHANNEL

GERMANY

ATLANTIC OCEAN

⬡ Paris

THE BASTILLE
(1698–1703)

FRANCE

SWITZERLAND

⬡ Pinerolo

SPAIN

PINEROLO
(?–1698)

ITALY

MEDITERRANEAN SEA

The Second Suspect: Molière

Over the years several historians have suggested one particularly interesting candidate for the man in the mask: the well-known playwright Molière.

This initially seems unlikely: Louis XIV had admired Molière from the time that he saw the playwright's farce *The Amorous Doctor* presented at court in October 1658. The king also approved the staging of Molière's *Tartuffe*, in spite of the disapproval of a religious faction (who were shocked by its presentation of a preacher as a hypocrite and lecher). But Molière won this battle in 1664—if Voltaire is right, three years after the man in the mask entered prison.

Molière died in 1673, at the age of 51, but we do not know with certainty when the man in the mask was actually imprisoned. It could even have been *after* Molière's death. Yet it must be admitted that Voltaire's description of the prisoner as being of "majestic height . . . and noble figure" hardly seems to fit the playwright in his 50s.

Playwright Molière

The Clue: The Mask

The likeliest key to the mystery is the necessity of the mask—no matter what it was made of. Why was the king so anxious that no one should see the prisoner's face? In the days before cameras, when accurate likenesses of even the most famous people were not widely seen, to be assumed instantly recognizable to the public meant that someone was very high in the pecking order. And no one in those days was higher or more recognizable than Louis XIV himself. This explains why the twin brother theory has always been so popular.

Furthering the case for the look-alike relative were the long-standing tales about Louis XIV's birth. His father, Louis XIII, did not like his wife, Anne of Austria, and, because he was not known to take mistresses, rumors floated that he must be either impotent or homosexual. There was therefore some anxiety about his ability to produce an heir to carry on the line. The queen's lover, many believed, was the great Cardinal Mazarin. Some suspect that the notorious Cardinal Richelieu was also her lover.

When Anne conceived the child who became Louis XIV, everyone was astonished. After 23 years of marriage and four stillborn infants, the birth of Louis was so astonishing, in fact, that many contemporaries believed the true father to be Cardinal Richelieu or another "stud" who had impregnated her for the good of the royal line. And what better stud could there have been than the handsome young captain of Richelieu's musketeers, François Dauger de Cavoye, who would demonstrate his potency by fathering six healthy sons on his wife?

Louis XIV, king of France

The Third Suspect: Eustace Dauger de Cavoye

After the fall of the Bastille in July 1789, a commission searching for information about the masked prisoner studied its archives. Certain letters from prison officials seemed to point to the eldest son of François de Cavoye. Eustace Dauger de Cavoye had earned a reputation as a hell-raiser early in his adult life.

Eustace got in his first serious trouble in 1659, when he was 22, for being present at a black mass where a pig was christened and then eaten. The regard in which his mother was held at court averted serious consequences for the youth. But when Eustace killed a page boy in a quarrel six years later, he was forced to sell his commission. Several years after that, he landed in Pinerolo prison, but no one knows why.

L'HOMME AU   MASQUE DE FER

L'homme au masque de fer, or *The Man in the Iron Mask*. A French political cartoon from 1789 shows an iron-masked prisoner in chains sitting on a bench while a guard enters his cell in the Bastille carrying a tray of food. Its original caption identified the prisoner as Louis de Bourbon, comte de Vermandois, an illegitimate son of Louis XIV, who had died in 1683 at the age of 16. There is no evidence to support this claim, and historians posit that revolutionaries spread stories such as these to show how decadent nobles ill treated their own.

Drawing of the exterior and an interior floor plan of the Bastille

The Motive

If Eustace were the Man in the Iron Mask, then it looks as if he indulged in a folly that turned out to be the last straw. Is it conceivable that Eustace tried to exert pressure on the king to release his younger brother, also named Louis, who had been imprisoned for four years in the Bastille? But what pressure? What did he know that the king would have wanted to keep secret?

Surely the great secret must have been that he and King Louis had the same father. Consequently the king was illegitimate and had no right to the throne. If Eustace dared to even hint at it, Louis would have made sure that he never talked. That would explain why the prison governor had orders to kill the prisoner if he tried to speak with anyone.

There remains one obvious question: if it were Eustace, why did the king not simply have him executed? The answer must surely be that the sons of the captain of the guard were the king's childhood playmates, and Louis must have had a certain feeling of affection for them. Eustace was safe . . . so long as he could not speak.

53

Andrew Crosse

The Man Who Was Dr. Frankenstein

(1837)

June 16, 1816, had been a rather cool and cloudy spring day on Lake Geneva, Switzerland, and the five people on holiday at the Villa Diodati had built a large fire and lit all of the candles. With little else to do to entertain themselves—in those days people ate dinner at four in the afternoon—they decided to relax with an evening of scary tales.

The host, poet George Gordon, Lord Byron, never traveled without a small leather-bound volume of ghost stories, mostly German, called *Fantasmagoriåa*. He opened the book and began to read aloud a story about a bridegroom whose bride turns into a rotting corpse as he tries to embrace her.

Fertile Minds

Byron's audience consisted of the poet Percy Bysshe Shelley; Shelley's future wife, 19-year-old Mary Godwin; Mary's stepsister, Claire Clairmont; and Byron's personal physician, John William Polidori. Claire was carrying Byron's child—she had seduced him by the simple expedient of writing to him and offering to go to bed with him.

When they were all ready to retire, Byron had a suggestion for them: each should try to write a ghost story. The suggestion proved extraordinarily fruitful, for it not only led Mary to write a disturbing tale of a reanimated corpse (inspired by a dream), but it also induced Byron to write a story fragment called "The Vampire," which triggered a literary trend that culminated, at the century's end, in Bram Stoker's *Dracula*.

As for Mary, she developed her famous dream of a mad scientist who created a horrible monster with yellow eyes. The tale became a great success when published (anonymously at first) as *Frankenstein, or, the Modern Prometheus* in 1818.

Villa Diodati, "birthplace" of Mary Shelley's *Frankenstein*

The Vampire

Byron's "The Vampire" concerned a Greek aristocrat who undergoes a mock death and swears his traveling companion to secrecy. Later the companion witnesses his former friend doing some highly immoral things but feels bound by his oath of silence . . .

The physician Polidori—who was envious of Byron—stole the piece. He turned Byron's work into a short novel called *The Vampyr*, which was published in a monthly magazine—and attributed to Byron. Later, the story was turned into a play that enjoyed immense success in London and Paris. (Polidori never made a penny.) London became mad for vampires, and novelist Bram Stoker capitalized. Polidori committed suicide a few years later.

Frontispiece of the 1831 edition of Frankenstein

The Monster Shocks London

In 1823 H. M. Miller turned *Frankenstein* into a play. The stage monster looked so horrible that ladies fainted on opening night, and the monster's makeup had to be toned down. The play went on to enjoy immense success at the Lyceum Theatre. Mary Shelley was not even consulted.

The Edison Stock Company made the first film version of *Frankenstein* in 1910. It was 10 minutes long. In 1915 the Ocean Film Corporation made a 60-minute version. But it was not until 1931 that Shelley's story finally came into its own with the Boris Karloff film, made in Hollywood by Universal Studios and directed by an Englishman, James Whale. Whale had already filmed *Dracula* with Hungarian actor Bela Lugosi. It was an instant success, and *Frankenstein* was an obvious choice as a sequel. Lugosi was the main candidate to star as the monster, but he disliked the idea of playing a grunting brute after the articulate and sinister Count Dracula.

The Most Famous Frankenstein

James Whale, fresh from Lugosi's refusal, happened to walk into the studio cafeteria at lunchtime when he spotted an English actor called William Pratt. Pratt was tall and in his mid-40s, with deep-set eyes and a strong face. He agreed to test for the part. The brilliant makeup artist James Pierce immediately saw possibilities in that powerful face and created from it the ghoulish and shambling creature we all know so well.

Pratt had already adopted the stage name Boris Karloff to shield his siblings, who worked in the foreign service, from the ignominy of having an actor in the family—and the name certainly suited the monster better than plain Bill Pratt.

As the monster Karloff was a sensation, fitting perfectly into a background of Gothic castles and bleak Teutonic landscapes. For the remaining 38 years of his life, Karloff was Hollywood's best-known villain.

What Mary Shelley (who died in 1851) would have felt about Hollywood's transformation of her best-known character into a symbol of evil is not difficult to guess. Her monster is a tragic, tormented human being, whose ambition—to love his fellow humans—is thwarted by his ugliness. Her monster is in no way evil.

As to the monster's creator, Victor Frankenstein, Shelley never intended him to be the mad scientist of the Hollywood films, but a kind of tragic, poetic idealist, more like Mary's husband than the frenetic genius Colin Clive played in the movie.

Boris Karloff in the 1931 film version of *Frankenstein*. Makeup artist James Pierce defined modern concepts of Shelley's monster with the look he created for Karloff's character.

The Man from Castle Frankenstein

Was Shelley's tragic mad scientist merely a creature of nightmare? Not entirely. She apparently based him upon two real "mad" scientists: Johann Konrad Dippel, an alchemist and inventor who was actually born in Castle Frankenstein, near Darmstadt, Germany, in 1673, and Andrew Crosse, an Englishman who claimed to have created life in his laboratory.

The son of several generations of Lutheran pastors, Johann Dippel reportedly questioned the catechism at the age of 9. As a student of theology he earned high regard as a brilliant thinker. This, according to one biographer, made him conceited and self-willed and caused his later problems. In his 20s he discovered alchemy and set out to earn riches by making gold (in which, predictably, he failed). But one can gauge his skill as a chemist by the fact that he invented the dye called Prussian blue. In 1707 Dippel studied medicine at Leyden in southern Holland. He became a doctor and achieved considerable success in Amsterdam.

Dippel made the mistake of getting involved in politics, and

The ruins of Castle Frankenstein

authorities eventually had him imprisoned for seven years for heresy. He moved to Norway, where the duke of Wittgenstein provided him with an alchemical laboratory. He became convinced that he had discovered an elixir of long life, which led him to prophesy in early 1734, when he was 51, that he would live until 1808. Unfortunately he died, probably of a stroke, in April of the same year.

The Other Frankenstein

Although the experiments that made him notorious took place more than two decades after Mary Godwin Shelley conceived her tale, she and her future husband had met the other candidate for the title of the "real" Dr. Frankenstein. Mary knew the man—Andrew Crosse—through a mutual friend. She and Shelley even attended Crosse's lecture on the results of his experiments with atmospheric electricity two years before she began writing her book.

Andrew Crosse became one of the most hated men in England because of his attempts to create life in his laboratory. In this endeavor he apparently succeeded, but at great cost. Shunned by the academy and his neighbors, he became a virtual prisoner in his own home. When he died 18 years later, the secret of how he had created life died with him. And the episode remains one of the strangest and most baffling in the annals of science.

Mary Shelley, creator of the Frankenstein monster

Electric Dreams

Andrew Crosse, born in 1774, had inherited wealth and the beautiful manor house Fyne Court, near Broomfield, in Somerset, England. As a schoolboy he became fascinated by electricity, and he spent most of his adult life experimenting with it.

It was 21 years after Mary Shelley wrote *Frankenstein* that Crosse performed the experiments that would make him famous—or infamous—throughout Europe and which earned him an entry in the *Dictionary of National Biography*.

Crosse was attempting nothing more blasphemous than creating crystals of silica. He made glass out of ground flint and potassium carbonate, and then dissolved it in hydrochloric acid. His idea was to allow this fluid to drip slowly through a lump of porous stone that had been "electrified" by a battery and to see whether it formed crystals.

After two weeks he observed something odd happening to the lump of red-colored stone (it was, in fact, a piece of iron oxide from the slopes of Mount Vesuvius, chosen merely because it was porous). Small white "nipples" began to appear on it. These nipples began to grow tiny hairs, or filaments. They resembled minute insects, but Crosse knew that this was impossible. On the 28th day, he examined the rock through a magnifying glass and was staggered to see that the filaments were moving. And after a few more days, there could be no possible doubt: the minuscule creatures were walking around. Under a microscope, he could see that they were tiny bugs, the smaller of which had six legs, while the larger ones had eight.

Silica crystals

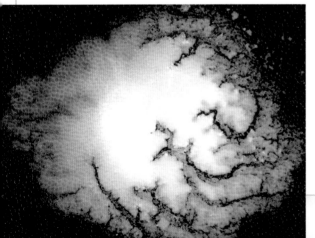

A New Species?

Crosse described his creatures as "the perfect insect, standing erect on a few bristles which formed its tail." They looked to him to be part of the genus *Acarus*. Further experiments showed that the tiny organisms were able to reproduce themselves, but none of them lived beyond the first autumn frost.

Crosse sent off a paper about his experiments to the London Electrical Society. An electrician named W. H. Weeks, who lived at Sandwich in Kent, repeated the experiments and announced his results in *Annals of Electricity* as well as in the *Transactions of the Society*: he too had "grown" the mites.

Crosse spoke of his results to a local newspaper editor, who published a friendly report in the *Western Gazette*. In no time at all, for better or for worse, Crosse's name was known throughout Europe.

Electron microscope image of a mite of the *Acarus* genus. Crosse thought that the "perfect insects" he'd spotted under his microscope were from this genus.

Let There Be Life

One of the most famous scenes in the film version of *Frankenstein* may be when flashes of lightning generate electricity that sparks life into the monster. That scene has as much in common with Crosse, who used electricity in his experiments, as it does with the Shelley book. In the novel, Dr. Frankenstein uses a combination of chemistry, alchemy, and electricity to produce life in his creature.

Black Magic?

Most people were inclined to believe that Crosse was some kind of magician. He was even blamed for a potato blight that swept England's West Country that year. Clergymen denounced him as an atheist and blasphemer, a "reviler of our holy religion," who had presumptuously set himself up as a rival to the God in whom he disbelieved.

Crosse did his best to defend himself, pointing out that he was a "humble and lowly reverencer of that Great Being" and insisting that he had made his discovery by pure chance. It made no difference. Indignant locals destroyed his fences. One outraged clergyman, the Rev. Philip Smith, led his congregation to a hilltop above Fyne Court and proceeded to read the ceremony of exorcism. Crosse's arrival on a horse interrupted the incensed preacher: the crowd instantly dispersed, no doubt convinced that Crosse could blight them with his magical powers.

Faraday, Too

In 1837 one of the greatest scientists of his day, Michael Faraday, defended Crosse at the Royal Institution. Faraday also claimed to have duplicated Crosse's experiments and produced the mites. Yet even this sterling recommendation failed to silence the critics.

When it dawned on Crosse that it was now practically impossible to make the public aware of what he had really said and done, he decided that the simplest course was to withdraw in dignified silence.

Faraday in his laboratory. Faraday attempted to defend Crosse and his work to the British science academy, but even this well-respected scientist could not quell Crosse's detractors.

"Surrounded by Death and Disease"

For the next 10 years Crosse led a bitter life. Both his wife and his brother fell ill and died in 1846. Crosse was a lonely man; most of his neighbors still shunned him. He was beset by financial worries—not, according to his own account, due to extravagance or excessive spending on scientific apparatus, but to his failure to pay enough attention to household expenditure, which he claimed had led to his being cheated. In a letter to the feminist writer Harriet Martineau in 1849—she wanted to write about his experiments—he described himself gloomily as "surrounded by death and disease." Yet it was in that year, when he was 65 years old, that he accepted an invitation to dinner and found himself sitting next to a pretty, dark-haired girl in her 20s who was fascinated by science and by Crosse himself. Cornelia Burns became his second wife soon after they met .

The last six years of his life were relatively happy; he went to visit Faraday in London and received friends at Fyne Court. But a deep streak of pessimism persisted; one day he told his wife that he was convinced that this world was hell and that we are sent here because of sins committed in a previous existence. At that moment there was a violent flash of electricity in the room. This was not God rebuking him for his lack of faith, but merely the result of falling snow causing a short circuit in some of his electrical equipment.

Crosse died of a stroke, at the age of 71, in 1855.

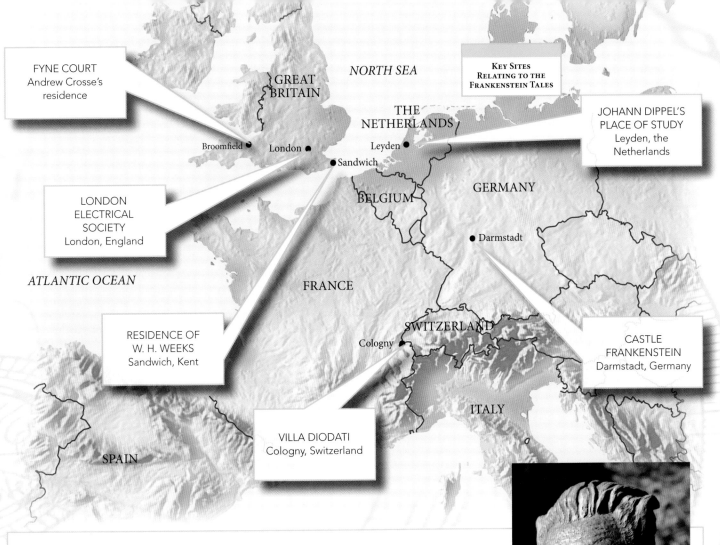

FYNE COURT
Andrew Crosse's
residence

JOHANN DIPPEL'S
PLACE OF STUDY
Leyden, the
Netherlands

NORTH SEA

GREAT
BRITAIN

THE
NETHERLANDS

Broomfield

London

Leyden

Sandwich

BELGIUM

GERMANY

LONDON
ELECTRICAL
SOCIETY
London, England

Darmstadt

ATLANTIC OCEAN

FRANCE

RESIDENCE OF
W. H. WEEKS
Sandwich, Kent

SWITZERLAND

Cologny

CASTLE
FRANKENSTEIN
Darmstadt, Germany

ITALY

VILLA DIODATI
Cologny, Switzerland

SPAIN

Wilhelm Reich

Why Did It Work?

One of the great puzzles of science is why some experiments work for some people but not for others. Wilhelm Reich (1897–1957) once placed dry sterile hay in distilled water. After a day or two it was full of tiny living organisms, some even visible to the naked eye. When Reich studied the experiment through a microscope he found that the cells at the edge of the hay disintegrated into "bladders" and that the bladders tended to cluster together. He became convinced that the bladders were the basic unit of life and called them "bions." Reich alleged that he was able to produce bions not only from organic substances like hay and egg white, but also from inorganic substances like earth and coke.

To silence skeptics who insisted that germs or minute living organisms from the air had contaminated his culture, he took the same precautions that Crosse took in his own experiments. He heated coke until it was red hot and then immersed it in a solution of potassium chloride; he claimed that the bions began to form immediately. These bions, he demonstrated, had an electrical charge, and were attracted to the anode or cathode of his apparatus. Reich finally concluded that his bions were not living cells but an intermediate form of life between dead and living matter.

Other scientists dismissed Reich as a crank, and he eventually landed in jail, where he died in 1957. Clearly, things had not changed much in the century between Crosse's death and Reich's.

Kaspar Hauser: The Boy from Nowhere

(1828–1833)

Kaspar Hauser

On Monday afternoon, May 26, 1828, a weary-looking youth appeared in the streets of Nuremberg, Bavaria. He was well built, but poorly dressed, and walked in a curious, stiff-limbed manner. He carried a letter addressed to the captain of the Fourth Squadron of the Sixth Cavalry Regiment. The shoemaker who found him took him to the regiment headquarters, but the youth was unable to answer questions, replying in a curious mumble. When Captain Wessenig arrived a few hours later, he found the place alive with excitement. No one could make heads or tails of their mysterious visitor. The youth had tried to touch a candle flame and screamed when his fingers burned. Offered beer and meat, he had stared at them uncomprehendingly, yet he had fallen ravenously on a meal of black bread and water. The only words the boy seemed to know were *Weiss nicht* ("I don't know"). Asked his name, the boy wrote, "Kaspar Hauser."

An Unlikely Visitor

The youth's letter read: "Honored Captain. I send you a lad who wishes to serve his king in the army. He was brought to me on October 7, 1812. I am but a poor laborer with children of my own to rear. Since then I have never let him go outside the house." The letter was unsigned.

Confounded, the cavalrymen locked him in a cell. Kaspar seemed perfectly content to sit there for hours without moving. He seemed to have no sense of time and only knew a few words. He could say that he wanted to become a *Reiter* (cavalryman) like his father—a phrase he had obviously been taught as if he were a parrot. Kaspar called every animal a horse, and when a visitor—one of the crowd who flocked to stare at him every day—gave him a toy horse, he adorned it with ribbons, played with it for hours, and pretended to feed it at every meal. He did not seem to know the difference between men and women, referring to both sexes as *Jungen* (boys).

Entrance to the house of Kaspar Hauser in Nuremberg, above, in a photograph taken in about 1860. At right, a contemporary illustration shows the shoemaker who found the boy presenting Kaspar to soldiers of the Fourth Squadron.

Reading in the Dark

One of the most curious things about Kaspar was his incredible physical acuteness. He began to vomit if coffee or beer was in the same room; the sight or smell of meat produced nausea. The scent of wine literally made him drunk, and a single drop of brandy in his water made him sick. His hearing and eyesight were abnormally acute; he could even see in the dark and would later demonstrate his ability by reading from a Bible in a completely black room. He could feel different magnetic charges and identify them with the north or south pole. He could distinguish different metals by passing his hand over them, even when they were covered with a cloth.

At first Kaspar had seemed to be intellectually impaired. But the attention of visitors made him visibly more alert day by day—exactly like a baby learning from experience. His vocabulary increased and his physical clumsiness vanished. He learned to use scissors, quill pens, and matches. And as his intelligence increased, his features altered. He had struck most people as coarse, lumpish, clumsy, and oddly repulsive; now his facial characteristics changed and become more refined.

At left, an 1839 painting of Hauser

A contemporary illustration shows Kaspar in his cell with his wooden horses when a man arrives to teach him rudimentary German.

Kaspar's Story

As he learned to speak, Kaspar gradually revealed his story. He stated that for as long as he could remember, he had lived in a small room, about 7 feet by 4 feet, with boarded-up windows. There was no bed, only a bundle of straw on the bare earth. The ceiling was so low that he could not stand upright. He saw no one. He would find bread and water in his cell each day. Sometimes his water had a bitter taste. If he drank this, he fell into a deep sleep, and when he woke up, he noticed that someone had changed his straw and cut his hair and nails while he had slept.

Kaspar's only toys had been three wooden horses. A man had once entered his room and taught him to write his name and to repeat phrases such as "I want to be a soldier" and "I don't know." One day Kaspar woke up to find himself wearing the old clothes in which he was later found; the same man who had taught him to speak came and led him outside. The man promised him a big, live horse when he became a soldier and had abandoned him somewhere near the gates of Nuremberg.

Overnight Celebrity

Suddenly Kaspar was famous, his case discussed throughout Germany. This must have worried whoever was responsible for turning him loose; his captor, or captors, had hoped that he would vanish quietly into the army and be forgotten; but now he was a national celebrity.

The town council decided he should be fed and clothed at the municipal expense, and housed him with the local schoolmaster, Friedrich Daumer. The town paid for thousands of handbills appealing for clues to his identity, even offering a reward. The police carefully searched the local countryside for his place of imprisonment, which was obviously within walking distance, but they found nothing.

A double statue of Kaspar Hausers in the old city center of Ansbach depicts him as the shuffling youth bearing his letter of introduction, foreground, and as a well-dressed gentleman, background left.

Trials and Tribulations

Then someone tried to kill him. On the afternoon of October 7, 1829, Kaspar was found in Daumer's cellar, bleeding from a head wound, with his shirt torn to the waist. Later he described being attacked by a man wearing a silken mask, who had struck him either with a club or a knife.

Kaspar was moved to a new address, with two policemen to guard him. But now the novelty had worn off, and many in Nuremberg objected to supporting Kaspar.

One day a wealthy Englishman, Lord Stanhope, came to interview Kaspar. The two seemed to take an instant liking to one another; they began to dine out in restaurants, and Kaspar was often seen in Lord Stanhope's carriage. Stanhope was convinced that Kaspar was of royal blood, and from 1831 to 1833 Stanhope presented Kaspar at many minor courts in Europe, where he never failed to arouse interest.

Philip Henry Stanhope, Fourth Earl Stanhope. Lord Stanhope gained custody of Kaspar late in 1831 and spent a great deal of time trying to trace the young man's origins. Even after he abandoned Kaspar in Ansbach, Stanhope continued to pay for Hauser's living expenses.

In 1833, back in Nuremberg, Stanhope asked permission to lodge him in the town of Ansbach, 25 miles away, where he would be tutored by Stanhope's friend, Dr. Johann Meyer, and guarded by a certain Captain Hickel. Stanhope himself disappeared back to England.

Kaspar was miserable. He hated lessons and longed for the old life of courts and dinner parties. He seems to have felt that Ansbach was hardly better than the cell in which he had spent his early years.

Kaspar's Death

On December 14, 1833, Kaspar staggered in from the snow to Meyer's house gasping: "Man stabbed . . . knife . . . Hofgarten . . . gave purse . . . Go look quickly." A hastily summoned doctor discovered that someone had stabbed Kaspar just below the ribs. Hickel rushed to the park where Kaspar had been walking, and found a silk purse containing a note, written in mirror writing. It said: "Hauser will be able to tell you how I look, whence I came and who I am. To spare him from that task I will tell you myself. I am from . . . on the Bavarian border . . . on the River . . . My name is M. L. O."

But Kaspar could not tell them anything about the man's identity. He could only explain that a laborer had delivered a message asking him to go to the Hofgarten. A tall, bewhiskered man wearing a black cloak had asked him, "Are you Kaspar Hauser?" and when he had nodded, the man handed him the purse. As Kaspar took it, the man stabbed him and then ran off.

Hickel revealed a fact that threw doubt on this story; there had only been one set of footprints—Kaspar's—in the snow. But when two days later, on December 17, Kaspar slipped into a coma, his last words were: "I didn't do it myself." A few days before Christmas, Kaspar died.

A contemporary print illustrates the death of Kaspar Hauser

Who Was He?

One of the many learned men who examined Kaspar while he was alive was the lawyer and criminologist Anselm Ritter von Feuerbach. He concluded that Kaspar must be of royal blood. The favorite royal suspect was Karl, grand duke of Baden. The story claims that Karl's stepmother, the Countess von Hochberg kidnapped Karl's only male progeny to secure the throne for her own son. Could Kaspar have been the son of the grand duke's?

Surely a more likely answer is that he was the illegitimate child of a respectable farmer's daughter, terrified that her secret would become local gossip. In that case, who was behind the attacks? It is possible that they just never happened? After the first attack, in Daumer's cellar, Nuremberg gossip suggested Kaspar's wound was self-inflicted. By the time of the second attack, his fame was in decline, and he was desperately unhappy about his situation.

Kaspar had emerged from obscurity to find himself the center of attention. But although he was 17 years old, he was developmentally a 2-year-old boy. And undoubtably, certain aspects of his story are unlikely. Would a masked man find his way into

Kaspar's gravestone reads, in Latin: Here lies Kaspar Hauser, riddle of his time. His birth was unknown, his death mysterious 1833. Another monument to him reads, "Here a mysterious one was killed in a mysterious manner."

the basement of Daumer's house, then merely hit Kaspar on the head with a club? As to the second attack, Hickel's assertion that there was only one set of footprints in the snow seems conclusive. And why was the mysterious letter written in mirror writing? Was it because Kaspar wrote it with his left hand, looking in a mirror, in order to disguise his writing? It is also unlikely that a paid assassin would write a letter at all. Is it not more likely that Kaspar, in a desperate state of unhappiness, decided to inflict a harmless wound but stabbed himself too deeply?

If so, Kaspar at least achieved what he wanted—universal sympathy and a place in history.

Jack the Ripper: identity unknown

Who Was Jack the Ripper?

(1888)

The five Jack the Ripper murders, which occurred between August 31 and November 9, 1888, achieved worldwide notoriety. They also presented police with a new kind of horror: a killer who struck at random. When the biggest police operation in London's history failed to catch the killer, the public hysteria was unprecedented. In the history of serial killer victims, Jack's five barely makes a blip; subsequent killers have murdered dozens before getting caught or disappearing. But Jack himself continues to present an irresistible mystery for one simple reason: his identity is still unknown.

The Victims

Although several other murders of women occurred in or near the Whitechapel district of London's impoverished East End that summer and fall of 1888, nearly all "Ripperologists" agree that five particular murders were definitely the work of the single killer who called himself Jack the Ripper.

The first victim, a 43-year-old prostitute named Mary Anne Nicholls, was found in the early hours of August 31, 1888, in Buck's Row, a slum street in Whitechapel. Her throat had been cut; in the mortuary doctors discovered that she had also been disemboweled.

The next victim was another prostitute, 47-year-old Annie Chapman. She was found a week after Nicholls, on September 8, spread-eagled in the backyard of a slum dwelling in the adjacent Spitalfields district. Her killer had ripped open her abdomen and removed her uterus. He'd also arranged the contents of her pockets around her in a curiously ritualistic manner—a characteristic act that forensics profilers have found to be typical of many serial killers.

The two murders engendered nationwide shock and outrage —nothing of this sort had ever happened before. That shock and outrage increased when, on the morning of September 30, 1888, the killer murdered two women in one night: Elizabeth Stride, 45, and Catherine Eddowes, 46. Within hours of the murders, someone claiming that he was the killer sent a letter to the London Central News Agency boasting of the "double event." He signed the letter, "Jack the Ripper."

As if in response to the sensation he was causing, the Ripper's next murder was by far the most gruesome. He killed and disemboweled a 24-year-old prostitute named Mary Jane Kelly; the mutilation that followed must have taken several hours.

And then the murders ceased. Most people believed that the killer had committed suicide or had been confined to a mental home.

The body of the final victim—Mary Jane Kelly—was completely eviscerated.

New Look at an Old Crime

From the point of view of the general public, the most alarming element about the murders was that the killer—almost certainly sexually motivated—seemed able to strike with impunity, and the police appeared to be completely helpless.

In 1988, a century after the Ripper murders, a television company in the United States produced a two-hour live special on the case. Two profilers from the Federal Bureau of Investigation (FBI), John Douglas and Roy Hazelwood, participated.

The Suspects

Douglas and Hazelwood sorted through a vast amount of evidence, including coroner's reports, witness statements, police files, and photographs. In addition they were presented with a list of five prime suspects, which included Queen Victoria's physician, Sir William Gull; heir to the throne, Prince Albert Victor; Roslyn Donston, a Satanist and occultist who lived in Whitechapel; Montague John Druitt, a melancholic schoolmaster who drowned himself a month after the last murder; and a psychotic Polish immigrant named Aaron Kosminski. Sir Melville Macnaghten, who became assistant chief constable at Scotland Yard soon after the murders, had listed the latter two as leading suspects in a memorandum dated February 23, 1894.

The FBI profilers dismissed most of these suspects on various grounds—for example, Gull had suffered a stroke that paralyzed his right side a year before the murders and would have been in no condition to prowl the streets. Prince Albert Victor had solid alibis: he wasn't even in London at the time of the murders.

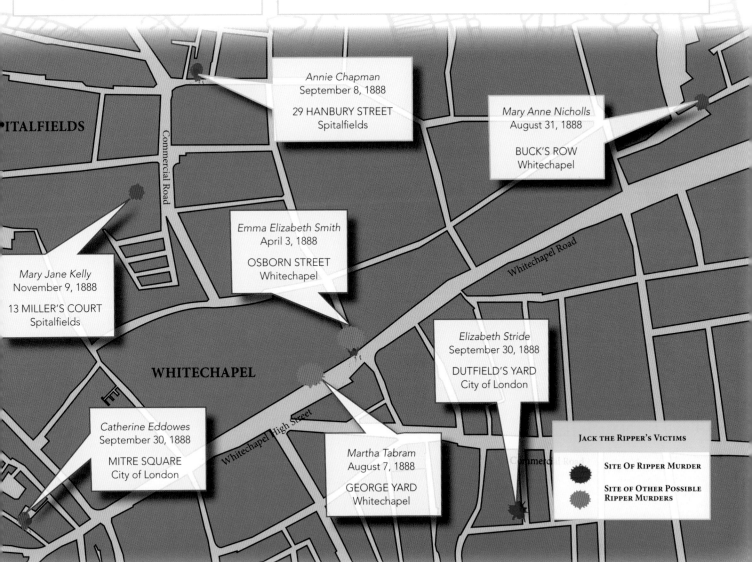

Annie Chapman
September 8, 1888

29 HANBURY STREET
Spitalfields

Mary Anne Nicholls
August 31, 1888

BUCK'S ROW
Whitechapel

SPITALFIELDS

Commercial Road

Emma Elizabeth Smith
April 3, 1888

OSBORN STREET
Whitechapel

Whitechapel Road

Mary Jane Kelly
November 9, 1888

13 MILLER'S COURT
Spitalfields

WHITECHAPEL

Elizabeth Stride
September 30, 1888

DUTFIELD'S YARD
City of London

Catherine Eddowes
September 30, 1888

MITRE SQUARE
City of London

Whitechapel High Street

Martha Tabram
August 7, 1888

GEORGE YARD
Whitechapel

Commercial Road

JACK THE RIPPER'S VICTIMS

SITE OF RIPPER MURDER

SITE OF OTHER POSSIBLE
RIPPER MURDERS

The Analysis

After analyzing the evidence Douglas and Hazelwood drew a forensics profile of the suspect, a technique now used regularly in law enforcement.

John Douglas explained that Jack was like a predatory animal who would be out nightly looking for weak and susceptible victims for his grotesque sexual fantasies. With such a killer, he said, one does not expect to see a definite time pattern because the murderer kills as opportunity presents itself. He added that such killers return to the scenes of their successful crimes.

Douglas also surmised that Jack was a white male in his mid-to-late 20s and of average intelligence. Douglas and Hazelwood agreed that Jack the Ripper wasn't nearly as clever as he was lucky. Hazelwood thought that Jack was single, never married, and probably did not socialize with women at all. He would have had a great deal of difficulty interacting appropriately with anyone, but particularly women.

A graffiti portrait of Jack the Ripper graces a wall in Spitalfields. The puzzling riddle of the Ripper's identity still intrigues us today.

Hazelwood also conjectured that Jack lived very near the crime scenes—such offenders generally start killing within close proximity to their homes. Hazelwood also rejected theories that draw a picture of an educated doctor or surgeon who carved up his victims with a skill that belied his medical training. He assumed that if Jack were employed, it would have been at menial work requiring little or no contact with others.

He went on to say that, as a child, Jack probably set fires and abused animals and that as an adult his erratic behavior would have brought him to the attention of the police at some point.

Douglas added that Jack seemed to have come from a broken home, where a dominant female raised him. She physically abused him, possibly even sexually abused him. Jack would have internalized this abuse rather than act it out toward those closest to him.

Filling Out the Profile

Douglas and Hazelwood continued filling in the details of Jack's character and habits. Douglas described Jack as socially withdrawn, a loner, having poor personal hygiene and a disheveled appearance. Such characteristics are hallmarks of this type of offender. He said that people who know this type of person often report that he is nocturnal, preferring the hours of darkness to daytime. When he is out at night, he typically covers great distances on foot.

Hazelwood said that Jack simultaneously hated and feared women. They intimidated him, and his feeling of inadequacy was evident in the way he killed. Hazelwood noted that the Ripper had subdued and murdered his victims quickly. There was no evidence that he savored this part of his crime; he didn't torture the women or prolong their deaths. He attacked suddenly and without warning, quickly cutting their throats.

The psychosexually pleasurable part came for him in the acts following death. By displacing or removing his victims' sexual and internal organs, Jack was neutering or desexing them so that they were no longer women to be feared.

Poster warning area residents of the murders in the East End

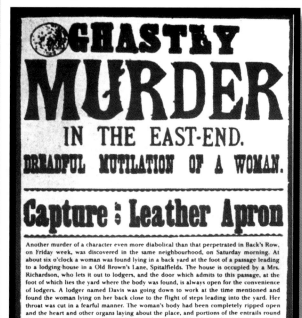

GHASTLY MURDER IN THE EAST-END. DREADFUL MUTILATION OF A WOMAN. Capture: Leather Apron

Another murder of a character even more diabolical than that perpetrated in Back's Row, on Friday week, was discovered in the same neighbourhood, on Saturday morning. At about six o'clock a woman was found lying in a back yard at the foot of a passage leading to a lodging-house in a Old Brown's Lane, Spitalfields. The house is occupied by a Mrs. Richardson, who lets it out to lodgers, and the door which admits to this passage, at the foot of which lies the yard where the body was found, is always open for the convenience of lodgers. A lodger named Davis was going down to work at the time mentioned and found the woman lying on her back close to the flight of steps leading into the yard. Her throat was cut in a fearful manner. The woman's body had been completely ripped open and the heart and other organs laying about the place, and portions of the entrails round the victim's neck. An excited crowd gathered in front of Mrs. Richardson's house and also round the mortuary in old Montague Street, whither the body was quickly conveyed. As the body lies in the rough coffin in which it has been placed in the mortuary - the same coffin in which the unfortunate Mrs. Nicholls was first placed - it presents a fearful sight. The body is that of a woman about 45 years of age. The height is exactly five feet. The complexion is fair, with wavy brown hair; the eyes are blue, and two lower teeth have been knocked out. The nose is rather large and prominent.

Knife believed to belong to the real Jack the Ripper. The murderer's *modus operandi* showed no technical skill that would indicate that he was a surgeon or had any particular knowledge of anatomy.

The Arsenic Suspect

James Maybrick

One of the must popular suspects of recent years was James Maybrick, the Liverpool cotton merchant who died of arsenic poisoning the year after the murders. A diary found in Liverpool in 1992 describes the events in gruesome detail, and its unnamed writer, who hints at being Maybrick, takes responsibility for the murders of Nicholls, Chapman, Stride, Eddowes, and Kelly, as well as two other women. Published as *The Diary of Jack the Ripper*, the entries certainly make Maybrick seem like a plausible Ripper. He was an arsenic addict (arsenic is a powerful stimulant in small quantities), and his frantic jealousy over his possibly unfaithful wife, Florence, 23 years his junior, might have unhinged him enough to make him strike out at any woman. But the handwriting of the diary was not remotely like Maybrick's, and that seems to exclude him as a suspect.

Doctor Dismissed

The comments of the FBI profilers are fascinating in part because of the number of suspects they exclude. The first book about the case, *The Mystery of Jack the Ripper* (1929), hypothesized that the killer was a certain Dr. Stanley, who committed the murders because his son had died of venereal disease acquired from the last victim, Mary Kelly. But Mary Kelly was suffering from no sexually transmitted diseases. And no medical register of the period lists a "Dr. Stanley."

In fact the murderer's methods showed no signs of medical skill. And Hazelwood and Douglas's theory of a mentally unstable, possibly psychotic, killer certainly fits the facts far better.

School's Out

Another major suspect was Montague John Druitt, mentioned earlier as the "melancholic schoolmaster" who drowned himself in the Thames. Druitt's name appears in *Mysteries of Police and Crime* (1898), a classic survey by Major Arthur Griffiths. Griffiths had known Sir Melville Macnaghten of Scotland Yard. In his memoirs Macnaghten mentions that there were three chief suspects, the leading one being the schoolmaster who drowned himself. Macnaghten does not name him, but a television interviewer, Dan Farson, succeeded in tracking down Macnaghten's notes on the case and learned the name of the suspect: M. J. Druitt.

But the notes, to Farson, seemed to exclude rather than point the finger at Druitt. "When I looked up the passage in Macnaghten," he explained, "I soon realized

that he was totally ignorant of the facts. He said Druitt was a doctor who lived with his family; in fact, he was a schoolmaster and a failed barrister who lived in chambers. He also said that Druitt drowned himself the day after the murder of Mary Kelly." Farson cites evidence against this, noting that the suicide took place three weeks later. He also cites a more plausible reason for Druitt's suicide: "His mother had gone insane, and he believed he was going the same way." So we must also dismiss Macnaghten and his suspect.

In pruning the list of suspects, Hazelwood and Douglas have come closer than anyone else has to solving the mystery of Jack the Ripper's identity.

Sir Melville Macnaghten of Scotland Yard

Lord Kitchener's Death—Accident or Murder?

(June 5, 1916)

Lord Kitchener

He was one of the most visible and controversial figures of World War I. The United Kingdom's secretary of war Field Marshal Horatio Herbert Kitchener, First Earl Kitchener, died on June 5, 1916, when the ship he was aboard, the HMS *Hampshire*, struck a mine and sank. Kitchener was en route to a meeting with the tsar of Russia to discuss plans to counteract some of the disasters suffered by the Russian armies in the previous year. One of the survivors, Fred Sims, recalled Kitchener standing impassively on deck, dressed in a greatcoat, awaiting the inevitable end. His body was never found.

A Famous Face

Kitchener's face—with its heavy drooping moustache and piercing eyes—was iconic in Great Britain, where it had appeared on various recruiting posters ("Your Country Needs You!"). Kitchener had been one of the country's great war heroes ever since he reconquered the Sudan in 1896 and avenged the death of General Gordon at Khartoum. After his conquest of the followers of the Mahdi in 1898 at Omdurman, Sudan, he was raised to the peerage as Baron Kitchener of Khartoum and Aspall. In the Boer War (1900–1902) Kitchener used fortified blockhouses and the systematic denudation of Boer lands to wear down the resistance of the guerrillas. His methods were severely criticized, but he was made a viscount and awarded $50,000 and the Order of Merit.

By the beginning of the war in 1914, Kitchener had been made an earl for distinguished services in India and Egypt. Appointed head of the War Office, he immediately laid plans to expand the British army from 20 to 70 divisions by recruiting men rather than the institution of a draft—hence the famous recruiting posters.

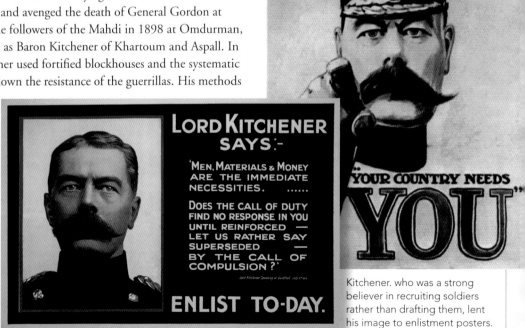

Kitchener. who was a strong believer in recruiting soldiers rather than drafting them, lent his image to enlistment posters.

Home-Front Enemy

Many had predicted that the "war to end all wars" would be over by Christmas 1914. Kitchener was one of few who predicted otherwise, foreseeing a long conflict. Kitchener was a difficult man and not easy to work with: he also had at least one political enemy. Chancellor David Lloyd George disliked Kitchener and felt that the British munitions industry needed a radical overhaul to compete with Germany in the war. He thought Kitchener was poorly suited to his role as overseer of munitions production, so he encouraged a powerful newspaper publisher, Lord Northcliffe, to play up the so-called Shell Scandal in the *London Times* and the *Daily Mail*.

Meanwhile, by Christmas 1914, incompetence and corruption had almost cost Russia the war. In June 1916 Russia was in serious trouble; money that should have been spent on munitions went into the pockets of government ministers. That summer Kitchener was dispatched to Russia to rein in Russia's spending. But first he stopped at Scotland's Scapa Flow—the United Kingdom's primary naval base during the Great War—to meet with Admiral Sir John Rushworth Jellicoe, who had recently led the British Fleet to victory in the Battle of Jutland. By now Kitchener was a tired and worried man who may have had presentiments of death.

A Fateful Journey

The HMS *Hampshire* was to depart Scotland on June 5 for northern Russia. But when the weather deteriorated, it seemed advisable to postpone sailing for 24 hours. Kitchener would not hear of it and the route was changed.

So the doomed cruiser *Hampshire* set sail at 4:40 PM with Kitchener in a cheerful mood. He had declined to wait while minesweepers swept the channel. Soon after the ship left Scapa Flow the storm struck, and a northwest gale whipped the sea to a fury.

HMS *Hampshire*

At about 7:45 PM the noise of the storm almost drowned out an explosion; one survivor later compared it to the sound of an lightbulb bursting. Then the lights failed, and the hiss of escaping steam filled the air. Rushing water trapped men in the engine room; some were scalded to death. Mutilated men staggered up onto the deck. The *Hampshire* had struck a mine. Witness saw Kitchener make his way to the deck, where he was last seen alive.

The news shocked Britain; homeowners drew their blinds and shops closed for the day. Army officers were ordered to wear mourning bands. When journalist Hannen Swaffer telephoned Lord Northcliffe to tell him of Kitchener's death, Northcliffe replied, "Good. Now we can get on with winning the war."

Sabotage?

The most popular theory called the ship's sinking sabotage. In February 1916, five months earlier, the *Hampshire* had been refitted in Belfast, Ireland. Kitchener had refused to allow Irish troops to wear a harp symbol on their uniforms, and it was reported that the Irish Republican Army had vowed to kill him.

In 1985 biographer Trevor Royle gained access to naval intelligence records. What he discovered confirmed the rumors that Kitchener's death had not been simply bad luck. In spring 1916 a German listening post at Neuminster had picked up a naval signal from a British destroyer to the Admiralty declaring that a channel west of Orkney had been swept clear of mines. When the same signal was repeated twice, the Germans realized that the navy must have some important reason for sweeping the channel and reporting to the Admiralty. Admiral von Scheer of

the German navy sent a U-boat commanded by Oberleutenant Kurt Beitzen to lay new mines in the recently cleared channel. One of these mines sank the *Hampshire*.

Royle discovered that naval intelligence had intercepted and read this signal from von Scheer (the British broke the German secret code). Also, on the day Kitchener was to sail, naval intelligence learned that the German submarine was still lurking in the area. Although three signals to this effect were sent to Admiral Jellicoe, for some reason Jellicoe allowed Kitchener to sail to almost certain death.

Was Lloyd George's scheming part of a plot to send a rival to his death? The evidence undoubtedly establishes that Kitchener's death can be laid at the door of Lloyd George and Jellicoe. But it seems unlikely that we can ever know for sure.

The Case of the Disappearing Mystery Writer

(1926)

Dame Agatha Christie

In 1926 Agatha Christie became embroiled in a bizarre mystery that sounds like the plot of one of her own novels. But unlike the fictional crimes unraveled by Hercule Poirot or Jane Marple, this puzzle has never been satisfactorily solved.

At the age of 36, Agatha Christie seemed an enviable figure. An attractive redhead, she lived with her husband, Colonel Archibald Christie, in a magnificent country house that she once described as "a sort of millionaire-style Savoy suite transferred to the country."

The Queen of Crime

The "Queen of Crime," as she came to be known, had been born Agatha Mary Clarissa Miller in Devon, England, in 1890. At the age of 24 she married Archibald Christie, an aviator in the Royal Flying Corps. During World War I, while Archie earned a reputation as a flying ace, Agatha worked in a hospital and a pharmacy. Shortly after the war ended, she gave birth to her only child, Rosalind, and a year after that she published her first novel, *The Mysterious Affair at Styles*. By 1926 the Christies looked to the world to be a happy couple, living comfortably in Sunningdale, Berkshire. Yet that year the couple's relationship—always a tumultuous one—hit a crisis.

A teenaged Christie in Paris, 1906

The Lady Vanishes

By this time, Christie had already authored several more volumes of detective fiction, but her latest, *The Murder of Roger Ackroyd*, a best-seller, had caused some controversy because of its "unfair" ending. Much to her readers' frustration, she used a plot device called an "unreliable narrator," who turns out to be the assistant to Hercule Poirot, Dr. James Sheppard. Although Sheppard does not lie throughout the novel, he omits information that later reveals his guilt. Nevertheless, the clues are imbedded in the novel for readers to find. Critics loved it.

Although a moderately well-known author, Christie was hardly a celebrity yet; few of her books achieved sales of more than a few thousand. Then, on the freezing cold night of December 3, 1926, she left her home and disappeared. Suddenly the entire country was speculating about her whereabouts.

Exit the Author

At 11:00 the next morning, a superintendent of the Surrey police received a report on a road accident at Newlands Corner, just outside Guildford. Agatha Christie's car, a Morris two-seater, had been found halfway down a grassy bank with its bonnet buried in a clump of bushes. There was no sign of the driver, but Christie had clearly not intended to go far, because she had left her fur coat in the car.

By midafternoon the press had heard of the disappearance and besieged the Christie household. From the start the police hinted that they suspected suicide. Her husband dismissed this theory, sensibly pointing out that most people commit suicide at home, and do not drive off in the middle of the night. But the police organized an extensive search of the area around Newlands Corner and deep-sea divers investigated the Silent Pool, a seemingly bottomless lake in the vicinity.

Christie's car, above, was found abandoned, with some of her possessions still inside but few clues as to her whereabouts.

Secret Stress

What nobody knew was that Christie's life was not as enviable as it looked. Her husband had recently fallen in love with a girl who was 10 years younger than Christie, Nancy Neele. Earlier that year Archie told Agatha that he wanted a divorce. To make matters worse, Christies's mother had recently died. Agatha was also sleeping badly, eating erratically, and moving furniture around the house haphazardly. She was obviously distraught, possibly on the verge of a nervous breakdown.

Agatha and Archibald Christie in 1919. Newspapers initially suspected Archie of foul play.

The Search Is On

The next two or three days produced no clues to her whereabouts. A report of women's clothes in a lonely hut near Newlands Corner, together with a bottle labeled "opium," caused a stampede of journalists. But it proved to be a false alarm; the opium turned out to be a harmless stomach remedy. Some newspapers hinted that Archibald Christie stood to gain much from the death of his wife, but he had a perfect alibi: he was at a weekend party in Surrey. Other journalists theorized that the disappearance was a publicity stunt. One acquaintance, Peter Ritchie-Calder, suspected that she had disappeared to spite her husband and bring his affair with Nancy Neele out into the open. Ritchie-Calder then read her novels to try to predict her next move. When the *Daily Mirror* offered a reward, reports of Christie sightings poured in. But they all proved to be false alarms.

The Plot Thickens

The mystery deepened when Christie's brother-in-law revealed that he had received a letter from her whose postmark indicated that it had been posted in London at 9:45 AM on the day after her disappearance, when she was presumably wandering around in the woods of Surrey.

An interview with her husband appeared in the *Daily Mirror* the following Sunday, in which he admitted, "that my wife had discussed the possibility of disappearing at will. Some time ago she told her sister, 'I could disappear if I wished and set about it carefully . . .'" It began to look as if the disappearance, after all, might not be a matter of suicide or foul play.

Newspapers closely chronicled Christie's disappearance, with some of them, such as the *Daily Mirror*, giving full front-page space to the story.

Lost and Found

On December 14, 11 days after her disappearance, the headwaiter in the Swan Hydropathic Hotel in Harrogate, North Yorkshire, looked closely at a female guest and recognized her from newspaper photographs as the missing novelist. He telephoned the Yorkshire police, who contacted her home. Colonel Christie took an afternoon train from London to Harrogate and learned that his wife had been staying in the hotel for a week and a half. She had taken a good room on the first floor at seven guineas a week and had apparently seemed "normal and happy," and "sang, danced, played billiards, read the newspaper reports of the disappearance, chatted with her fellow guests, and went for walks."

Agatha was reading a newspaper story about her own disappearance when her husband approached her. "She only seemed to regard him as an acquaintance whose identity she could not quite fix," said the hotel's manager. Archibald Christie told the press: "She has suffered from the most complete loss of memory, and I do not think she knows who she is." A doctor later confirmed that she was suffering from amnesia. But Ritchie-Calder later remembered how little her behavior corresponded with the usual condition of amnesia. When she vanished, she had been wearing a green knitted skirt, a gray cardigan, and a velour hat, and carried a few pounds in her purse. When she was found, she was stylishly dressed and had £300 on her. She had told other guests in the hotel that she was a visitor named Teresa Neele from South Africa.

The Old Swan Hotel, formerly known as the Swan Hydropathic Hotel

The Case of the Best-Seller

The twist ending, such as the one Christie used in *The Murder of Roger Ackroyd*, greatly influenced the detective novel genre.

There were unpleasant repercussions. A public outcry, orchestrated by the press, wanted to know who was to pay the £3,000, which the search was estimated to have cost, and Surrey taxpayers blamed the next big increase on her. Her next novel, *The Big Four*, received unfriendly reviews, but nevertheless sold 9,000 copies—more than twice as many as *The Murder of Roger Ackroyd*. And from then on (as Elizabeth Walter has described in an essay called "The Case of the Escalating Sales"), her books sold in increasing quantities. By 1950 all of her books were enjoying a regular sale of more than 50,000 copies, and the final Miss Marple story, *Sleeping Murder*, had a first printing of 60,000.

Agatha Christie at work on a novel during the 1950s. Cynics say that Christie's disappearing act boosted her sales and kept her writing.

Christie's second husband, archaeologist Max Mallowan

The Mystery of Success

Agatha Christie divorced her husband (who wed Nancy Neele) and in 1930 married Professor Sir Max Mallowan. But for the rest of her life she refused to discuss her disappearance and would only grant interviews on condition that it was not mentioned. Her biographer, Janet Morgan, accepts that Christie had a nervous breakdown, followed by amnesia. Yet this is difficult to fully accept. Where did she obtain the clothes and money to go to Harrogate? Why did she register under the surname of her husband's mistress? And is it possible to believe that her amnesia was so complete that, while behaving normally, she was able to read accounts of her own disappearance, look at photographs of herself, and still not even suspect her identity?

Ritchie-Calder, who got to know her very well later in life, remains convinced that "her disappearance was calculated in the classic style of her detective stories." A television play produced after her death even speculated that the disappearance was part of a plot to murder Nancy Neele. The only thing that is certain about "the case of the disappearing mystery writer" is that it may have helped her become the best-selling fiction author of all time.

Strange Places

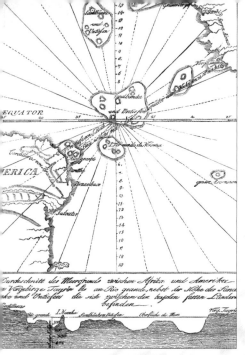

Map of Atlantis, showing mid-Atlantic

Atlantis: The Mystery of the Vanishing Continent

(9800 BCE)

Atlantis has been described as the greatest of all historical mysteries. Plato, writing about 350 BCE, was the first to speak of the great island that had vanished "in a day and a night," sinking beneath the waves of the Atlantic.

Plato's account in his dialogues *Timaeus* and *Critias* has the absorbing quality of good science fiction. The story, as recounted in *Timaeus* by poet and historian Critias, tells how Solon, the famous Athenian lawgiver, went to Sais in Egypt about 590 BCE and heard the story of Atlantis from an Egyptian priest.

Beyond the Pillars

According to the priest, Atlantis was already a great civilization when the Greeks founded Athens, which Plato dates to about 9600 BCE. Atlantis was then "a mighty power that was aggressing wantonly against the whole of Europe and Asia, and to which your city [Athens] put an end." Atlantis, said the priest, lay "beyond the pillars of Hercules" (the Strait of Gibraltar) and was larger than Libya and Turkey put together. Deserted by their allies, the Athenians fought alone against the Atlantians and finally conquered them. But at this point violent floods and earthquakes destroyed both the Athenians and the Atlantians, and Atlantis sank beneath the waves in a single day and night.

The Legend

In the second dialogue, the *Critias*, Plato goes into great detail about the history and geography of the lost continent. The Atlantians were great engineers and architects; their capital city was built on a hill, surrounded by concentric bands of land and water, joined by immense tunnels large enough for a ship to sail through. The city was about 11 miles in diameter. A huge canal connected the outermost of these rings of water to the sea. Behind the city farmers worked on a plain 230 by 340 miles. Behind the plain were mountains with many wealthy villages, fertile meadows, and all kinds of crops and livestock.

The Rock of Gibraltar, one of the pillars of Hercules, in foreground, with North Africa in the distance

Destruction

Eventually the Atlantians began to lose their wisdom and virtue, and became greedy, corrupt, and domineering. Then Zeus decided to teach them a lesson. So he called all the gods together . . .

And there, frustratingly, Plato's story breaks off. He never completed the *Critias* or wrote the third dialogue of the trilogy, the *Hermocrates*.

Most scholars have assumed that Atlantis was a folktale; even Plato's pupil Aristotle is on record as disbelieving it. Yet this seems unlikely. The *Timaeus* dialogue was one of Plato's most ambitious works; his translator Jowett called it "the greatest effort of the human mind to conceive the world as a whole which the genius of antiquity has bequeathed to us." So it seems less likely that Plato decided to insert a fairy tale into the middle of it and more likely that he wanted to preserve the story for future generations.

In the late nineteenth century, U.S. congressman Ignatius Donnelly became fascinated by Atlantis, and the result was the book *Atlantis, the Antediluvian World* (1882), which became a best-seller and has remained in print ever since. Donnelly asks

Artist's impression of the mythological city-state of Atlantis

whether Plato was recording a real catastrophe and concludes that he was. He points out that modern earthquakes and volcanic eruptions have caused tremendous damage that equals the kind Plato describes.

Donnelly also studied flood legends from Egypt to Mexico, pointing out similarities, and indicated all kinds of affinities connecting artifacts from both sides of the Atlantic. British prime minister William Gladstone was so impressed by the book that he tried to persuade the cabinet to fund a ship to trace the outlines of Atlantis. (He failed.)

Was Atlantis Santorini?

In the late 1960s archaeologist Angelos Galanopoulos propounded what is perhaps the most credible theory of the destruction of Atlantis, which he based upon the discoveries of Professor Spyridon Marinatos about the island of Santorini, or Thera, in the Mediterranean. Around the year 1500 BCE a tremendous volcanic explosion ripped apart Santorini and probably destroyed most of the civilization of the Greek islands, the coastal regions of eastern Greece, and northern Crete. This, Galanopoulos suggests, was the catastrophe that destroyed Atlantis. But surely the date is wrong? The destruction of Santorini took place a mere 900 years before Solon, not nine *thousand*.

This is the essence of Galanopoulos's argument—he believes that a scribe accidentally multiplied all of the figures in Plato's dialogue by 10. Galanopoulos points out that all of Plato's measurements seem far too large. The 10,000-stadia ditch around the plain would stretch around modern London 20 times. The width and depth of the plain behind the city, 23 by 34 miles, would be a more reasonable size than 230 by 340 miles. If all of Plato's figures are reduced in this way, then Santorini begins to sound

altogether more like Atlantis—although Galanopoulos suggests that the Atlantian civilization stretched all over the Mediterranean and that Crete itself was probably the Royal City. And how could such a mistake come about? Galanopoulos suggests that the Greek copyist mistook the Egyptian symbol for 100—a coiled rope—for the symbol for 1,000—a lotus flower.

There is only one major objection to all this: Plato states clearly that Atlantis was beyond the Pillars of Hercules. But Galanopoulos argues that the Pillars of Hercules could well refer to the two extreme southern promontories of Greece, Cape Matapan and Cape Malea, rather than the Strait of Gibraltar.

And this, on the whole, seems one of the most compelling theories of Atlantis so far.

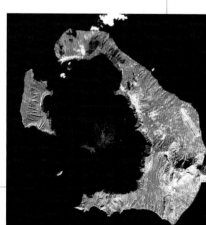

Aerial view of Santorini

A contemporary map of the Roanoke area

What Happened to the Roanoke Colony?

(1590)

In 1584 Sir Walter Raleigh sent an expedition to North America to choose a likely location to establish a permanent settlement. The expedition leaders chose what is now the Outer Banks of North Carolina as an ideal spot. The short history of Roanoke, the first English colony in the New World, was marred by savagery, xenophobic fear, and bigotry—almost all being displayed by the "civilized" Englishmen and not by the "primitive" local Algonquian Indians.

The subsequent mysterious disappearance of all of the Roanoke colonists was a grim start to European colonization of North America.

Pirate Nation

The gentleman-explorer Sir Walter Raleigh established the Roanoke colony. Queen Elizabeth I gave Raleigh a commission to create a colony in the New World, but she gave him only 10 years to do so. Considering the difficulties involved—the stormy 3,000 miles of the Atlantic Ocean, the danger of possibly hostile American Indians, and the threat of the definitely hostile Spanish conquistadores, who were already established in the Caribbean and South America—this was a huge task.

By the early 1580s England was all but at war with Spain: the Spanish Catholics regarded the English Protestants as foul heretics, while the comparatively poor English viewed the wealth of gold and silver that Spain was shipping from the Americas with considerable envy. English sailors were just waiting for war to be declared to begin officially sanctioned privateer raids against the Spanish treasure fleets. And a port colony in what would later be named North Carolina would be an ideal base.

Sir Walter Raleigh

Savage Attacks

In spring 1585, 75 men, mostly veteran soldiers, landed on what they named Roanoke Island to start building the fledgling colony. Unfortunately these men took a military attitude toward local American Indians. The Carolina Algonquian tribes were initially very welcoming, but matters soured after some of the English colonists visited a local settlement, departed amicably, and then discovered that a silver cup had gone missing. Believing that the Algonquians had stolen the cup and determined to send a firm message to "primitive savages," the English marched back, burned the tribal leader at the stake, and then sacked and burned the village. The silver cup was not found in the ravaged settlement.

After an uncomfortable year on Roanoke—with no sign of promised supply ships and angry natives all around them—the soldier-colonists hitched a ride home with the passing pirate fleet of Sir Francis Drake. On arriving a month later to discover the colony abandoned, Raleigh's supply ships left a 15-man holding force and then sailed away.

The next batch of colonists, 117 in all, arrived the following year. This group discovered that the 15 men left by the previous year's expedition had vanished; the newcomers found only the buried bones of one man. The friendly Croatan tribe, from nearby Hatteras Island, reported that unknown natives had attacked the men and that nine survivors had set off up the coast in an open boat, never to be seen again. It was with this ominous beginning that the Roanoke Colony was settled in earnest on July 22, 1587.

Happy Birthday

On August 18, 1587, colonist Eleanor Dare gave birth to a daughter she called Virginia: the first English child to be born in the Americas. Shortly thereafter Indians killed a man called George Howe as he fished for crab in Albemarle Sound. Convinced that this was the first salvo of an impending attack, the colonists sent their governor, John White (Virginia Dare's maternal grandfather), back to England to recruit additional soldiers. He necessarily took their only ship with him, leaving the remaining 116 Roanoke colonists stranded.

But the start of the Anglo-Spanish War and the attack of the Spanish Armada on the British navy, delayed Governor White's return by almost three years. When he finally returned on August 18, 1590—his granddaughter's third birthday—he found the colony completely abandoned.

The Roanoke colony's only ship departs for England as the colonists bid their governor, John White, farewell. White was the last Englishman to see the Roanoke colonists alive.

Lost

Few clues remain about what happened to the Roanoke colonists, but we can make some assumptions.

John White found no bodies or graves in the abandoned colony, making it unlikely that local tribes had massacred the inhabitants; why would raiders carry away the bodies of their victims? The then-common European prejudice that American Indians were all cannibals was certainly untrue of the Carolina Algonquian peoples.

Another possibility is that Spanish conquistadores captured and enslaved the colonists—as they had every right to do during wartime. But Spanish records indicate that Spain didn't even know that the Roanoke colony existed.

John White did find two words carved into trees at the colony site: CROATAN and CRO. This might suggest that the isolated colonists had either been kidnapped by or taken under the protection of the Croatan tribe. The Croatan had been the only friendly tribe left in the area in 1587, so one might hope that it was the latter. But the Croatans had moved inland by 1590, beyond the reach of the grieving White and his crew.

Later English colonists reported an oddly "white" strain in some Carolina Algonquians, but any hope of solving the Roanoke mystery with modern DNA studies is all but lost. The Carolina Algonquian tribes were largely obliterated within a few generations by European diseases and weapons, brought to the New World by subsequent waves of colonists.

The site of the mysterious Roanoke colony as it appears today. The scant ruins of the colony are now a popular tourist attraction.

Modern climatological studies indicate that the period between 1587 and 1589 was one of severe drought, the worst in North America for 800 years. Perhaps the starving Roanoke colonists threw themselves on the mercy and charity of local natives?

The Oak Island Money Pit

(1795 to present)

Oak Island

Mahone Bay, Nova Scotia, contains 365 islands. In summer 1795, a youth named Daniel McGinnis decided to explore one of them. Soon he came upon an oak tree with a ship's tackle block hanging from one of its lower branches. Sure that he had stumbled upon the trail of some buccaneer's treasure hoard, he decided to investigate further.

McGinnis rushed home, seeking the aid of two close friends, John Smith and Anthony Vaughan. The next day, he led the group, shovels in hand, to the marked oak tree. The diggers soon hit rock. Clearing the dirt, they found themselves in a 13-foot-wide flagstone-covered circle.

Peeling the Layers

Rather than finding buried treasure under the flagstone layer, McGinnis and his companions merely found another layer. At a depth of 10 feet they came upon a platform of oak logs. They dragged them out and at 20 feet came upon another layer of logs, and then another at 30 feet. Finally they decided to give up and dejectedly paddled home.

Frustration

McGinnis married and moved to the island, which he christened Oak Island. Soon after a new friend of his, Simeon Lynds, became intrigued by the find. Lynds raised some capital and in 1803 formed the Onslow Company, which included the original diggers, McGinnis, Smith, and Vaughan. They began work on what they now called the Money Pit.

In digging its two tunnels, the Onslow Company came upon a new barrier of oak logs every 10 feet, a layer of charcoal at 40 feet, a layer of hard putty at 50 feet, and a layer of coconut fiber at 60 feet. At 90 feet they discovered a stone inscribed with mysterious hieroglyphic-type writing. Only a few feet below that, they struck a hard surface that seemed to stretch right across the shaft. Was it a treasure chest? The men made this discovery late on a Saturday evening. They did not work on Sunday. Smith later said that they spent that day deciding how many shares each man was to receive.

The sight that met their eyes as they arrived on the Monday morning must have seemed to them like a nightmare: all but about 30 feet of the 90-foot shaft was filled with muddy water. Distraught, the treasure hunters again decided to give up.

Nova Scotia

Gold River

Western Shore

Oak Island

Mahone Bay

Aspotogan Peninsula

Indian Point

Mahone Bay

Big Tancook Island

ATLANTIC OCEAN

MAHONE BAY, CANADA

Lunenburg

Forty Years On

In 1849 a new syndicate, the Truro Company, tried again. Digging to a depth of 86 feet, workers were glad to find no sign of flooding. But on Sunday after church, they returned only to find the pit filled with water.

A horse-driven drill managed to descend to 106 feet but brought up only mud and stones. The company decided to dig yet another shaft and try to tunnel a way in from underneath. The excavators reached a depth of 109 feet without encountering water, but as they started to dig toward the main pit, a deluge poured in on them, and once again a group of treasure hunters barely escaped with their lives.

From the Sea

One of the drenched men observed that the water tasted salty. Watching the water level in the pit over a 12-hour period, the group saw that it rose and fell with the tide in the bay—the water was coming from the sea.

Now they shifted their attention to the nearest beach, Smith's Cove, 500 feet to the northeast. And as the tide went out they observed that the sand "gulched water like a sponge being squeezed." They realized that the Truro Company's second tunnel had inadvertently unplugged a waterway, which the pit's designers had dug from the main pit to Smith's Cove. As quickly as the treasure hunters pumped water out of the tunnel, the sea would refill it.

Digging revealed a huge human-made sponge of coconut fiber that stretched for 150 feet. The company found five box drains that led to a funnel-shaped sump just above the high-water mark. The water passed along a downward-sloping passage for the 500 feet to the Money Pit, reaching it just below the 90-foot level.

The searchers were elated; such elaborate precautions suggested an immense treasure. Now all that remained was to block the passage . . .

They built a dam, but the tide destroyed it. Another attempt to block the tunnel failed as the familiar rush of water flooded in. After this most recent blow, the Truro Company gave up the search.

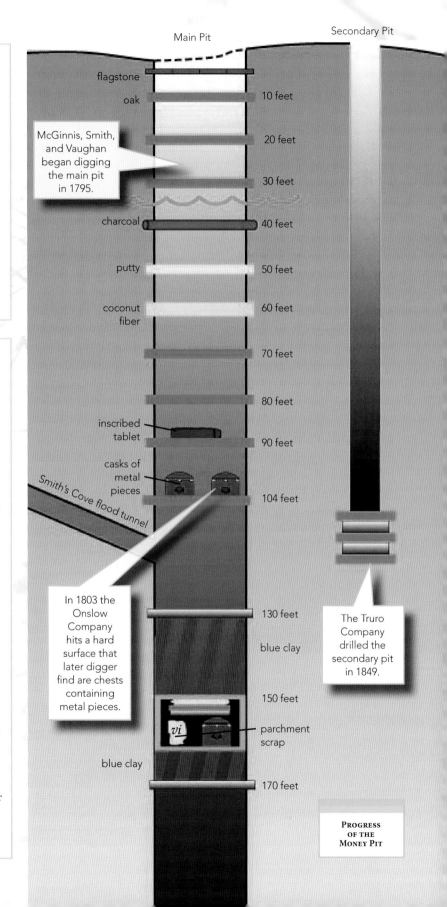

Main Pit

Secondary Pit

flagstone

oak

10 feet

McGinnis, Smith, and Vaughan began digging the main pit in 1795.

20 feet

30 feet

charcoal

40 feet

putty

50 feet

coconut fiber

60 feet

70 feet

80 feet

inscribed tablet

90 feet

casks of metal pieces

Smith's Cove flood tunnel

104 feet

In 1803 the Onslow Company hits a hard surface that later digger find are chests containing metal pieces.

130 feet

blue clay

The Truro Company drilled the secondary pit in 1849.

150 feet

vi

parchment scrap

blue clay

170 feet

PROGRESS OF THE MONEY PIT

A Death

In 1859 history repeated itself. Even with a workforce of 63 men, the newly formed Oak Island Association was unable to stem the flood. In 1861 steam pumps replaced manual pumps. The boiler promptly burst, scalding a worker to death. Work was again suspended.

In the ensuing years searchers made many more attempts, most of them digging additional shafts around the Money Pit. In 1866 a new syndicate attempted to dam up Smith's Cove, but unusually high tides defeated it. At one point workers actually discovered the site where the flood tunnel entered the Money Pit. This new discovery should have solved the problems. Workers need only block the tunnel to prevent more seawater from entering. Unfortunately shafts so honeycombed the entire area that the water could now enter from several other directions.

Yet Another Attempt

In 1891 a group calling itself the Oak Island Treasure Company tried again. It intended to "use the best modern appliances for cutting off the flow of water through the tunnel." Unfortunately their modern equipment made no difference because the treasure hunters once again attempted to cut off the flow of water at the Money Pit end.

Finally the company did what it should have done at the start: dig at the Smith's Cove end. At about 15 feet below the surface the diggers encountered a tunnel. They placed a charge of dynamite in the hole. When it detonated, a sudden rush of turbulence erupted in the water of the Money Pit, 450 feet away. The flood tunnel had almost certainly collapsed. Yet when the group attempted to pump out the pit, the water rushed back in just as quickly. The group surmised that there was a second flood tunnel, a great deal lower than the first.

The company did make significant finds during its search: between 130 and 151 feet and between 160 and 171 feet it found blue clay consisting of clay, sand, and water. The clay, forming a watertight seal, appeared to be the same "putty" encountered at the 50-foot level of the pit. What was even more intriguing was what lay hidden in the gap between the putty layers: a cement vault, 7 feet high with 7-inch thick walls. Drilling into the vault revealed a layer of wood, followed by a void of several inches, and then an unknown substance. Next came layers of soft metal, a few feet of metal pieces, and then more soft metal. Most perplexing was what the searchers found attached to the drill auger—a fragment of sheepskin parchment with the letters "vi," or "ri" in handwritten script.

Encouraged, the company sank six more shafts in its attempt to block off the newly suspected second flood tunnel; it abandoned each in turn as water gushed in. It was pointless to continue. The company had spent more than $225,000 on the operations; even if it finally recovered the treasure, there would be no guarantee that it would reimburse all the members for such enormous costs.

More Dead Ends

During the next 30 years various parties made several more attempts to excavate the Money Pit. Each attempt made it less likely that anyone would ever recover the treasure. The original site was little more than a quagmire.

In 1937 a wealthy New Jersey business owner, Gilbert D. Hedden, spent two seasons digging and drilling and reached the discouraging conclusion that the treasure chests had broken up in the waterlogged soil. He decided that if he could block off the second flood tunnel, the quagmire would slowly dry out.

Hedden decided against searching between the Money Pit and the sea. Instead he tried logic. Why had the pirates never returned for their treasure? The likeliest possibility was that the pirates had died at the end of a rope, and the vital clue might be contained in court transcripts. Hedden soon found the man who seemed to fit his theories: Captain Kidd.

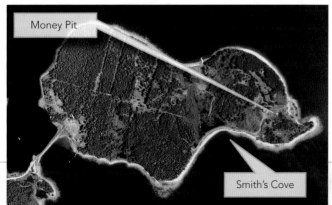

Money Pit

Smith's Cove

Aerial view of Oak Island. Smith's Cove is an inlet on the southeast end of the small island. The cove supplies the water that fills at least one of the tunnels that were added to flood the main pit 500 feet northeast.

On the Trail of the Privateer

In fact William Kidd had not been a pirate but a privateer, a sailor whose government pays him to attack enemy ships. In 1696 King William III of England had commissioned Kidd to suppress piracy and confiscate pirate loot. But Kidd was a weak and ambitious man who found attacking merchant ships easier than pursuing pirates. Authorities sent him back to England, where he was tried and executed.

On the eve of his execution Kidd was said to have made the speaker of the House of Commons an offer: Kidd would lead the authorities to his buried treasure worth 100,000 pounds.

In a 1935 book by Harold Wilkins, *Captain Kidd and his Skeleton Island*, Hedden came upon a map purporting to be Kidd's treasure island. It had an obvious similarity to Oak Island. In high spirits Hedden set off for England to interview Wilkins, who said that he'd drawn the map from memory after seeing the original in a private collection. Like all of his predecessors, Hedden had reached a dead end.

Illustration of Captain Kidd and his crew burying their loot. In the late 1930s treasure hunter Gilbert D. Hedden thought that he'd stumbled upon evidence that the Money Pit stored Kidd's hoard.

Wild Goose Chase

Next came Edwin H. Hamilton, a machine engineer who drilled down to 180 feet, deeper than anyone before him. He made an interesting discovery: the mouth of the second flood tunnel joined the Money Pit from the same side as the first one.

After Hamilton abandoned his excavations, Robert Restall, an ex-circus stunt rider, met his death in the Money Pit when exhaust gas from a pump filled the shaft. His 22-year-old son and two other men died trying to save him.

Then, in 1965, Robert Dunfield, an American petroleum geologist, once again tried the brute-force approach and brought in a gigantic clam digger and bulldozers. He could not keep the tunnels from flooding.

In 1970 Daniel Blankenship formed the Triton Alliance to explore the Money Pit. In 1976 it dug Borehole 10-X, a 237-foot tube of steel sunk 180 feet northeast of the pit. The digging uncovered several artificial cavities. A camera lowered to 230 feet revealed completely unexpected images: a severed hand floating in the water, three chests, an assortment of tools—and a human body. Divers sent to investigate these amazing finds met strong currents and such poor visibility that they had to turn back. Not long after, the hole collapsed, obliterating the Money Pit.

So the mystery remains: who built the Money Pit?

Rupert Furneaux's book *The Money Pit* suggests that British army engineers at the end of the Revolutionary War constructed it to hide the garrison's war chests, which contained money to pay the British army. If that's the case, the army retrieved the money and took it back to England. This seems to be the likeliest explanation for the total failure of all the syndicates to find the slightest sign of treasure. Still the Triton Alliance continues the quest.

Mystery of the Moving Coffins

(1812–1820)

Christ Church, Oistin, Barbados

On August 9, 1812, pallbearers carried the coffin of the Hon. Thomas Chase, a slave owner on the Caribbean island of Barbados, down the steps of the family vault in the Christ Church cemetery in the town of Oistin. As they moved aside the heavy slab and the lamplight illuminated the interior, it became clear that something strange had happened. One of the three coffins already occupying the vault lay on its side. Another lay head-downward in a corner. But no sign of forced entry supported the obvious theory of desecration. Even so, the local white population had no doubt that black laborers were responsible for the violation; Thomas Chase had been a ruthless man. In fact the last coffin laid in the vault—only a month before Chase's—was that of his daughter, Dorcas Chase. According to rumor, she starved herself to death because of her father's brutality.

The Unquiet Grave

Four years went by; then two members of the Chase family were buried within seven weeks of each other, both of them in lead coffins. Each time, the burial party found the coffins tumbled, but there was no evidence of human entry. Even the heavy lead-encased coffin of Thomas Chase, which took eight men to lift, had moved. A wooden coffin—that of Thomasina Goddard, the first occupant of the vault—had disintegrated into planks, apparently as a result of its rough treatment. The planks were tied together roughly with wire, and the coffin was placed against the wall. After each burial, the coffins were carefully lined up and the vault firmly sealed.

   The story had now become something of a sensation in the islands. A local magistrate and Rev. Thomas Orderson of Christ Church made a careful search of the vault, trying to figure out how the vandals had got in. There was undoubtedly no secret door; the stone floor, walls, and ceiling were solid and uncracked. Orderson also exonerated floods as the culprit. Although the vault lay two feet below ground level, it had been excavated out of solid limestone; floods would have marked the stone. Besides, it was unlikely that heavy lead-encased coffins would float. Orderson dismissed the theory held by the local black population that the tomb had been cursed.

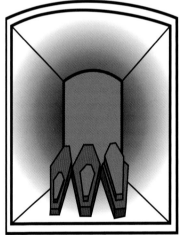
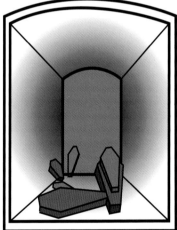

The positions of the coffins before and after the vault was opened for Thomas Chase's internment. When his daughter, Dorcas, died in 1812 her coffin was placed beside the other occupants: the wooden coffin of Thomasina Goddard, interred in 1808, and a child's lead coffin interred in the same year. The child's coffin was standing head downward in a corner and Dorcas's was on its side.

Trouble in the Tomb

By the time the next burial took place, there was a great deal of public interest. In July 1819 when pallbearers carried the cedar coffin of Thomazina Clarke into the vault, an audience of nearly 100 had gathered to watch. The cement took a long time to remove from the door—it had been used in abundance to reseal the vault—and even when it had been chipped away, the door refused to yield. Considerable effort revealed that the coffin of Thomas Chase was now jammed against it, 6 feet from where it had been placed. All the other coffins were disturbed, with the exception of the wire-bound coffin of Thomasina Goddard. This seemed to underscore the notion that flooding was not the answer—would lead-encased coffins float while wooden planks lay unmoved?

The governor, Lord Combermere, now ordered an exhaustive search. But it only verified what Orderson proclaimed: vandals could not have forced their way in, there was no hidden trapdoor, and no entrances for floodwater. Before the tomb was resealed, the governor ordered that the floor be sprinkled with sand, which would show footprints. Then once again laborers cemented the door shut. Combermere then pressed his private seal into the wet cement.

Interior of the Chase Vault today

An inscription still identifies the Chase vault, although the coffins left it in 1820.

Abandoned

Eight months later, the governor decided to investigate whether their precautions had been effective. A party of nine, including the governor, the rector, and two masons made their way to the vault. They verified that the cement was undisturbed and the seals intact. Yet, once again, the place was in chaos. The child's coffin lay on the steps that led down into the chamber, while Thomas Chase's coffin was upside down. Only Thomasina Goddard's bundle of planks remained undisturbed. The sand on the floor was still unmarked. Once again the masons struck the walls with their hammers, looking for a secret entrance. And finally, when it seemed obvious that the mystery was insoluble, Lord Combermere ordered that the coffins be removed and buried elsewhere. After that the tomb remained empty.

The Mystery Remains

None of the many writers on the case have been able to supply a plausible explanation. Flooding would have disarranged Thomasina Goddard's coffin and moved the sand on the floor. No earthquakes during the period were reported. And vandals could not have broken in without leaving any traces.

Yet a "supernatural" explanation is just as implausible. It has been suggested that the disturbances began *after* the burial of a woman believed to have committed suicide; the suggestion is that the other "spirits" refused to rest at ease with a suicide. Moving coffins might suggest such a poltergeist, but all investigators agree that a poltergeist needs some kind of "energy source"—often an emotionally disturbed adolescent living on the premises. And an empty tomb can provide no such energy source.

Many locals believed there was some kind of voodoo at work—some magical force deliberately conjured by a witch seeking revenge on hated slave owners. It sounds unlikely, but it is the best explanation ever offered.

The Secrets of Rennes-le-Château

(1885)

Church of Sainte-Marie-Madeleine

Rennes-le-Château is a tiny village on the French side of the Pyrenees in the region of Languedoc. In the first millennium BCE it was a prosperous town, known to the Phoenicians and the Romans, who called it Reddae. For more than 1,000 years it thrived in relative obscurity. In the fourteenth century CE half the town was destroyed in a siege; the plague carried off most of the rest of the inhabitants. Since then Rennes-le-Château has been a mere village.

In 1885 a new priest arrived in the village: 33-year-old Bérenger Saunière, known as a rebel. His superiors had sent Saunière to Rennes-le-Château, pretty well the end of the world, as a kind of punishment. He was a pauper when he arrived, but a strange discovery inside the church of Sainte-Marie-Madeleine sent him to Paris—and Saunière returned, mysteriously, showered in wealth.

The Discovery

For the first three years of Saunière's stay in Rennes-le-Château, as his account books show, he was very poor indeed. In 1888 he started some repairs on the church of Sainte-Marie-Madeleine. Workers lifted the top of the high altar and discovered that one of the two pillars on which it rested was hollow. Hidden inside were three wooden tubes, each containing a roll of parchment. The parchments seemed to be in some kind of code. Saunière showed them to the bishop of Carcassonne, who sent him to Paris to consult experts at the church of Saint Sulpice.

When Saunière returned to Rennes-le-Château he was a rich man. He built the villagers a mountain road and a water tower, and had the church elaborately but strangely decorated with such oddities as an enormous lame demon carrying the font of holy water. Over the door he had inscribed, TERRIBILIS EST LOCUS ISTE ("Dreadful is this place").

Encoded Treasure

The Asmodeus font

Where had Saunière's sudden wealth come from? The only clue is that the code on the parchments contained the words, "Teniers and Poussin hold the key." And while in Paris, Saunière had purchased for himself reproductions of two pictures: *The Temptation of Saint Antony* by David Teniers the Younger and *The Shepherds of Arcadia* by Nicolas Poussin.

The lame demon has been identified as Asmodeus, guardian of King Solomon's legendary treasure. And so it has been speculated that the coded manuscript led Saunière to a treasure—possibly the treasure of the Cathars, a heretical sect associated with this region, whose last adherents were burned alive in 1243 after a siege at the mountain of Montségur. It is said that three men escaped the siege and that they carried with them the "treasure of the Cathars." Others believe, however, that the treasure was a group of holy books.

Secret Societies

In recent years Henry Lincoln, an English scholar, has thrown new light on the mystery. With the use of a computer, he claims to have decoded Saunière's manuscript and discovered the hidden secrets of the paintings by Teniers and Poussin, particularly the latter, which pictures a tomb close to the village of Rennes-le-Château.

Lincoln is convinced that Saunière's secret was simple. Rennes-le-Château was once called Aereda and was an important center of the Knights Templar, the order dedicated to guarding the Temple of Jerusalem. Lincoln has uncovered evidence that the Templars were connected with another secret order known as the Priory of Sion, also connected with the Temple of Jerusalem. There seems to be strong evidence that this secret society continued down the ages, and that the Rosicrucians, a fellowship of mystic-philosopher-doctors dedicated to studying nature, the physical universe, and the spiritual realm, which formed in seventeenth-century Germany, were actually the Priory of Sion, who were simply using a new name.

In short, it looks as if Saunière stumbled upon some secret of the Rosicrucians and that the money he received came from them.

One of the two versions of the *Shepherds of Arcadia* that Nicolas Poussin painted in the 1630s, which may hold important clues to the secret of Rennes-le-Château

Heresy in Rennes-le-Château

There is still a great deal of mystery involved. In 1910 Saunière's bishop suspended him as a priest, but Saunière continued to say Mass in the chapel he built himself. When Saunière died of a stroke in 1917, he made a confession that deeply shocked the priest who heard it. Some say Saunière confided that he'd found evidence to prove that Jesus did not die on the cross, but instead escaped to France; in fact to Rennes-le-Château. This would imply that the whole foundation of Christianity is unsound: no crucifixion, no vicarious atonement for the human race.

Perhaps it is just as well that the ultimate mystery of Rennes-le-Château remains unsolved.

Engraved memorial stone on the tomb of Father Saunière

The Mystery of Eilean Mòr—the Island of Disappearing Men

(December 15, 1900)

Flannan Lighthouse today

In the empty Atlantic, 17 miles to the west of the Hebrides, lie the Flannan Islands, the largest and most northerly of which is called Eilean Mòr. Its name has become synonymous with an apparently insoluble mystery of the sea.

Although Hebridean shepherds often ferried their sheep over to the islands to graze on the rich grass, they themselves never spent a night there, claiming that the islands were haunted. The waters of the area are dangerous, and in 1895 the Northern Lighthouse Board (NLB), the lighthouse authority for Scotland and the Isle of Man, announced plans to erect a lighthouse on Eilean Mòr. The lighthouse finally opened in December 1899 and for the next year its beam could be seen reflected on the rough seas between the Isle of Lewis and the Flannans.

Then, 11 days before Christmas in 1900, the light went out.

Tidy House

The weather was too stormy for the NLB steamer *Hesperus* to investigate immediately, though everyone voiced concern for the three men tending the lighthouse: James Ducat, Donald McArthur, and Thomas Marshall. Finally, on December 26, *Hesperus* could make her way to the island. In the heavy swell she had to make three approaches before she was able to moor by the lighthouse's eastern jetty. No flags had answered the steamer's signals, and her crew saw no sign of life.

Harbormaster Joseph Moore rushed to investigate. He found doors closed, the clock in the main room stopped, and the ashes in the fireplace cold. Afraid, Moore waited for two seamen to join him before venturing upstairs. All they found, however, were neatly made beds in the tidy sleeping quarters.

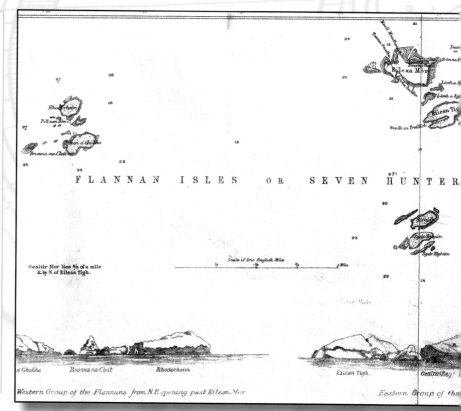

The Investigation

The *Hesperus* returned to the Isle of Lewis with the mystery unsolved. Two days later investigators landed on Eilean Mòr, and tried to reconstruct what had happened. An investigation proved that the light had not failed for lack of oil; the wicks were trimmed and the lights were all ready to be lit. The last entry in the record of James Ducat, the chief lighthouse keeper, was dated December 15 at 9:00 AM, the day the light went out. Everything was in order; clearly, the men had completed their basic duties for the day. Whatever happened to the men occurred, therefore, between the time they finished their daytime duties and darkness, when they regularly lit the lamp.

At first it looked as if the solution was straightforward. On the western jetty they found a number of ropes entangled around a crane that was 65 feet above sea level. A tool chest kept in a crevice 45 feet above this was missing. It looked as if the gale had sent a 100-foot wave crashing into the island, sweeping the tool chest—as well as the three men—away. Also missing were Ducat's and Marshall's oilskin raincoats, water-resistant garments worn only when they visited the jetties. So the investigators had a plausible theory. Ducat and Marshall had feared that the crane was damaged in the storm; they had struggled to the jetty in their oilskins, then been caught by a sudden huge wave. But in that case, what had happened to the third man, Donald McArthur, whose oilskins remained in the lighthouse?

The windswept island of Eilean Mòr, shown at the top right of the map, left, is part of the Flannan Isles, also known as the Seven Hunters Isles. Today, only seabirds, such as the northern gannet, shown below, inhabit the remote and rocky island.

Unsuitable Theories

All of these theories were dashed when someone pointed out that the 15th had been a calm day; the storms had not started until the following day. Perhaps Ducat had simply entered the wrong date by mistake? Investigators had to abandon that hypothesis, too, when Captain Holman of the steamship *Archer* reported that he had passed close to the islands on the night of December 15, and that the light was already out.

Other hypotheses, too, have been suggested and discarded. If one man were in danger of drowning, the other two might have also drowned saving him—but surely they would not have taken the time to don oilskins first. Moreover, if someone had fallen in, the rescuers would have thrown him a lifebelt and rope (provided on the jetties for just such an emergency), instead of jumping in themselves.

One last theory was that one of the three men had gone insane and pushed the others to their deaths, then thrown himself into the sea. It is just possible—but there is little evidence to support it.

Vanished

The British broadcaster Valentine Dyall suggested the most plausible explanation in his book *Unsolved Mysteries* (1954). He recounts the experience of Scottish journalist Iain Campbell, who witnessed a freak wave some 70 feet above the jetty on Eilean Mòr in 1947. It lingered for a minute, then subsided. The lighthouse keeper told him that this curious "upheaval" occurs periodically and that several men had barely avoided being dragged into the sea. Such an eruption could certainly have caught off-guard the three lighthouse keepers in 1900.

But it is still hard to understand how all three men could be involved in such an accident. McArthur was not wearing his oilskins, so it is highly unlikely that he was on the jetty (and he was probably in the tower itself). Even if his companions were swept away, would he have been foolish enough to rush to the jetty and fling himself in to save them?

One thing is clear: on a calm December day at the turn of the century, a tragedy snatched three men off Eilean Mòr and left few clues to the mystery.

The Bermuda Triangle

The Bermuda Triangle
(1918 to present)

On the afternoon of December 5, 1945, five Avenger torpedo bombers took off from Fort Lauderdale, Florida, for a routine two-hour patrol over the Atlantic. By 2:15 PM the planes of Flight 19 were well over the Atlantic, following their usual patrol route. The weather was warm and clear. At 3:45 PM the control tower received a message from Lt. Charles Taylor: "This is an emergency. We seem to be off course. We cannot see land . . . repeat . . . we cannot see land."

Despite the setting sun, the men couldn't identify their direction and could only say that everything looked strange, including the ocean. The situation grew desperate. Unless the planes could return to land quickly, they would run out of fuel. A giant Martin Mariner flying boat, with a crew of 13, took off at 6:27 PM on a rescue mission. Twenty-three minutes later, observers watched a bright orange flash light up the eastern sky. Neither the Martin Mariner nor the Avengers ever returned. Six airplanes vanished completely, as other planes and ships have vanished in the area that has become known as the Devil's Triangle, or the Bermuda Triangle.

Vincent Gaddis Sounds the Alarm

The disappearance of Flight 19 was not the first such event in the area, nor would it be the last. Over the next two decades, at least 15 additional disappearances in the 50-mile region between Florida and the Bahamas cost more than 200 lives.

One of the first people to realize that all this amounted to a frightening mystery was journalist Vincent Gaddis. In February 1964 his article "The Deadly Bermuda Triangle" appeared in *Argosy* magazine, and bestowed the now familiar name on that mysterious stretch of ocean. A year later, in a book about sea mysteries called *Invisible Horizon*, Gaddis included a long list of ships that had vanished in the area, beginning with the *Rosalie,* which vanished in 1840, and ending with the yacht *Connemara IV* in 1956. In the final chapter Gaddis entered the realm of science fiction and speculated on a space-time continuum, implying that some of the missing planes and ships had vanished down a kind of fourth-dimensional plughole.

U.S. Navy Avenger torpedo bombers—the ill-fated planes of Flight 19

The USS *Cyclops*

Flight 19 vanished just after World War II, but the closing months of World War I saw an even more spectacular disappearance. In January 1918, the USS *Cyclops*—a navy cargo ship—sailed to Brazilian waters to fuel British ships in aid of the war effort. On February 16 the *Cyclops* and her 306 crewmen left from Rio de Janeiro for the return voyage home. After having been last seen at Barbados on March 3 and 4, she disappeared in the Bermuda Triangle. No trace of the ship nor any of her crew was ever found, and the *Cyclops* remains the single most devastating non-combat loss in U.S. naval history.

The U.S. Navy launched the *Cyclops* in 1910. The ship, which carried a cargo of heavy manganese, was lost at sea in 1918. No wreckage nor any trace of the crew were ever found.

Ivan Sanderson Makes a Map

Scottish naturalist and writer Ivan Sanderson felt that Robert Gaddis's spacetime theory was going to too far into the realm of science fiction to adequately explain what was happening in the Bermuda Triangle. Relying on his scientific training, Sanderson marked a number of areas where disappearances had occurred on a map of the world. There was, for example, another "Devil's Triangle" south of the Japanese island of Honshu where ships and planes had vanished.

Below are various versions of the triangle's boundaries. Since Sanderson first drew a map of the Bermuda Triangle, other writers and researchers have redrawn its boundaries.

Always the Innovator

Christopher Columbus may have been the first person to record an encounter with the forces of the Bermuda Triangle. During a 1492 journey in the area, he wrote in his log that his compass acted strangely, and he described seeing weird lights in the sky.

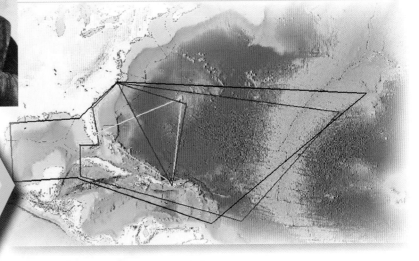

Berlitz Hits the Jackpot

Sporadic attempts to investigate the Bermuda Triangle and explain its peculiar effects occurred for the next three years, but the general public remained largely in the dark. That changed in 1974, when Charles Berlitz, a well-regarded linguist and creator of a successful language-learning course, once again rehashed the story of the Bermuda Triangle in a new book. Berlitz persuaded a commercial publisher, Doubleday, to publish it, and the book promptly jumped to the top of the best-seller lists. Berlitz was the first man to turn the mystery into a worldwide sensation, and to become rich on the proceeds.

Skeptics were roused to a fury, blasting the public with articles, books, and television programs debunking the Bermuda Triangle. They adopted the commonsense approach: the disappearances were all due to natural causes, particularly to freak storms. Yet the sheer quantity of disappearances in the area, most of them never even yielding a body or a trace of wreckage, somewhat disputes this explanation.

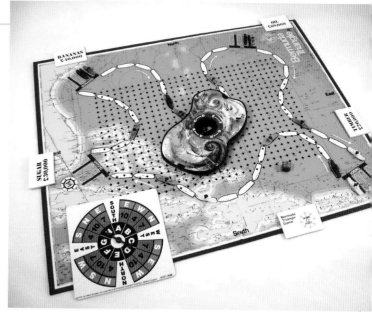

The overwhelming success of Charles Berlitz's book *The Bermuda Triangle* set off a popular-culture craze. Whether one was a believer or a skeptic, consumers in the mid-1970s could find plenty of new material on the mystery. There were also products that exploited the phenomenon for fun, such as the Milton Bradley board game The Bermuda Triangle, introduced in 1976. It came complete with a magnetic cloud that could move or destroy a player's "ship" as it made its way from port to port.

Those Who Escaped

Is there, then, an alternative which appeals to common sense? One such theory rests on the evidence of some of those who have escaped the Bermuda Triangle. In November 1964 charter pilot Chuck Wakely was returning from Nassau to Miami, Florida. He had climbed up to 8,000 feet when he noticed a faint glow around the wings of his plane. This increased steadily, and all his electronic equipment began to fail. Then slowly the glow faded, and his instruments once again functioned normally.

In 1966 Captain Don Henry was steering his tug from Puerto Rico to Fort Lauderdale on a clear afternoon. He heard shouting, and hurried to the bridge. There he saw that the compass was spinning clockwise. A strange darkness came down, and the horizon disappeared. A later report stated that, "The water seemed to be coming from all directions." And although the electric generators were still running, all electric power faded away. An auxiliary generator refused to start. The boat seemed to be surrounded by fog. Fortunately the engines were still working, and suddenly the boat emerged from the fog. To Henry's amazement, the fog was concentrated into a single solid bank, and only within this area was the sea turbulent; outside the area the sea remained calm. Henry remarked that the compass behaved as it did when a large deposit of iron affects the needle.

Divine Retribution?

In December 2008 a plane carrying 11 passengers disappeared en route to Mayaguana Island in the Bahamas. The twin-engine plane took off from the Dominican Republic on December 15. The pilot, Adriano Jimenez, was flying with only a student licence. In addition there were reports that he had stolen the plane.

Jimenez sent out an emergency signal approximately 35 minutes after taking off and then disappeared from radar. The U.S. Coast Guard scoured an area of about 5,300 square miles but turned up nothing before suspending its search.

The Magnet Theory

Earth is, of course, a gigantic magnet, and magnetic lines of force run around its surface in strange patterns. Birds and animals use these lines of force for migrating, or "homing" behavior. But there are areas of the earth's surface where birds lose their way because the lines form a magnetic anomaly or vortex. The *Marine Observer* for 1930 warns sailors about a magnetic disturbance in the neighborhood of the Tambora volcano, near Sumbawa, which deflected a ship's compass by six points. Dr. John de Laurier of Ottawa camped on the ice floes of northern Canada in 1974 in search of an enormous magnetic anomaly 43 miles long, which he believed originated about 18 miles below the surface of the earth. De Laurier's theory is that such anomalies occur where the earth's tectonic plates rub together—an occurrence that also causes earthquakes.

A Disturbance in the Force

The central point is that our earth is not like an ordinary bar magnet, whose field is symmetrical and precise; it is full of magnetic "pitfalls" and anomalies, possibly due to movements in its molten iron core. Such movements would in fact produce shifting patterns in the earth's field and bursts of magnetic activity. If they are related to fault zones, then we would expect them to occur in definitive areas, just as earthquakes do. A magnetic disturbance would cause compasses to spin, rather like a huge magnetic meteor roaring up from the center of the earth. On the sea it would produce violent turbulence, affecting the water in the same way the moon affects the tides, but in an irregular pattern, so that the water would appear to be coming "from all directions." Clouds and mist would be sucked into the vortex, forming a "bank" in its immediate area. And electronic gadgetry would probably go haywire.

All this reminds us why simplistic explanations of the Bermuda Triangle—books contending that the mystery is a journalistic invention—are not only superficial but dangerous. They discourage the investigation of one of the most interesting scientific enigmas of our time.

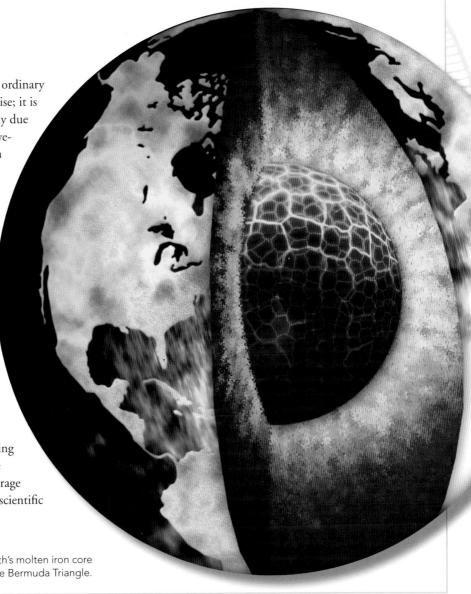

The magnetic force emanating from the earth's molten iron core may explain the strange disturbances in the Bermuda Triangle.

Strange Happenings

Can a human spontaneously ignite?

Spontaneous Human Combustion

(1400s to present)

On the morning of July 2, 1951, Pansy Carpenter, owner of the Allamanda Apartments in Saint Petersburg, Florida, noticed a strange odor. She tried the door of a tenant's apartment—67-year-old Mary Reeser—and shrieked: the metal doorknob was searingly hot. Stepping through the open door, Carpenter saw, through the haze of superheated air, what was left of Mary Reeser.

Mary Reeser

Fire had reduced Reeser, a robust woman; the well-stuffed armchair in which she had been sitting; and the side table beside it to a pile of fine ashes interspersed with blackened, heat-eroded chair springs. The carpet bore a 6-foot circle burned away around the woman's remains. The ashes still glowed red-hot.

A moist, slightly sticky black soot coated everything above a line 4 feet from the floor. Below that demarcation, the room was virtually undamaged—heat had slightly darkened only the paint on the wall immediately behind the armchair.

Plastic fittings above the smoke-line had melted like candle wax, but a pile of newspapers, just outside the scorched circle, was not even browned. And just outside the area of burned carpet lay a severed, but wholly untouched left foot, still inside its slipper.

Reeser had simply turned to ash, evidently burning not like a bonfire, but like a smoldering cigar.

Explaining the Impossible

There was no sign of gasoline or any other accelerant on Reeser's remains—in fact there was no evidence of suicide or any foul play in the strange burning.

The official explanation was that Reeser had dropped a cigarette onto her rayon night-clothes, which had ignited, killing her within seconds. The fat in her body then fueled the fire until she was just ash.

But this explanation created more questions than it answered. Chief among its critics was Wilton Krugman, professor of physical anthropology at the University of Pennsylvania. He wrote:

I find it hard to believe that a human body, once ignited, will literally consume itself. . . . [It will] burn itself out, as does a candlewick, guttering in the last residual pool of melted wax.

Only at 30,000°F-plus (over 16,600°C) have I seen bones fuse—or melt, so that it ran and became volatile. These are very great heats—they would sear, char, scorch, or otherwise mar or affect everything within a considerable radius. What I'm driving at is this: The terrific destruction of Mrs. Reeser's body (bones included) must have been accompanied by such heat that the room itself should have been burned much more than it was.

Investigators sift through the ashy remains of Mary Reeser.

A Horrific History

It may be that spontaneous human combustion (SHC)—human beings bursting into flame for no traceable reason—has occurred repeatedly, if very rarely, throughout history. Some of our ancestors thought that people who turned to a pile of ashes had incurred the anger of the gods and been struck by a thunderbolt. But could they have actually been victims of an unknown physical process within the body?

Documented examples of apparent SHC are rare, yet they crop up in history books with disturbing regularity. Indeed there are dozens of recorded cases.

For example, Thomas H. Bartholini's 1654 pamphlet, *Historiarum Anatomicarrum Rariorum*, mentions "a knight [called] Polonus, during the time of good Queen Bona Sforza [who reigned in Milan from 1469 to 1476], consumed two ladles of strong wine, vomited a flame and was thereupon totally consumed."

Nichole Millet, the alcoholic wife of an innkeeper in Rheims, France, had spontaneously combusted on February 20, 1725. A contemporary report noted that "a part of the head only, with a portion of the lower extremities and a few of the vertebrae, had escaped combustion. A foot and a half of the flooring under the body had been consumed, but a kneading-trough and a powder tub, which were very near the body, had sustained no injury."

More recently, in 1997, in County Kerry, Ireland, the community nurse who regularly visited him found the charred remains of 76-year-old John O'Connor in his living room. His head, upper torso, and feet were unburned, and there was almost no fire or smoke damage to the furniture.

Witnessing the Flames

Rarely it seems, does anyone witness another person spontaneously combust. One case is that of Jeannie Saffin of Edmonton, London. On the afternoon of September 15, 1982, 82-year-old Jack Saffin noticed a flash of light as he and his daughter, 61-year-old Jeannie, sat in their kitchen. When he turned to ask Jeannie if she'd seen it too, he saw that flames had enveloped her face and hands. He dragged her to the sink in an effort to douse the flames and shouted to his son-in-law to come help. When EMTs arrived to take Jeannie to the hospital they saw that flames had not damaged the kitchen.

Jeannie, who was mentally disabled, died of severe burns eight days later. The police who investigated the case found no evidence of accelerants or even a reasonable source for the flames—in fact they could find no cause at all for Jeannie's combustion.

Theories

Charles Dickens, in his 1853 novel *Bleak House*, killed off the villainous miser Krook with spontaneous combustion. Although heavily criticized by some scientists for "giving currency to vulgar error," Dickens was unrepentant. He had reported on a case of apparent SHC as a young journalist and felt the subject needed proper scientific investigation.

Unfortunately, given the rarity of apparent SHC cases (and its downright weirdness), little scientific research has been conducted on the subject. It has been noted that being elderly, overweight, and alcoholic seems to increase one's risk of such a death, but this is by no means always the case.

Suggested explanations range from ball-lightning strikes to static electricity buildup to, of course, the perennial wrath of God. But no conclusive proof exists.

At present the only theory to enjoy any level of scientific acceptance is the "wick effect." It suggests that something—such as a cigarette—ignites the victim's clothes. The resulting flame releases melted fat from the dead victim's flesh into the cloth of the clothes, and this then burns steadily, like a candlewick, until fire reduces all of the fat, and the body, to greasy ashes.

Illustration of the fiery death of Krook, a rag and bottle merchant, in Dickens's *Bleak House*

Crop Circles: UFOs, Whirlwinds, or Hoaxers?

(1678 to present)

Inside a crop circle

On August 14, 1980, farmer John Scull, of Westbury in Wiltshire, England, found a field of his oats crushed to the ground in three large circles, each 60 feet in diameter. Close examination of the flattened cereal revealed that the circles had not been made at the same time—that in fact, the damage had been spread over a period of two or three months, probably between May and the end of July of that year. The edges of the circles were sharply defined, and all the grain within the circles was flattened in the same direction, creating a clockwise swirling effect around the centers. None of the oats had been cut—merely flattened. The effect might have been produced by a very tall, strong man standing in the center of each circle and swinging a heavy weight around on a long piece of rope.

A Hoax Unearthed

Now the national press began to cover the phenomena, and the British public soon became familiar with the strange circle formations. Unidentified Flying Object (UFO) enthusiasts appeared on television explaining their view: that the phenomena could be explained only by flying saucers. Skeptics preferred the notion of fraud. This latter view seemed to be confirmed when circles found at Bratton turned out to be a hoax sponsored by the *Daily Mirror*; a family named Shepherd had been paid to duplicate other Bratton circles. They did this by entering the field on stilts and trampling the crops underfoot. But, significantly, the hoax was quickly detected by Bob Rickard, the editor of an anomaly magazine, the *Fortean Times,* who noted the telltale signs of human intruders.

One of the many Wiltshire, England, crop circles

Summer Whirlwinds?

Dr. Terence Meaden, an atmospheric physicist, suggested that the circles had been produced by a summer whirlwind. Such wind effects are not uncommon on open farmland. But Dr. Meaden had to admit that he had never seen or heard of a whirlwind creating circles.

Moreover, it was noted that the center point on all three circles was off center by as much as 4 feet. The swirling patterns around these points were therefore oval, not circular. This seemed to contradict another theory, namely that vandals had caused the damage; vandals would hardly go to the trouble of creating precise ellipses.

The Mowing Devil

Did crop circles first appear in 1678? This British pamphlet, or "chapbook," tells a fable about a miserly farmer, too cheap to pay a laborer to cut his oats. "That the Devil himself should Mow his oats before he [the worker] should have anything to do with them!" said the farmer. But he would pay for invoking the name of the wicked one. That night, the oat field seemed to be on fire, but the next morning, the oats had been cut in circles, with every stem placed neatly. This frightened the cheap farmer so much that he was too afraid to gather the harvest.

A Pattern Forms

On August 19, 1981, another three-circle formation appeared in a wheat field below Cheesefoot Head, near Winchester in Hampshire. These circles had been created simultaneously and, unlike the widely dispersed circles in Wiltshire, were in close formation—one circle measured 60 feet across with two 25-foot circles on either side. But the sides of these circles had the same precise edges as the Wiltshire circles, and again, the swirl of the flattened plants was slightly off center, creating ellipses.

A group of three circles appeared in a wheat field in the Hampshire village of Cheesefoot Head in 1981, and many others have since formed there. One researcher spoke to a retired area farmer who said that crop circles have been appearing in Cheesefoot Head fields since 1922.

Increasing Complexity

Over the next two years the number of circles in Great Britain increased, as did their complexity. And in the next decades, the circles would show up in more places and in many forms. There were crop circles with "rings" around them—flattened pathways several feet wide that ran around the outer edge in neat circles. Some even appeared with two or three such rings. Quintuplet formations and "singletons" also continued to appear.

It began to look as if whoever—or whatever—was creating the circles took pleasure in taunting the investigators. When believers in the whirlwind theory pointed out that the swirling had so far been clockwise, a counterclockwise circle promptly appeared. When it was suggested that a hoaxer might be making the circles with the aid of a helicopter, a crop circle was found directly beneath a power line. When an aerial photographer named Busty Taylor mentioned that he would like to see a formation in the shape of a Celtic cross, a Celtic cross appeared the next day. And, as if to rule out all possibility of natural causes, one "sextuplet" in Hampshire in 1990 had keylike objects sticking out of the sides, producing the impression of an ancient pictogram.

What Can They Mean?

In a 1990 symposium, The Crop Circle Enigma, John Michell made the important suggestion that the crop circles have a meaning, which "is to be found in the way people are affected by them." In conjunction with this idea, Michell noted that "Jung discerned the meaning of UFOs as agents and portents of changes in human thought patterns, and that function has been clearly inherited by crop circles."

An aerial view of the crop circle formation at Avebury Manor, Wiltshire, which appeared in July 2008. Some observers interpret the pattern as if it were an ancient pictogram depiction of our solar-system as it will appear December 21, 2012—the date many believe is the last day of the Maya calendar.

Crop circles originally cropped up in Great Britain, but they now appear all over the world, such as this one in the Vaud canton of Switzerland, in 2008. The mysterious circle of unknown origin swirls through a wheat field, attracting the curious to come investigate its patterns.

The Culprits Revealed?

In 1999 a gentleman from Southampton, England, came forward to take credit for at least some crop circles. Douglas Bower told the BBC that he, along with his friend David Chorley, had used a wooden plank to flatten crops and create the circles. He also said that the two men had been making the circles since 1991. Bower even demonstrated his technique for the cameras.

But rather than putting the matter to rest, Bower's confession ignited the fury of some who remained convinced that the circles were the work of extraterrestrial beings.

Their Range Expands

Today it seems that an entire industry has grown up around crop circles. Web sites and books about the subject abound. Those who want to learn more can watch one of several documentaries and at least one feature-length film—the 2002 *Signs*, starring Mel Gibson. Enthusiasts can also participate in any of several conferences around the world, including the annual Glastonbury Symposium in the United Kingdom or the Independent Crop Circle Researchers' Association conference in the United States.

The most recent development in the world of crop circles has nothing to do with their origin, but rather with commerce: today, companies ranging from Nike and Microsoft to Shredded Wheat have advertised their wares in fields across the world.

The Devil's Footprints

(1855)

The Devil's cloven hooves

On the morning of February 8, 1855, Albert Brailsford, the principal of the village school in Topsham, Devon, walked out of his front door to find that it had snowed in the night. He was intrigued to notice a line of footprints—or rather hoofprints—running down the village street. At first glance they looked like the ordinary hoofprints of a shod horse. A closer look revealed that this was impossible: the prints ran in a continuous line, one in front of the other. If it had been a horse, then it must have had only one leg and hopped along the street. And if the unknown creature had two legs, then it must have placed one carefully in front of the other, as if walking along a tightrope. Odder still, the prints—each about 4 inches long—were only about 8 inches apart. Each print was very distinct, as if it had been branded into the frozen snow with a hot iron.

Over Hill, Over Dale

Brailsford alerted his neighbors, and soon a party of villagers was following the tracks southward through the snow. The villagers halted in astonishment when the hoofprints ended at a brick wall. They were even more baffled when someone discovered that the prints continued on the other side of the wall and that the snow atop the wall was undisturbed. The tracks also approached a haystack and continued on the other side of that, although the hay remained neat and tidy. The prints passed under gooseberry bushes and were even seen on rooftops. It looked as if some practical joker had decided to set the village of Topsham an insoluble puzzle.

The excited investigators tracked the prints for mile after mile over the Devon countryside. The prints wandered erratically through a number of small towns and villages. If it had been a practical joker, he would have had to cover about 100 miles, much of it through deep snow. Moreover, he would surely have hurried forward to cover the greatest distance possible. Yet the steps wandered, often approaching front doors, then going away again. At some point the creature had crossed the estuary of the river Exe; it looked as if it crossed between Lympstone and Powderham. Yet there were also footprints in Exmouth, farther south, as if it had turned back on its tracks. There was no logic in its meandering course.

The Devil's Hoof

In places it looked as though the horseshoe had a split in it, suggesting a cloven hoof. There had been rumors at that time of a "devil-like" figure on the prowl in Devon. In the middle of the Victorian era, few country people doubted the existence of the Devil. Men armed with guns and pitchforks followed the trail; when night came villagers locked their doors and kept loaded shotguns at hand.

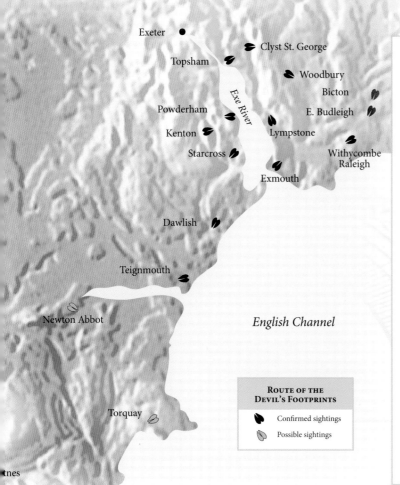

Exeter
Clyst St. George
Topsham
Woodbury
Bicton
Exe River
E. Budleigh
Powderham
Lympstone
Kenton
Starcross
Withycombe Raleigh
Exmouth

Dawlish

Teignmouth
English Channel
Newton Abbot

ROUTE OF THE DEVIL'S FOOTPRINTS

Confirmed sightings

Possible sightings

Torquay

tnes

The Story Hits the Papers

A week later the story reached the newspapers. The *London Times* of February 16, 1855, carried an account of the hoofprints. The next day the *Plymouth Gazette* followed suit and mentioned one clergyman's theory that the creature had been a kangaroo—he was apparently unaware that a kangaroo has claws. A report in the *Exeter Flying Post* made the slightly more plausible suggestion that the animal was a bird. Nevertheless, a correspondent in the *Illustrated London News* pointed out that no bird leaves a horseshoe-shaped print.

Great bustards

Also in the *Illustrated London News*, on March 3, the great naturalist and anatomist Richard Owen announced dogmatically that the footmarks were those of hind foot of a badger, without explaining why the badger hopped acrobatically on one hind foot. Another correspondent, who signed himself "Ornither," was quite certain that a huge bird called the great bustard, whose outer toes were rounded, made the prints. But that still failed to explain why it walked 100 miles.

A Runaway Balloon?

Many theories arose to account for the hooflike prints, but for the superstitious, a simple, but far-fetched, answer was the most persuasive: the cloven hooves of the Devil himself had burned their marks into the snow. Nonetheless perhaps the likeliest hypothesis is one put forward by author Geoffrey Household, who edited a small book on the matter:

I think that Devonport dockyard released, by accident, some sort of experimental balloon. It broke free from its moorings, and trailed two shackles on the end of ropes. The impression left in the snow by these shackles went up the sides of houses, over haystacks, etc. . . . A Major Carter, a local man, tells me that his grandfather worked at Devonport at the time, and that the whole thing was hushed up because the balloon destroyed a number of conservatories, greenhouses, windows, etc.

Household goes on to say that the balloon finally came down at Honiton.

But a glance at the map of the footprints shows that they meandered in a kind of circle between Topsham and Exmouth. Would an escaped balloon drift so erratically? Surely its route would tend to follow a more or less straight line, in the direction of the prevailing wind—which, moreover, was blowing from the east.

The fact that it took a week for the first report to appear in print means that certain vital clues were lost forever. Now the only certainty seems to be that the mystery will never be solved.

What source would account for the hoofprints on rooftops?

The Midwest Hellfire

(1871)

The Great Chicago Fire, view from the west

In the nineteenth century the Midwestern "Bible Belt" of the United States had more than its share of hell-and-damnation preachers, and many of them were predicting that the judgment and punishment visited on Sodom and Gomorrah would soon fall on all sinners. At the same time, the rolling farmlands and prairies of the Midwest have often been called "God's own country," largely because of the ubiquity and fervency of Christian worship in those states.

Strange, then, that it was not New York, San Francisco, or some other "Godless metropolis" that saw a catastrophe of both unexplained cause and Biblical destructiveness. It was the Midwest—at the height of the nineteenth-century Christian revival—that saw Hell come to Earth.

Jack-in-the-Box Inferno

The autumn of 1871 was hot and dry across the Midwest. From July into October the region had suffered a relentless drought. In the prairies to the south and west, from the booming new city of Chicago to the dense forests of northern Michigan, no rain had fallen, and in spite of the Great Lakes, humidity was at an all-time low. The desiccated atmosphere was dusty and harsh, the plants were parched brown, and Chicago's ever-present wind offered no relief. City dwellers, unprepared for a drought lasting into the winter months, could only hope for rain, and they prayed that no fires would break out before the weather broke.

At 9:25 PM on the evening of October 8, 1871, Fire Marshall Williams and his crew were called to a blaze on DeKoven Street in Chicago's lumber district. Although only a single barn, belonging to Patrick O'Leary, was on fire, Williams had good reason to fear that the conflagration might spread. Just the previous day, four whole blocks of the city had burned down, the wooden buildings igniting like dry tinder. As the firemen fought the O'Leary blaze they noticed the wind beginning to rise and worked frantically to bring the flames under control before sparks spread it far and wide.

Williams later reported that when the fire was halted "it would not have gone a foot further; but the next thing I knew they came and told me that St. Paul's Church, about two blocks north, was on fire." Once again, Williams doused the blaze before it could spread to neighboring buildings, but "the next thing I knew the fire was in Bateham's planing-mill."

Chicago residents streamed onto city bridges as they tried to escape the flames engulfing entire buildings.

Judgment Day

The fire spread relentlessly: sparks from existing fires sometimes leapt whole blocks to settle on some distant building. The firefighters were familiar with this pattern, but this time the "leaps" seemed impossibly long. It was almost, said one, as if the sparks were coming down from the sky rather than from the burning houses.

The increasing gale fanned the fires, spread the sparks, and eventually grew strong enough to turn the water jets from the fire hoses into ineffectual drizzles. As the number of fires increased, any hope of getting them under control was finally abandoned. The Great Chicago Fire soon engulfed entire districts. Six-story buildings were reduced to ashes in less than five minutes. The hair, eyebrows, and clothes of firefighters smoldered in the heat.

Temperatures climbed high enough to melt stone blocks, while several hundred tons of pig iron, piled on the riverbank 200 feet from the flames, fused into a solid mass.

While many people streamed out of the city, others, trapped by walls of flame, were forced to take shelter in the cold waters of Lake Michigan. At the same time thousands of terrified animals, penned in Chicago's huge stockyards, broke free and stampeded through the streets, adding to the panic and confusion. Many of the scorched and blinded residents of Chicago were convinced that Judgment Day had arrived.

Map of Chicago, 1871. The darker area shows the destroyed districts.

Unnumbered Deaths

The unprecedented conditions produced unlikely phenomena: an onrushing wall of fire turned due south and ran half a mile *into* the howling gale; reporters noted that some buildings seemed to catch fire from the inside rather than the outside. One newspaperman said it looked "as though a regiment of incendiaries were at work. What latent power enkindled the inside of these advanced [distant] buildings while externally they were untouched?" One witness later said he believed that there was some unknown "food for fire in the air, something mysterious as yet and unexplainable. Whether it was atmospheric or electric is yet to be determined."

For 27 hours the fire burned unchecked. Flames destroyed more than 17,500 of the city's tightly packed wooden buildings, and 100,000 people were made homeless. The lost property was eventually estimated at $200 million—a near unimaginable figure in the nineteenth-century United States, when a house could be purchased for $50. Yet, incredibly, only 250 bodies were recovered. Even so, as historian Herbert Asbury later pointed out, this figure did not represent the final death toll: "At least as many more were believed to have been consumed by the fire, which in places reached temperatures as high as 3,000 degrees Fahrenheit." Those temperatures can reduce a body to ash and bits of bone.

The Forgotten Catastrophe

The Great Chicago Fire was the worst city blaze in U. S. history, but it was not the worst fire disaster. The near total destruction of a major metropolis (started, it was rumored, by Mrs. O'Leary's cow kicking over a lamp) has, in the history books, almost entirely eclipsed a firestorm that ravaged eight states, destroyed countless acres of farmland, forest, and prairie, and killed more than 2,000 people. It is doubly strange that historians have neglected this disaster because it took place on the same night as the Great Chicago Fire, across most of the surrounding states.

Late in the evening, a little before O'Leary's Chicago barn caught fire, a gale began to blow across the prairie from the southwest. Over the next few hours high winds pushed fires across Illinois, Iowa, Indiana, Wisconsin, Michigan, Minnesota, North Dakota, and South Dakota. Witnesses spoke of torrents of flame cascading from above and suffocating fogs of thick, black smoke that poured from a howling, crimson sky.

The luckiest of the stricken states were the Dakotas, Indiana, Illinois (outside Chicago), and Iowa. Here no human casualties were reported, but the loss of timberland and crops to flash fire was devastating.

Given the conditions, that there were no known fatalities in these states was little short of miraculous. Near the town of Yankton in South Dakota, for example, a wall of flame 30 feet high was seen sweeping before the wind as fast as a "fleet horse could run," devouring everything in its path.

Scorched Earth

Minnesota was less fortunate. The counties of Carver, Wright, Meecher, and McLeod were inundated with flame, and the cities of Saint Paul and Minneapolis were both under dire threat during the night. Fifty state residents were reported killed by burning or suffocation.

Michigan, with its great forests, was half destroyed by fire. To the east of the state, between Saginaw Bay and Lake Huron, the fire reduced an area of some 1,400 square miles to scorched earth. Blazing forests cut off the towns along the shores of this area, and their inhabitants were forced to take to the water to escape. (Rescue boats out of Detroit were still picking up survivors several days later.) Eleven townships were partially destroyed and 12 more were completely lost in this area alone. Searchers later dug 50 bodies from the ashes.

To the west, down the shore of Lake Michigan, the towns of Muskegon, Manistee, Glen Haven, and Holland were set ablaze. The latter two towns were all but destroyed, and, around Holland, more than 200 farmsteads saw their land reduced to a burned waste.

In the center of Michigan, the city of Saginaw suffered $100,000 worth of fire damage, and the whole of the Saginaw Valley, south to Flint, was set ablaze. Only the combined male populations of Midland, Bay City, and Lansing managed to keep the blaze in check. Nonetheless the counties of Gratiot, Iosco, Alpena, and Alcona were devastated.

Dry prairie grass burns easily. In fact occasional fires play an important ecological role by removing trees and clearing dead grasses. In autumn 1871, however, conditions were ripe for unprecedented catastrophe.

Nowhere to Hide

Wisconsin was hardest hit. An area of at least 400 square miles between Brown County in the north and Marinette on Green Bay in the south was devastated, losing nine towns and four entire counties. Although this was less than a quarter the land damage suffered by Michigan, more than 1,000 people lost their lives in this area. About half of these were later found to have died not from burns, but from asphyxiation. The fires were so tremendous that they sucked the oxygen from the atmosphere and filled one of the greatest open prairies in the world with enough smoke to kill.

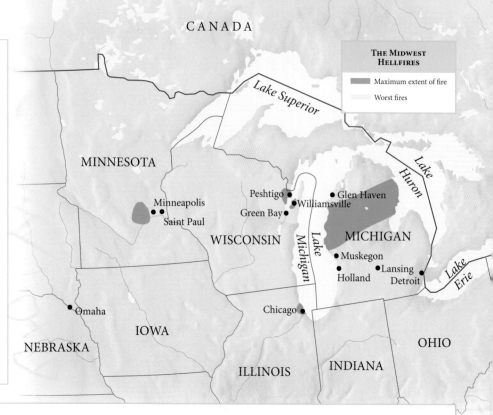

CANADA

THE MIDWEST HELLFIRES

▨ Maximum extent of fire
▨ Worst fires

Lake Superior

Lake Huron

Lake Erie

Lake Michigan

MINNESOTA

Minneapolis
Saint Paul

Peshtigo
Williamsville
Green Bay
Glen Haven

WISCONSIN

MICHIGAN

Muskegon
Holland
Lansing
Detroit

Omaha

Chicago

IOWA

NEBRASKA

ILLINOIS

INDIANA

OHIO

The Heart of the Firestorm

Of the 78 inhabitants of the village of Williamsonville, Wisconsin, only 4 survived that night. In the town of Menekaune, dozens of people who could not reach the relative safety of the bay died amid the blazing houses. At Williamson's Mills almost every member of 14 families perished; 32 people desperately threw themselves down the settlement's well—all were found dead. In the Sugar Bush settlements more than 260 people were killed; many were found suffocated but otherwise unmarked in areas some distance from the flames.

It was, however, in the town of Peshtigo that the most terrible losses of the night were incurred. In 1871, Peshtigo was a growing metropolis of more than 2,000 people. It maintained 15 hotels and shops, several factories, and 350 homes. By the morning of October 9, not a single building remained.

Survivors later told of a cloudless evening with a wind strong enough to shake the wooden houses. Around 9:30 PM a red glare came into view to the southwest; it expanded and filled the sky as it approached with the storm. A swelling rumble that soon reached the pitch of continuous thunder accompanied the crimson light. In the last moments before the catastrophe, sharp reports like distant cannon shots were heard—these were later identified as explosions of methane as the firestorm passed over neighboring marshes. In the last seconds the whoosh and crash of igniting and falling trees filled the air. Then the firestorm engulfed Peshtigo.

An illustration from the November 25, 1871, edition of *Harper's Weekly* magazine shows the confusion and chaos as frantic humans and terrified animals try to find shelter from the fast-moving inferno.

A Dome of Fire

One of the few survivors of the great blaze in Peshtigo gave this description of the first few moments of the destruction:

In one awful instant a great flame shot up in the western heavens, and in countless fiery tongues struck downward into the village, piercing every object that stood in the town like a red-hot bolt. A deafening roar, mingled with blasts of electric flame, filled the air and paralyzed every soul in the place. There was no beginning to the work of ruin; the flaming whirlwind swirled in an instant through the town. All heard the first inexplicable roar, some aver that the earth shook, while a few avow that the heavens opened and the fire rained down from above. The tornado was but momentary, but was succeeded by maelstroms of fire, smoke, cinders and red-hot sand that blistered the flesh.

The superheated blast ripped the roofs from the houses, setting them ablaze before they hit the ground. Unshielded buildings, animals, and people exploded into flame where they stood. Even the citizens who were protected from the direct blast of the storm were choked by black whirlwinds of smoke or suffocated as the burning air seared their lungs.

One house on the edge of town was whipped straight up into the air. Witnesses said that the walls of flame around the town met to form a dome of fire, and that at about 100 feet above the ground the flying house burst into flames and was torn to pieces.

Below, the Peshtigo River, which runs through the town. The mural at left, which can be seen at the Peshtigo Fire Museum, shows the town residents jumping into the river during the height of the firestorm.

BEFORE THE FIRE · 1871 DURING THE FIRE · AFTER THE FIRE

Panic

After the first onslaught, Peshtigo's firestorm slackened a little. Several firefighters even tried to deploy a fire hose, but it burst into flames and was reduced to melted rubber before they could start pumping the water.

For those who were not already dead or incapacitated, the only hope of survival was reaching the watery safety of the Peshtigo River, which ran through the center of the town. Finding a way there, however, was a problem. Nearly every town landmark was ablaze. Smoke filled the rushing air like black fog. Nowhere in the open was safe, as wild gusts of wind hurled tongues of fire as if from a flamethrower. Finally, those who did not cover their mouths when they breathed risked scorching their lungs too badly to ever take another breath.

Two mobs of terrified evacuees met in the middle of the wooden bridge that spanned the river. In the grim confusion the groups fought to pass one another, both convinced that the far side must be safer than the inferno that they were trying to escape. As panicked people strove to find a path to safety, the bridge, which was itself in flames, buckled and collapsed.

One man managed to keep his head in the surrounding panic. Seeing that his sick wife could never make it to the river on foot, he and their five children pushed her, bed and all, out of the house and into the rushing water. They had trouble keeping her head above the surface, but the entire family survived.

Nothing but Ashes

Those who made it to the river were not out of danger. In those days, when bathing in public was still considered indecent, few men and almost no women knew how to swim. The flaming, smoke-laden air above the water was difficult to breathe, and the current swept burning debris toward the bobbing heads. Because this was a rural community, terrified horses and cows ran loose; many people died from trampling.

Outside the town an impenetrable wall of burning woodland blocked escape. Many people sought refuge in the few brick buildings, but these quickly turned into ovens, and the bones of the dead were later found amid the heat-shattered rubble. Only one group, which staggered into the swampy ground to the east of the town, managed to escape by lying flat in the hot and brackish, but protecting, water.

One farmer on the edge of town shot his family and then himself before the surrounding flames could close in. In another area, a desperate mother dug a hole in the earth with her bare hands, placed her baby in it, and then shielded the child with her own body. She burned to death; her baby suffocated.

In the early morning hours the firestorm abated. By dawn most of the fires were dying, but only because almost everything in the area had been reduced to ash or slag. Survivors suffering from burns, lacerations, and exposure saw a blackened landscape stretching as far as the eye could see. The final death count in Peshtigo was 1,152—more than half the town's population.

The State Historical Society of Wisconsin erected a memorial to the victims of the Peshtigo Fire at the Peshtigo Fire Cemetery.

Burning Air

Because the Great Chicago Fire commanded all national attention, it was several weeks before anything other than local help was offered to survivors in the rural areas. The governors of Michigan and Wisconsin were both forced to issue special proclamations begging for assistance. It was months before the terrible damage could be fully assessed. Indeed in some areas fires continued to burn for more than three weeks. Ashes from the conflagration were blown as far eastward as the Azores in the mid-Atlantic Ocean.

The official explanation for the calamity was a windstorm that carried sparks—originally from bush fires in the southern prairies, then from the fires caused by the storm itself.

Yet this theory seemed somehow inadequate. It failed to explain the sheer violence of the firestorm. Over recent centuries droughts have been recorded worldwide—some going on for decades—but nowhere have high winds and flying sparks created a conflagration like the one that struck the Midwest in 1871. Accounts such as that of Peshtigo seem to imply that the very air was ablaze. Witnesses of spontaneously combusting buildings in Chicago could only suggest invisible incendiaries or a mysterious "food for fire in the air," as a cause. Moreover, the high incidence of death by suffocation, not only outdoors, but often far from burning areas, suggested to many that there may have been some deadly quality in the wind itself . . .

A chunk of blackened white pine, which survived the Peshtigo Fire

Spanish White Heat

Could there be any basis for suspecting that the catastrophic fires of autumn 1871 were caused by some rare atmospheric event? Or any of the other several unexplained heat blasts that have been recorded since the Great Midwest Firestorm?

The Spanish province of Almeria suffered a plague of bizarre fires, beginning on June 16, 1945. Throughout that day, around the town of La Roda, white clothing spread out to dry suddenly burst into flames. This had never been known to happen before, nor was any other shade or color of cloth affected.

During the next 20 days, more than 300 unexplained fires broke out in the area. Not just laundry, but farmhouses, barns, threshing bins—even the clothes on people's backs burst into flame without visible cause. What was remarkable, though, was that in almost every case the object damaged had been white.

The government dispatched a team of scientists to the area, but when they unpacked a box containing their instruments it burst into flame. The rather disgruntled experts eventually reported that the fires might have been triggered by Saint Elmo's

The intense heat blast that sent temperatures skyrocketing in Spain's Almeria province seemed to affect only white objects or fabrics. Laundry spread to dry on the ground and hung on lines burst into flames with no visible source of ignition.

fire (a harmless and heatless electrical discharge) or underground mineral deposits. The director of Spain's National Geographic Institute connected the two theories when he noted that "the land [around La Roda] is a particularly good conductor of electricity." He could not, however, explain why the area had only recently been plagued by incidents of spontaneous combustion if it were naturally prone to them. Obviously, even if they were on the right track, some unknown catalytic force was at work.

The Portuguese Furnace Blast

On July 6, 1949, something described as "an inferno-like blast" hit the town of Figueira, approximately 235 miles north of Lisbon on the central coast of Portugal. It took place was early morning—a time when most Portuguese housewives were out doing the day's shopping, and few others were about. Suddenly, without warning or any apparent cause, the air temperature soared to an unbearable level: a naval officer who was working near the harbor reported a thermometer leaping from 100°F to 158°F in only a few seconds.

The heat blast was reported to have felt like "tongues of flame." Hundreds of people were knocked senseless, while others prayed in terror or searched fruitlessly for somewhere cooler. Cattle and donkeys panicked, and thousands of poultry fell

dead. The Mondego River, which discharges into the Atlantic at Figueira, steamed and even dried up at several shallow points. The Spanish press reported that in one place "millions of fish died in the mud that was rapidly becoming a sand bed." Then, approximately two minutes after it hit, the heat wave passed like the lifting of a curtain.

But the mystery inferno had merely moved inland. Thirty miles from the coast, the town of Coimbra was roasted a short while later; there the scorching again lasted two minutes before passing, this time for good. No unusual winds, sun effects, or tectonic movements were noted immediately before, during, or after the event. The searing heat simply swept in from the clear sky over the sea, then vanished.

Star Wars?

The Spanish press reported that on July 5, 1949—the day *before* the Portuguese heat blast in Figueira—a "great column of whirling wind of a luminous brown color struck a small settlement with a violent roar and kindled flames that leapt 30 feet high." Unfortunately the newspaper did not give the name of the settlement, and the report therefore cannot be confirmed.

This event, however, seems to have been the climax of the spontaneous combustion plague in the Iberian Peninsula. Several minor fires were reported over the next few days, but by July 10, the phenomenon had apparently ceased altogether.

These stories might remind the modern reader of the heat blast that devastated Hiroshima after the dropping of the atomic bomb, minus, of course, the following air blast and radiation sickness. Indeed, UFOlogists have speculated that the Figueira and Almeria heat blasts might have been caused by aliens demonstrating their super-weapons for inscrutable reasons of their own. Certainly no known human technology at that time could have produced such short-lived, but intense heat waves. Even today, orbital lasers that could create such effects are only at the theoretical stage of development.

Discounting these unverifiable notions, there is still the possibility of freak atmospheric effects or even of another kind of intruder from space . . .

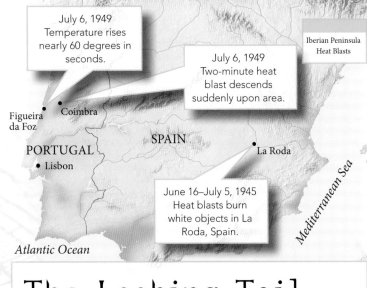

Iberian Peninsula Heat Blasts

July 6, 1949
Temperature rises nearly 60 degrees in seconds.

July 6, 1949
Two-minute heat blast descends suddenly upon area.

June 16–July 5, 1945
Heat blasts burn white objects in La Roda, Spain.

Figueira da Foz • Coimbra

PORTUGAL
• Lisbon

SPAIN

• La Roda

Mediterranean Sea

Atlantic Ocean

The Lashing Tail From Space

A few years after the Great Chicago Fire, Minnesota congressman and author Ignatius Donnelly made an interesting observation in his book *Ragnarok*. He noted that Biela's comet, during its close brush with the earth's gravity field in 1846, had split into two parts. The shattered comet was due to return in 1866, but, to the astonishment of astronomers, it failed to appear. Then in November 1872 (just over a year after the Great Midwest Firestorm), it reappeared unexpectedly in a spectacular and meteoric display. This might seem irrelevant to the events of 1871, except that the comet was missing its tail during the 1872 visit.

A comet is made up of a head of solid ice and a long tail of gases, ice particles, and space dust resembling the wake of a ship. Donnelly suggested that the 1846 brush with the earth had detached Biela's tail, and that after the split, the comet's head had been diverted into a slightly different orbital path, and the material of the tail continued orbiting the sun. Donnelly's theory was that, 25 years later, on the night of October 8, 1871, the remains of the tail returned and plunged into the atmosphere over the Midwest. The burning, demon wind that ravaged eight states, he suggested, was a direct result of the atmospheric impact and superheating of a cloud of space debris.

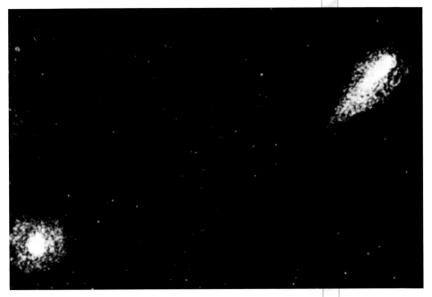

Comet Biela, illustrated in 1846 by an observer

The Tunguska Event
(1908)

Trees flattened by the Tunguska explosion

On June 30, 1908, the inhabitants of Nizhut-Karelinsk, a small village in central Siberia, watched a bluish white streak of fire cut vertically across the sky. What began as a bright point of light lengthened over a period of 10 minutes until it seemed to split the sky in two. Then it shattered to form a monstrous cloud of black smoke. Seconds later a terrific roaring detonation set buildings to trembling.

They did not know it at the time, but those villagers had witnessed the greatest natural disaster in earth's recorded history. If the object that caused what is now known as "the Great Siberian Explosion" had arrived a few hours earlier or later it might have landed in more heavily populated regions, taking millions of lives.

The Aftershocks

As it later turned out, the village of Nizhut-Karelinsk, was actually 200 miles away from the "impact point," and yet the explosion had shaken debris from the roofs of buildings. A Trans-Siberian express train stopped because the driver was convinced that the cars had derailed; seismographs in the town of Irkutsk indicated that an earthquake had struck.

The shock wave traveled around the globe twice before it died out, and its general effect on the weather in the northern hemisphere was far-reaching. During the rest of June it was so light out that it was quite possible to read the small print in the *London Times* at midnight.

For some months the world was treated to spectacular dawns and sunsets, as impressive as those that had been seen after the great Krakatoa eruption in 1883. From this, as well as the various reports of unusual cloud formations over the following months, it was clear that the event had thrown a good deal of dust into the atmosphere.

Kulik Investigates

It was not until World War I had been fought and the Russian Revolution had overthrown the tsarist regime that news of the extraordinary events of that June day finally reached the general public. In 1921, as part of Lenin's general plan to place the Soviet Union at the forefront of world science, the Soviet Academy of Sciences commissioned mineralogist Leonid Kulik to investigate meteorite falls on Soviet territory. It was Kulik who stumbled upon the few brief reports in 10-year-old Siberian newspapers that finally led him to suspect that something extraordinary had happened in central Siberia in summer 1908.

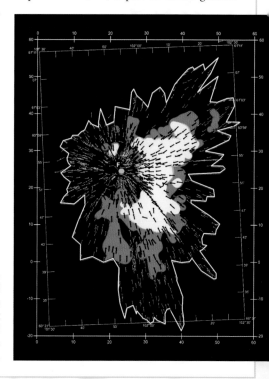

In 1999 a team from the Russian Academy of Sciences plotted a new map of the fallen tree coordinates. From this image it determined that at least one, and possibly two, massive objects exploded over Siberia in 1908.

Disaster Averted, Unnoticed

Kulik found the newspaper accounts of the event confusing and contradictory.

The reports described the ground opening up to release a great pillar of fire and smoke that burned brighter than the sun. Distant huts were blown down and reindeer herds scattered. A man plowing in an open field felt his shirt burning on his back, and others described being badly sunburned on one side of the face but not the other. Many people claimed that the noise had temporarily deafened them, others suffered the long-term effects of shock. Yet, almost unbelievably, not a single person had been killed or seriously injured. Whatever it was that produced the explosion had landed in one of the few places on earth where its catastrophic effect was minimized. A few hours later, and it could have obliterated Saint Petersburg, London, or New York. Even if it had landed in the sea, tidal waves might have destroyed whole coastal regions. On that June day the human race had escaped the greatest disaster in its history— and didn't even know it.

Finally Kulik discovered that a local meteorologist had made an estimate of the point of impact, and in 1927 the Academy of Sciences gave him the necessary backing to find the site where the "great meteorite" had fallen.

Leonid Kulik, the Russian mineralogist who first investigated the mysterious Tunguska event

Journey into Siberia

The Siberian forest is one of the least accessible places on Earth. Even today it remains largely unexplored; whole areas have been surveyed only from the air. What settlements there are can be found along the banks of its mighty rivers, some of them miles in width. The winters are ferociously cold; in the summer the ground becomes boggy, and the hum of mosquitoes fills the air. Kulik was faced with an almost impossible task: to travel by horses, sleds, and rafts with no idea of exactly what he was looking for or where to find it.

In March 1927 he reached the tiny village of Vanovara, about 100 miles from the estimated blast site. From there he set off, accompanied by two local guides who had witnessed the event. After many setbacks the three men arrived in April on the banks of the Mekirta River—the closest river to the impact point. In 1927 it formed a boundary between untouched forest and almost total devastation.

Even today, more than a century after the explosion, the Tunguska area is oddly barren

Even in 1927, nearly two decades after the event, rows of downed trees covered thousands of square miles of formerly dense forest.

The Cauldron

The second expedition followed the line of broken trees for several days until they came to a natural amphitheater in the hills and pitched camp there. They spent the next few days surveying the surrounding area; Kulik reached the conclusion that "the cauldron" as he called it, was the center of the blast. All around, the fallen trees faced away from it, and yet, incredibly, some trees actually remained standing although stripped and charred, at the very heart of the explosion.

The full extent of the desolation was now apparent: from the river to its central point was a distance of 37 miles. So the blast, Kulik calculated, had flattened more than 4,000 square miles of forest.

Still working on the supposition that a large meteorite had caused the explosion, Kulik began searching the area for its remains. He thought he had achieved his objective when he discovered a number of pits filled with water; he naturally assumed that fragments of the exploding meteorite had made them. But the holes were drained and found to be empty. One even had a tree stump at the bottom, proving it had not been made by a blast.

Utter Devastation

On that April day Kulik stood on a low hill and surveyed the destruction caused by the Tunguska explosion. For as far as he could see to the north, perhaps a dozen miles, not a single full-grown tree of what had once been dense forest remained standing. Every single one of them had been flattened by the blast. He also noticed an important fact: the flattened trees all lined up precisely facing the same direction, pointing southeast toward the horizon. It was obvious to him that this was just the edge of the devastation; the blast must have been far larger than even the wildest reports had suggested.

Kulik was eager to continue his exploration of the disaster and to search out its epicenter, but his two guides were terrified and refused to go on. So Kulik was forced to return to Vanovara with them. It was not until June that he managed to return with two new guides.

Aerial photo of the area around the Tunguska site. Scientists at the University of Bologna now suspect a small lake, Cheko, to be the impact crater that Kulik couldn't find.

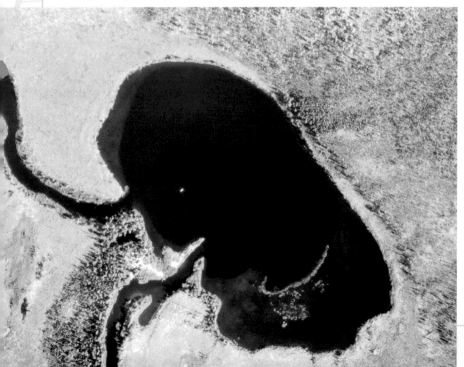

No Crater

Kulik was to make four expeditions to the area of the explosion, and until his death he remained convinced that an unusually large meteorite had caused it. Yet he never found the iron or rock fragments that would provide him with the evidence he needed. In fact he never succeeded in proving that anything had even struck the ground. There was evidence of two blast waves—the original explosion and the ballistic wave—and even of brief flash fires, yet there was no crater.

The lack of a crater only deepened the riddle. A 1938 aerial survey showed that only 770 square miles of forest had been flattened and that original trees were still standing in the spot where the crater should have been. This evidence suggested that the explosion was caused not by an enormous meteor but rather by a bomb.

June 30, 1908
An unknown object explodes over a sparsely populated area of Siberia, leveling trees for thousands of square miles. A massive explosion of this size would have leveled the metropolitan areas of major cities, such as Moscow, Paris, London, and New York.

EUROPE

Saint Petersburg

Moscow

Ural Mountains

RUSSIA

Siberia

Vanovara

PACIFIC OCEAN

KAZAKHSTAN

Irkutsk

Mongolia

CHINA

Mysterious Meteorite

Even the way that the object fell to Earth was disputed. More than 700 eyewitnesses claimed that it changed course as it fell, saying that it was originally moving toward Lake Baikal before it swerved. Falling heavenly bodies have never been known to do this, nor is it possible to explain how it could have happened in terms of physical dynamics.

Another curious element about the explosion was its effect on the trees and insect life in the blast area. Trees that had survived the explosion had either stopped growing, or were shooting up at a greatly accelerated rate. Later studies revealed new species of ants and other insects that are peculiar to the Tunguska blast region.

A meteoroid pierces the earth's atmosphere.

The Sky is Falling

It was not until some years after Kulik's death in a German prisoner-of-war camp that scientists began to see similarities between the Tunguska event and two other, more catastrophic, explosions: the destruction of Hiroshima and Nagasaki with thermonuclear devices. Our knowledge of the atom bomb helps us to understand many of the mysteries that baffled Kulik.

There was no crater at Tunguska because the explosion had taken place above the ground, as is the case with an atomic bomb. The standing trees at the central point of the explosion confirmed this. At both Nagasaki and Hiroshima buildings directly beneath the blast remained standing, because the blast spread sideways. Genetic mutations in the flora and fauna around the Japanese cities resemble those witnessed in Siberia, while blisters found on dogs and reindeer in the Tunguska area can now be recognized as radiation burns.

Atomic explosions produce disturbances in the earth's magnetic field, and even today the area around the Tunguska explosion has been described as being in "magnetic chaos."

Professor Alexis Zolotov, leader of the 1959 expedition to Tunguska, calculated that, whatever the object was—a meteor or comet—it was about 130 feet in diameter, and exploded approximately 3 miles above the ground with a force of 40 megatons—2,000 times greater than the atomic bomb at Hiroshima.

UFO Mysteries

(1947 to present)

Pilot Kenneth Arnold

The history of modern UFOlogy, or the study of unidentified flying objects, begins on June 24, 1947. That's when Kenneth Arnold was flying his private plane near Mount Rainier in Washington State and saw nine shining disks moving against the background of the mountain. He estimated their speed at about 1,000 miles per hour and later said that the disks swerved in and out of the peaks of the Cascades with "flipping, erratic movements." Arnold told a reporter that the objects moved as a saucer would "if you skipped it across the water."

The next day Arnold's story appeared in newspapers all over the United States. Soon reports flooded in of other "flying saucer" sightings, and the U.S. Air Force initiated an investigation, known as Project Sign. Ten days after the sighting, the air force announced confidently that Arnold had been hallucinating.

Then, on January 7, 1948, Captain Thomas Mantell—who was piloting a P-51 fighter jet, chased a round, white object in the sky. At 30,000 feet, Mantell seems to have blacked out and his plane went into a fatal dive. This episode probably did more than any other to publicize UFOs in the late 1940s.

Project Blue Book

From the files of Project Blue Book: a 15-year-old boy shot this photo of a UFO flying over his San Bernadino, California, home in the 1950s.

Air force investigations of UFO sightings continued, and in 1952 Project Blue Book was born. Although this project lasted nearly 20 years and collected more than 12,600 reports of UFOs, its attitude throughout the life of the investigation remained skeptical. Project Blue Book dismissed all but 6 percent of the reports as explainable by natural causes. J. Allen Hynek, an astrophysicist asked to take part in the project, began as skeptic but became convinced that this residue of cases that could not be dismissed as hoaxes, illusions, or honest mistakes. "Blue Book," says Hynek in *The UFO Experience,* "was a cover-up."

It struck early students that Arnold's UFO sighting was surely not the first-ever sighting of strange objects in the sky. A search of newspaper files revealed many older ones. As early as 1800 an "airship" was seen hovering over Baton Rouge. Charles

Fort's 1919 *Book of the Damned* devotes a chapter to reports of strange lights in the sky; these include the famous "False Lights of Durham," seen over the city of Durham in northeast England in 1866. A commission headed by Admiral Collinson investigated the lights. Typically, it "reached no conclusion."

One important feature of the sightings that later emerged was that the objects were often cigar-shaped, rather than circular; and the cigar-shaped objects were larger than the smaller saucers. In fact many observers have reported seeing the small saucers emerging from the cigar-shaped object, implying that this latter object is the parent craft.

Hynek was one of a small number of serious, responsible students of the UFO phenomenon who emerged in the early 1950s; others included Jacques Vallee, Donald Keyhoe, M. K. Jessup, and Aimé Michel. Keyhoe, who inaugurated his own study project, was convinced that beings from other planets who had been studying Earth for the past 200 years piloted the saucers. He and many others suggested that the first sighting occurred soon after the explosion of the first atomic bomb.

Roswell

The Roswell Incident is one of the most hotly disputed stories in UFO mythology. On a July evening in 1947, a fast-moving, glowing object hurtled through the sky above ranch foreman Mac Brazel as he rode out to check his sheep. The object seemed to crash, and the following day Brazel found shiny metal foil and wreckage in a desert area north of Roswell, New Mexico. The U.S. Air Force soon moved in and removed the debris, then announced that it had been merely a crashed weather balloon. This caused widespread incredulity, and rumors spread that an alien spaceship had crashed and been seized by the government.

A sign marks the UFO crash site near Roswell, New Mexico, and also advertises the UFO Museum in Roswell. The area has become famous as the nexus of UFOlgists.

But Where Did They Come From?

Renowned British astrologer Sir Fred Hoyle claimed that the saucers had been around since the beginning of time. This view is taken by Raymond Drake as well, whose books *Gods and Spacemen in the Ancient East* and *Gods and Spacemen in the Ancient West*, examine ancient texts for mentions of objects that sound like Ezekiel's wheel of fire.

Some writers are convinced that UFOs are hostile. Their view is that sightings are of reconnaissance vehicles preparing an invasion of Earth. Others, including noted UFOlogist Brinsley Le Poer Trench, believe that there could be two groups of "sky people," one very ancient and friendly, the other more recent and sinister in its intentions. The "antis" like to point out that car engines and other electrical equipment seem to stall in the presence of UFOs—one writer blames them for the massive New York power failure of 1965.

Inevitably some of the speculation seems to cross the line into pure fantasy. For instance Frank Scully, a Hollywood journalist who wrote for the magazine *Variety*, suggested that the saucers came from Venus and were driven by magnetic propulsion (a book he wrote was later denounced as a hoax by *True* magazine). UFO researcher George Adamski claimed he had shaken hands with a charming Venusian in the California desert and was taken for a trip into space. Antonio Boas, a Brazilian farmer, claims that he was taken aboard a saucer where two "little men" took blood samples, and a beautiful naked "girl" with no lips seduced him— obviously for scientific purposes. Adamski himself states that most "contactee" claims are pure fantasy—giving precise figures of 800 "genuine" cases out of 3,000.

Many contactees have reported hearing the voices of spacemen inside their heads. Dr. George Hunt Williamson's *Secret Places of the Lion* describes how spacemen contacted him through automatic writing, telling him they arrived on Earth 8 million years ago and built the Great Pyramid 24,000 years ago; a spacecraft is hidden under its base, according to Williamson.

Good News or Bad?

As UFO reports continue, many from ordinary people with no desire for publicity, there has been increasing acceptance of the phenomena. Carl Jung, who began by advancing a theory that the saucers were "projections" from the collective unconscious, ended by recognizing that the saucers seemed to be more "factual" than that. In 1969 Air Marshal Sir Victor Goddard lectured in London and suggested that UFOs could come from a parallel world; this view has become increasingly popular.

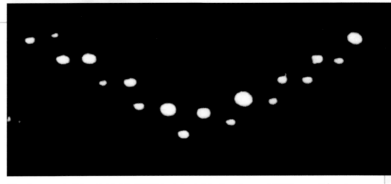

The famous Lubbock Lights UFO incident. During August 1951, on at least 14 occasions, lights hovered over the town of Lubbock, Texas. Hundreds of witnesses saw them, including four respected college professors: a geologist, a chemist, a physicist, and a petroleum engineer. Four photographs of the lights exist. Project Blue Book proclaimed that there was a perfectly natural explanation for the lights—but it never revealed what that "natural" cause was.

Collective Memories and Lines of Energy

UFO crash simulation. Perhaps an alien craft will someday crash on Earth—and finally provide irrefutable evidence of extraterrestrial life.

Many writers have pointed out that UFOs are seen most frequently at the crossing point of ley lines (lines where Earth's energy is allegedly concentrated). For example, there have been hundreds of sightings over Warminster, in the United Kingdom. In fact an entire book, *The Warminster Mystery* by Arthur Shuttlewood, published in 1973, is devoted to those sightings. Shuttlewood's book, like John Michell's 1969 book *The Flying Saucer Vision*, points out the association between UFO sightings and ancient sacred sites. In the 1973 book *The Dragon and the Disc*, F. W. Holiday notes the similarity between the shape of disc barrows—Bronze-Age burial mounds that are common in Wiltshire in the United Kingdom—and saucers. He also suggests how frequently UFO sightings are associated with "ghosts"—as when a blood-soaked figure staggered out of a hedge near Warminster and vanished. In his 1978 book, *The Undiscovered Country*, Stephen Jenkins conducts a lengthy and highly convincing investigation into the connection between UFOs, ley lines, and supernatural occurrences. Holiday, too, believes that saucers, like lake monsters, should be regarded as some kind of partly supernatural phenomenon, associated with racial memory, as it is called by Jung.

118

Now You See It, Now You Don't

One of the most striking elements of UFOs is the ambiguity of the whole phenomenon. The evidence looks very convincing; yet all hopes of reaching some final, positive conclusion recede when we try to pin it down. Case in point: medical and parapsychological researcher Andrija Puharich describes how psychic Uri Geller went periodically into trances. In these trances, voices of "extraterrestrials" spoke through his mouth, identifying themselves as members of "The Nine," a group of space people whose aim, they said, was to guide the Earth through a difficult period in its history and prevent humankind from destroying itself. There is much solid evidence that the phenomena really took place, and Puharich himself is a highly regarded scientific investigator; yet the events seem so weird and inconsequential that it is difficult to take them seriously. Puharich broke with Geller, and afterward the communications continued, as recounted by Stuart Holroyd in his 1977 book *Prelude to a Landing on Planet Earth*. The "alien communicators" declared that they intended to land on Earth in force and were eager to prepare humankind for this event . . .

but the date for the landing passed without incident. John Keel, another investigator of UFO phenomena, speaks a great deal about the "men in black" who often warn people to keep silent about their glimpses of UFOs. His books are full of "hard evidence," including names, dates, and signed statements. It seems clear that something is going on, but whether that something is contact with extraterrestrial intelligence seems doubtful.

In *The Invisible College*, published in 1975, Jacques Vallee suggested that the phenomena may be basically "heuristic," that is, intending to educate the human race about a new consciousness. He points out that it is impossible to decide whether UFOs are genuine and, if they are genuine, where they originate: in outer space, in other dimensions, or in the human mind itself. Yet the repetitiveness of the phenomenon and its unpredictability seem to prepare the human mind for something startling; or, at the very least, to remain open-minded. Alternatively, it could be a manifestation of right-brained human unconscious trying to prevent us from becoming jammed in a two-dimensional left-brain reality.

Are They Out There?

By the end of the 1970s much of the public curiosity about UFOs had dissipated, but research into the phenomenon continues. In France SEPRA (Service of Expertise on Atmospheric Phenomena) was set up in 1983 to officially study UFOs. After the organization folded in 2004, its head, Jean-Jacques Velasco, published *UFOs . . . the Evidence*, in which he states unambiguously that UFOs do exist. In fact of the approximately 5,800 cases SEPTRA studied, Velasco reports that at least 14 percent were extraterrestrial in origin.

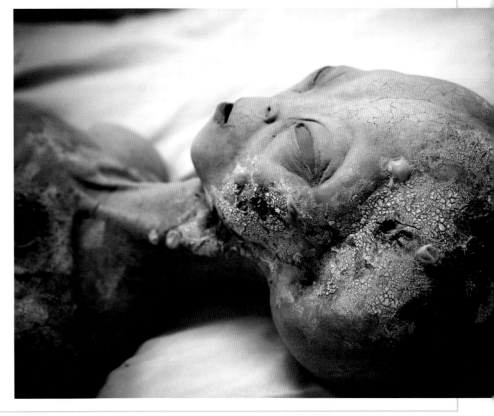

A model of an alien that was allegedly autopsied by the U.S. government after the 1947 Roswell, New Mexico, incident. If UFOs are real, one must conclude that extraterrestrial beings, the creators and operators of the UFOs, also exist.

Alien Abductions

(1953 to present)

Have you been abducted by aliens? The question is less absurd than it sounds, for there are thousands of people who believe they have been taken to alien spacecraft but had their memories tampered with so that they no longer recall what happened.

In 1989 the late John Mack, a psychiatrist and professor at Boston University, had been asked by a psychiatrist friend if he would like to meet Budd Hopkins. Mack asked, "Who's he?" When told that Hopkins was a New York artist who tried to help people who believed they had been taken into spaceships, Mack replied that Hopkins must be crazy, and so must the "abductees."

But Mack was a reasonable, open-minded sort of person, and a few months later he agreed to meet Hopkins. And Mack learned, to his amazement, that all over the United States there are people who claim that they have been taken from their beds by little gray-skinned aliens with huge black eyes, transported aboard a UFO, subjected to medical examination, and then released with the memory of the experience obliterated. But under hypnosis, they could frequently recall the experience in great detail.

Are they trying to contact us?

Is It Mental Illness?

Mack's natural suspicion was that their "memories" of the abduction were somehow implanted by the leading questions asked by the hypnotist. He also suspected that such people were neurotics who needed some drama to brighten their lives, and that they had probably derived their ideas about little gray aliens from television or books like Whitley Strieber's 1987 best-seller *Communion*. But when he met some of the abductees, he was struck by their normality; none of them seemed psychiatrically disturbed. Moreover a large percentage of these people had no previous knowledge about abductees and little gray men. There was an interesting sameness about their descriptions of the inside of the spacecraft, their captors, and what happened to them. Clearly they were telling what they felt to be the truth.

When Hopkins suggested that he should refer cases from the Boston area to Mack, Mack agreed. Between spring 1990 and the publication of *Abduction* four years later, Mack saw more than 100 "abductees" who ranged in age from 2 to 57. They came from every group of society: students, house-wives, writers, business people, computer industry professionals, musicians, even psychologists.

Dr. John Mack, perhaps more than anyone else, lent credibility to stories of alien abductions.

The Case of Catherine

A typical case was that of Catherine, a 22-year-old music student and nightclub receptionist. One night in February 1991, she suddenly decided to go for a drive after working at the nightclub. When she arrived home, she was puzzled to discover that it was so late: 45 minutes seemed to be missing. She was also suffering from a nosebleed—the first in her life. The next day she saw on television that a UFO had been seen in the Boston area. Someone recommended that she see John Mack.

After several sessions of hypnosis, memories of abduction began spontaneously to emerge. She recalled that her first abduction had occurred when she was 3, and another when she was 7. Finally she recalled what had happened in the missing three-quarters of an hour. She had found herself driving into some woodland, where she experienced a kind of paralysis. Aliens took her out of her car and guided her into a UFO, where her abductors began to remove her clothes. When she asked them angrily why they didn't just rent some pornography, they looked blank, and it dawned on her that they didn't know what pornography was.

Her abductors took her into an enormous room in which there were many tables upon which were lying human beings. She was made to lie on a table, and an instrument was inserted into her vagina. When the instrument was removed, there was, on the end of it, what seemed to be a three-month-old fetus. (Three months earlier, she had found herself driving along deserted roads in the middle of the night. She pulled in at a rest stop and, although she had no further memory of what happened, she believes she may have been impregnated at that time and that the aliens may have been engaged in some kind of breeding experiments.)

Her attitude toward the aliens was at this time one of rage, but, during the course of the sessions with Mack, she came to take a more balanced view, suspecting that the aliens may be "more advanced spiritually and emotionally than we are." She finally became one of the most active members of Mack's support group, reassuring others who found the abductee experience terrifying.

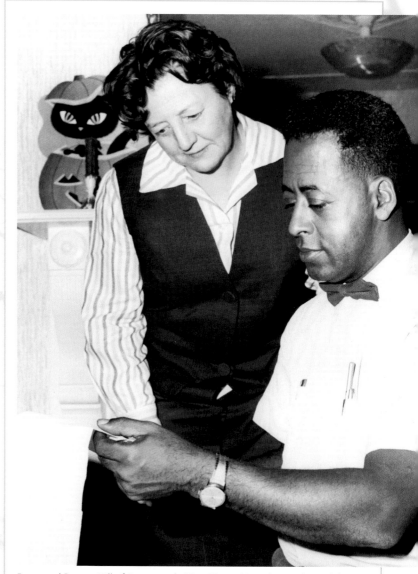

Betty and Barney Hill of Portsmouth, New Hampshire, above, claimed that on a trip home from Canada in 1961 they were abducted and held aboard a UFO.

A Compelling Story

If some abduction tales sound wildly implausible, others are oddly convincing. In September 1961 Betty and Barney Hill were driving to their New Hampshire home from Canada when they spotted a UFO. Both of them blacked out and, two hours later, woke up in the car. Under hypnosis, both recalled being taken aboard a "saucer" where they were examined. John G. Fuller's book about their experience, *The Interrupted Journey*, is one of the more convincing contactee records and includes precise transcripts of hypnotic sessions.

An Intelligent Universe?

We might conclude from all these abductions that the Earth may be in some imminent danger to which we all must be immediately awakened. But Mack's view was that the abduction experience "opens the consciousness" of those concerned, and that his own experience of working with abductees "provides a rich body of evidence to support the idea that the cosmos, far from being devoid of meaning and intelligence, is informed by some kind of universal intelligence, one to which human intelligence is akin and in which it can participate."

Coverage in the Press

In December 2005 a couple from Houston, Texas, said that they were abducted by aliens on more than one occasion. Clayton Lee claimed to have been probed by the aliens, which took some of his DNA and left him with a scar on his side. Donna Lee contended that the aliens also removed a fetus from her body. A local television station broadcast a session that Donna Lee had with a hypnotist who was trying to help her retrieve memories of the incident. During the session Lee became upset, screaming, "They're touching me! Quit touching me!"

This was not the first, nor would it be the last time alien abductions were explored on television. Several documentaries, including one broadcast on the highly regarded science show NOVA, which included interviews with Carl Sagan and John Mack.

Common Threads

If alien abductions are nothing more than hokum, then why do the abductees' personal accounts share so many common elements? In a 1998 article in *Skeptical Inquirer* magazine, psychologist Dr. Susan Blackmore discussed some of those shared attributes:

> The experience begins most often when the person is at home in bed (Wright 1994) and most often at night (Spanos, Cross, Dickson, and DuBreuil 1993). . . . There is an intense blue or white light, a buzzing or humming sound, anxiety or fear, and the sense of an unexplained presence. A craft with flashing lights is seen and the person is transported or "floated" into it. Once inside the craft, the person may be subjected to various medical procedures, often involving the removal of eggs or sperm and the implantation of a small object in the nose or elsewhere. Communication with the aliens is usually by telepathy. The abductee feels helpless and is often restrained, or partially or completely paralyzed.

What could explain these shared experiences?

Nearly every abductee who has recall of the abduction has described a similar experience, including seeing a blindingly intense light and feeling afraid before being transported to the alien spacecraft for seemingly biological experimentation.

Cultural Memories

In her 2005 book, *Abducted: How People Come to Believe They Were Kidnapped by Aliens*, psychologist Dr. Susan Clancy argues that the abduction memories actually come from our popular culture—television shows, movies, comic books, newspapers. In addition she explains that alien abduction stories began to emerge only after such stories were featured on television and in movies, starting in about 1953.

Dr. Susan Clancy, a Harvard University psychologist, interviewed many people who claimed to have been abducted by aliens and concludes that their experiences are not real.

How Many?

Unlike the UFO issue—which most feel does not really concern nonbelievers—the idea of abduction has all the signs of being something that should concern everyone. A poll conducted over three months by the Roper organization in 1991 indicated that hundreds of thousands of Americans believed they had undergone the abduction experience.

Sleep Paralysis

Some researchers of abduction incidents posit that people who have claimed to have been abducted by aliens were actually suffering from a condition called sleep paralysis, a state in which a person is awake and can see and hear, but cannot move. Sleep paralysis is common among those suffering from narcolepsy—a condition in which a person falls asleep unexpectedly and uncontrollably. The paralysis can trigger anxiety, fear, and even hallucinations in which the sufferer feels that someone is in the room with them.

Take the Survey

For those who suspect that they may have been abducted, the Web site of the Alien Abduction Experience and Research Organization offers an online quiz. Here are just a few of the 25 questions: Do you secretly feel you are special or chosen? Do you dream about seeing UFOs, being inside UFOs, or interacting with UFO occupants? Have x-rays or other procedures revealed unexplainable foreign objects lodged in your body?

Twin Identities
(1970s to present)

Identical twins

In 1979 Barbara Herbert, a 39-year-old woman from Dover, England, approached social worker John Stroud for help in searching for her twin sister. Their mother had abandoned the girls at the beginning of World War II, and they had been separately adopted. With John Stroud's help, she traced the midwife who had delivered them. Eventually Herbert learned that her twin was named Daphne Goodship and lived in Wakefield, Yorkshire.

When Barbara and Daphne finally met, both were wearing a beige dress and a brown velvet jacket. This proved to be merely the first of an astonishing series of coincidences. Both women were local government workers, as were their husbands; both had met their husbands at a dance at the age of 16 and married in their early 20s in the autumn; both had suffered miscarriages with their first baby, and then had two boys followed by a girl; both had fallen downstairs at the age of 15 and suffered from weak ankles as a result; both had taken lessons in ballroom dancing; and both had the same favorite authors. Altogether, John Stroud listed 30 coincidences of this sort. Some of them were likely due to identical genetic predispositions. But accidents like falling downstairs or miscarriages could hardly be explained by their genes.

The Jim Twins

Around the same time, a pair of identical male twins appeared on *The Johnny Carson Show*. When Jim Lewis of Lima, Ohio, was nine years old, he discovered that he had an identical twin who had been adopted at birth. Thirty years later, he set out to find him and learned his twin, Jim Springer, lived in Dayton, Ohio. As soon as they met, they discovered a string of the same kind of preposterous coincidences that had amazed Barbara and Daphne.

Both had been named Jim; both had married a girl named Linda, then divorced and married a girl named Betty; both had called their sons James Allan, although Lewis spelled the name with only one "l"; both had owned dogs named Toy; both had worked part-time as deputy sheriffs; both had worked for McDonald's and as gas-station attendants; both spent their holidays at the same seaside resort in Florida and used the same beach—a mere 300 yards long; both drove a Chevrolet; both had a tree in the garden with a white bench around it; both had basement workshops where they built frames and furniture; both had had vasectomies; both drank the same beer and chain-smoked the same cigarettes; both had gained 10 pounds at the same point in their teens, and lost it again; and finally, both enjoyed stock-car racing but disliked baseball.

Their case was published in *Science*, the journal of the American Association for the Advancement of Science.

Not Clones

A clone has identical DNA to its original, but recent studies have revealed that identical twins do not share identical genes or DNA.

More Synchronicity

Professor Tim Bouchard, a psychologist who had been studying twins at the University of Minnesota, was so fascinated by the Jim twins that he raised a grant to study identical twins separated at birth. John Stroud soon heard about his research, and sent some of his identical twins to America. (John Stroud and Tim Bouchard acquired the same number of identical twins to study—sixteen pairs.) Bouchard quickly realized that the coincidences in the lives of the "Jim twins" were the rule, rather than the exception.

The "Jim twins," James Lewis, left and James Springer, right, with Professor Tom Bouchard at the University of Minnesota. After they were reunited in 1979, at the age of 29, the twins agreed to take part in a research study on the environment's effect on development.

Deep Connection

Recent research provides more fodder for speculation about the bond between identical twins. For instance, identical twins who grew up separately have similar IQs, even closer (on average) than those of fraternal twins who grow up together. When one of a pair of identical twins dies, the remaining twin often experiences deep survivor's guilt and prolonged grief. They may also have difficulties in forming intimate relationships. The kind of suffering felt by surviving twins is so specific that in 1986, Florida therapist Michael Caruso formed a support group called Twinless Twins.

The Power of Twins

Twins have always been a part of myth and legend. Greek and Roman mythology gave us several sets of twins: Castor and Pollux were Greek gods who aided shipwrecked sailors. Their names were also given to the twin stars in constellation Gemini. In Roman mythology, twin brothers Romulus and Remus—sons of Mars, god of war—founded Rome.

Destinies in Duplicate?

What can we make of such preposterous coincidences? It is not entirely surprising that identical twins share the same health problems, the same tastes in clothes, and the same speech rhythms. After all, identical (or "monozygotic"—MZ for short) twins have nearly identical genes and DNA. But coincidences like the same jobs, the same dates, and the same towns are obviously impossible to explain genetically. Even the assumption that MZ twins remain in telepathic contact fails to explain how they could fall downstairs at the same time or both have miscarriages. Research continues, yet the mystery remains.

Charles Fort and Frogs that Fall from the Sky

(2000s)

"'Tremendous numbers of little toads, one or two months old . . . were seen to fall from a great thick cloud that appeared suddenly in the sky that had been cloudless.'—an occurrence in August 1804, near Toulouse, France, according to a letter from Prof. Pontus to M. Arago."

This cryptic little paragraph, from Charles Fort's 1919 *Book of the Damned*, is typical of Fort's no-nonsense style. So is this one: "'A shower of frogs which darkened the air and covered the ground for a long distance is the reported result of a recent rainstorm at Kansas City, Missouri.'—*Scientific American*, July 12, 1873."

Fort does not believe in trying to prove anything. He simply dumps a pile of weird facts in front of the reader and leaves it at that. This may explain why his books never achieved popularity in his own lifetime (1874 to 1932). It was not until the late 1940s—the age of UFOs and space travel—that he was suddenly recognized as the patron saint of the unexplained.

Can tiny frogs fall from the sky?

The Life of a Maverick

Charles Hoy Fort was the eldest son of a wealthy and bad-tempered New York businessman. He grew up with a keen sense of injustice and a dislike of both his parents, which evolved into a dislike of anyone in authority.

At the age of 22, he began supporting himself by writing stories in a style that owed something to Mark Twain. He also cultivated a taste for oddities—books about the Great Pyramids, Atlantis, and the canals of Mars. His first nonfiction book, which he wrote in his mid-30s, was called simply *X*. In it he argued that our civilization is controlled from Mars. In his next book, *Y*, Fort espoused the Hollow Earth theory—the belief that Earth's core is hollow, and perhaps, inhabited. He also described a civilization inside the South Pole. Both manuscripts were rejected and later lost.

In 1916, when Fort was 42, a small inheritance enabled him to devote his days to writing another book, originally called *Z*.

From an early age, Charles Fort showed a keen interest in the unexplained, and devoured books on such topics as the such as the mysterious Great Pyramids.

Things that Fall from the Sky

Fort began to spend his days in the public libraries of New York, searching the periodicals for reports of strange and unexplained events. It struck him that although scientific journals often reported curious happenings, no one wanted to explain them.

Particularly numerous were reports of things falling from the sky: not just meteorites, but showers of coal, fish, frogs, sand, stones, and even blood. Most sounded too silly to be significant. But Fort pointed out that peasants in the fields near Luce, France heard a violent crash like a thunderclap and saw a great stone object hurtle down from the sky on September 13, 1768. The French Academy of Sciences asked the great chemist Antoine Lavoisier for a report on the occurrence; but Lavoisier was convinced that stones never fell out of the sky, and reported that all the witnesses were mistaken or lying. It was not until the nineteenth century that the Academy finally accepted the reality of meteorites. By that time Lavoisier had been dead a long time—he had died by the guillotine during the French Revolution.

Unlike Fort, scientist Antoine Lavoisier, at left with his wife, dismissed claims of odd objects, such as stones, falling from the sky. In his study of the phenomenon, he concluded that the witnesses were unreliable—and probably outright liars.

More Strange Events

The Book of the Damned was a collection of hundreds of unexplained events; it made Fort's reputation among literary men. But it failed to reach a wider public because Fort did not make the slightest attempt to tell a story or entertain his readers.

But the facts are certainly astonishing enough. He describes, for example, a series of strange events that took place in the early 1860s. In July of that year, a great meteorite covered with ice crashed to the earth in Dharamsala, in northern India, and was described by the British Deputy Commissioner in the area. But how could a meteorite, which becomes red hot as it falls through our atmosphere, be covered with ice?

The following evening, the Commissioner saw lights moving in the sky as they were fire balloons. At the same time, a newspaper in Benares, 800 miles to the southeast of Dharamsala, carried a report of a shower of live fish. At Farrukhabad—which lies midway between Dharamsala and Benares—a red substance allegedly rained from the clouds. In 1861, after an earthquake in Singapore followed by days of torrential rain, live fish were found swimming in pools left in the streets. The popular theory that the rain had caused a river to overflow seemed to be contradicted when fish were found in a courtyard surrounded by a high wall.

Fort maintains that strange lights, much like the aurora borealis, or northern lights, shown above, appear before the strange showers of objects.

What's Going on Up There?

Fort suspected that these phenomena were somehow connected with space; there were luminous effects in the sky, like an aurora borealis, at the time of these curious events. There was a period of darkness during daylight hours, a dark spot on the sun, and an earthquake as well. We may know a great deal about the surface of our planet, but we know very little about the billions of miles of space through which Earth travels. Fort's biographer, Damon Knight, was inclined to take the same view after he had gone to the trouble of making a vast card index of all the odd events described in Fort's books; he made graphs that showed when these events occurred. He discovered an immediate correlation between storms, objects seen in the sky or falling from the air, and objects seen in space (like sunspots and comets). For example all of them

reached a peak in 1887 and again in 1892. Knight suggests tentatively that such events could be connected with forces exerted by heavenly bodies—the forces astrologers believe in.

But Fort made no attempt to present a coherent argument in *The Book of the Damned* or the three volumes that followed it. He suggests on one page that there was some sort of floating continent hovering in the sky over India in 1860, and on the next, that there is a sort of universe parallel to ours, but in another "dimension." The reader may get the feeling that Fort takes neither idea seriously. His aim was to provoke "anger and distress" in scientists, and force them to more fully examine their assumptions. He succeeded in neither objective; scientists simply ignored him.

The Fort Society

After his death in 1932, Fort's work was largely forgotten, except by a small circle of admirers who formed a Fortean Society. Fort's work began to attract attention again in the late 1940s, after pilot Kenneth Arnold sighted flying saucers near Mount Rainier in Washington state. As the flying saucer cult gained momentum, Fort was remembered again for his work on the topic years earlier. For example in *The Book of the Damned* he cited the astronomer

E. W. Maunder, of Greenwich Observatory. In November 1882 Maunder observed a kind of aurora, and in the midst of it, a great circular disc of greenish light that passed across the moon.

In the same book, Fort suggests that there have been many "visitors" to Earth, and even—probably his most famous idea— that humankind might be the "property" of such aliens. But Fort never committed himself to any single theory.

Genesistrine

The closest Fort comes to a general theory is in a passage from *The Book of the Damned* about a region of space he calls Genesistrine. Although obviously tongue-in-cheek, it is worth quoting, if only to demonstrate why Fort's work remains unread:

Genesistrine.

The notion is that there is somewhere aloft a place of origin of life relatively to this earth. Whether it's the planet Genesistrine, or the moon, or a vast amorphous region super-jacent to this earth, or an island in the Super-Sargasso Sea, should perhaps be left to the researches of other super—or extra—geographers. That the first unicellular organisms may have come here from Genesistrine—or that men or anthropomorphic beings may have come here before amoebae: that, upon Genesistrine, there may have been an evolution expressible in conventional biologic terms, but that evolution upon this earth has been—like evolution in modern Japan—induced by external influences; that evolution, as a whole, upon this earth, has been a process of population by immigration or by bombardment. Some notes I have upon remains of men and animals encysted, or covered with clay or stone, as if fired here as projectiles, I omit now, because it seems best to regard the whole phenomenon as a tropism—as a geotropism—probably atavistic, or vestigial, as it were, or something still continuing long after expiration of necessity; that, once upon a time, all kinds of things came here from Genesistrine, but that now only a few kinds of bugs and things, at long intervals, feel the inspiration.

Fort would have been delighted with the age of television. It would have satisfied his "craving to annoy" in front of an audience of millions.

As recently as 2004, tiny fish that look like minnows or smelts, have rained on British towns.

Recent Rains

In the 1st century BCE, author and philosopher Pliny the Elder wrote about rains of frogs and fishes. Occasional storms of animals—usually fish or frogs but sometimes even turtles—continued over the centuries. Recent years have brought more strange showers.

In early August 2000 the seaside town of Great Yarmouth in Norfolk, England, lived through a rainy day, which was not so strange. What *was* unusual were that smelts—tiny fish about two inches long—were falling with the rain. Although the town's cats were pleased, residents were merely puzzled.

Then, in mid-August 2004, it happened again. This time, tiny fish, probably minnows, fell in the town of Knighton, Wales, about 175 miles east of London.

A Logical Explanation

Although showers of frogs and fish may sound like freak occurrences, those who study such events will tell you that they're not as puzzling as they once were.

Waterspouts—tornados that form on water—and even strong winds can pick up objects in the water, including small animals, and deposit them several miles away.

Strange Monsters

A sea serpent

Sea Monsters: Unknown Giants of the Deep

(100 CE to present)

On October 10, 1848, the *London Times* reported the following: "When the *Daedalus*, frigate, Captain M'Quhae, which arrived on the 4th [of October], was on her passage from the East Indies between the Cape of Good Hope and St. Helena, her captain, and most of her officers and crew, at four o'clock one afternoon, saw a sea serpent."

A conference was hastily called at the British Admiralty, which concluded that an immediate investigation was required.

The *Daedalus* Serpent

The Admiralty contacted Captain Peter M'Quhae to find out whether there was any substance to the story. To their embarrassment, M'Quhae replied that despite certain glaring inaccuracies, the *Times* story was essentially correct.

His story was as follows: At 5:00 P.M. on August 6, 1848, while the HMS *Daedalus* lay between the Cape of Good Hope and Saint Helena, one of the midshipmen reported a strange creature swimming slowly toward them off the starboard bow.

Most of the crew were at supper. There were only seven men on deck, including the captain, the watch officer, and the ship's navigator. All of them witnessed what M'Quhae described as "an enormous serpent." Judged to be about 100 feet long, it swam in a straight line past the frigate, apparently oblivious to its existence. The captain judged it to be traveling at a rate of 12 to 15 miles an hour and explained that it had remained within the range of their spyglasses for nearly 20 minutes. Although the afternoon was showery and dull, M'Quhae stated that it was still bright enough to see the creature clearly; he said that it swam close enough that "had it been a man of my acquaintance I should have easily recognized his features with the naked eye."

A nineteenth-century print shows a gigantic sea serpent swimming alongside a sailing ship. In those days, the public met reports of sea monster sightings with a mixture of skepticism and credulity.

The Serpent Described

M'Quhae described the large, distinctly snakelike head projecting just above the waves on a neck about 15 inches thick, followed by 60 feet or so of serpentine back, which crested above the surface of the water. The color was uniformly dark brown, apart from the throat, which was a yellowish white. To M'Quhae it seemed to slip through the water effortlessly, without the aid of fins or the undulatory swimming typical of snakes and eels. (This odd fact may be explained by the mane of hair or seaweed that ran along its back; this may have obscured its means of propulsion.) At no point did the creature open its mouth to reveal "large jagged teeth" (as the *Times* had reported). The witnesses had all agreed that it appeared neither frightened nor threatening but rather that it was traveling forward "on some determined purpose." M'Quhae had made a sketch of the creature which, at an admiral's request, he converted into a larger drawing to accompany his statement.

To the Admiralty's credit, it quickly made the controversial report publicly available. On October 13 the *Times* printed the report in full, and 15 days later the *Illustrated London News* printed several pictures of the "Daedalus sea serpent" based on M'Quhae's drawing. The "purposeful" sea monster became a subject of (sometimes heated) national debate.

THE SEA-SERPENT.

Nineteenth-century print of a sea serpent. Tales of long, sinuous sea monsters similar to the one sighted by the *Daedalus* crew have always been found among seafaring peoples.

An original illustration of the 1848 *Daedalus* sea serpent. According to Captain M'Quhae, the monster had ". . . something like the mane of a horse, or rather a bunch of seaweed, washed about its back."

The Danish Monster

One contribution to this debate came as a letter in the *Literary Gazette*, which pointed out that the description of the *Daedalus* monster was remarkably like that of a sea serpent described by the Danish Bishop Pontoppidan in his influential zoological study, *A Natural History of Norway* (1753). The letter continued: "One might fancy the gallant Captain had read the old Dane, and was copying him, when he tells of the dark-brown color and white about the throat, and the neck clothed as if by a horse's mane or a bunch of sea-weed, the exact words of the historian." M'Quhae maintained a dignified silence.

An illustration from Bishop Pontoppidan's *A Natural History of Norway* shows sailors taking aim at a gargantuan dark-colored sea serpent with a horselike mane, .

Owen the Debunker

Sir Richard Owen, an anatomist, naturalist, paleontologist of immense reputation, and curator of the Hunterian Museum, came forward to lead the crusade of *Daedalus* sea serpent debunkers. Owen was considered by many people to be the greatest living authority on zoology. Pugnaciously conservative, he would later become Darwin's most bitter and most venomous opponent.

Owen began by sending the *Times* a copy of a lengthy letter he had written to a friend who had inquired whether the *Daedalus* sea serpent might not be a survival of the Saurian age—one of the most popular theories that had emerged during the controversy.

Owen dismissed M'Quhae's suggestion that the creature was a giant sea snake, implying that the captain should leave scientific deductions to the experts. After a careful consideration of M'Quhae's statement, Owen concluded that the creature was almost certainly a mammal of some sort, and—since his analysis was based on the preconceived idea that the sighting was of some species already known to science—he went on to suggest one that might fit the bill: the *Phoca proboscidea,* or elephant seal. The elephant seal may grow to 20 feet in length, and is native to the seas around Antarctica.

A male southern elephant seal. Sir Richard Owen suggested the *Daedalus* crew had mistaken one of these enormous aquatic mammals for an amphibious sea serpent.

European Sightings

In fact there had been hundreds of sightings of sea serpents before 1848, starting in ancient Greece and Rome. For example, Roman writer Pliny the Elder tells of a sighting of a fish-stealing sea serpent. Bernard Heuvelmans's book *In the Wake of the Sea Serpents* (1968) lists about 150 sightings between 1639 and 1848. In total, Heuvelmans quotes 587 sightings between 1639 and 1966.

One of the 1966 sightings was made by two Englishmen, John Ridgeway and Chay Blyth. Ridgeway wrote in *A Fighting Chance,* "I was shocked to full wakefulness by a swishing noise to starboard. I looked out into the water and suddenly saw the writhing, twisting shape of a great creature. It was outlined by the phosphorescence in the sea as if a string of neon lights were hanging from it. It was an enormous size, some 35 feet or more long, and it came towards me quite fast. . . . It headed straight at me and disappeared right beneath me. . . . I was frozen with terror at this apparition."

Heuvelmans concludes his chapter—and his sightings—with a report by two vacationers near Skegness in eastern England in 1966, who saw "something like the Loch Ness monster" one hundred yards out to sea: "It had a head like a serpent and six or seven pointed humps trailing behind."

GLOUCESTER SERPENT
Sighted by townspeople, 1817

SEA CAVE SERPENTS
Described by Olaf Mansson, 1555

NORTH ATLANTIC OCEAN

NORWAY

GREAT BRITAIN

SKEGNESS SIGHTING
Spotted by tourists, 1960s

EUROPE

NORTH AMERICA

Massachusetts

CARTEIA SERPENT
Sighting in Carteia, modern San Roque, Spain, c. 100 CE

SPAIN

CAPE ANN SERPENT
Sighted by English sailors, 1639

AFRICA

TENERIFE SERPENT
Serpent spotted nearby by *Alecton* crewmembers, 1861

DAEDALUS SERPENT
Spotted by HMS *Daedalus* crew, 1868

SOUTH ATLANTIC OCEAN

FAMOUS SEA SERPENT SIGHTINGS

New England Sea Serpents

The first reported New World sea serpent prowled the shores of Cape Ann, Massachusetts, in 1639. To the English sailors who saw the creature, it resembled a giant snake "coiled like a cable on the rock." Nearly a century later another sea creature appeared in a Massachusetts harbor. First spotted by two women in August 1817, who reported seeing something strange in the water off what is now Pavilion Beach in Gloucester Harbor. For nearly a month, the creature appeared every day, until nearly everyone in the town had witnessed what was described as a 40-foot-long chocolate covered creature with a marlinlike horn on its head cruising the harbor. The witnesses all agreed that it moved very fast, with a vertical undulation.

The Cape Ann sea serpent

Early Monsters

As early as 1539 a Swedish bishop named Olaf Mansson published a map of the north that clearly showed two sea serpents. In *A History of the Goths, Swedes, and Vandals,* published in 1555, Mansson describes a "serpent 200 feet long and 20 feet thick" that lives in the sea caves off Bergen. This story, accompanied by terrifying pictures of serpents devouring ships, was cited by many subsequent encyclopedias. Two hundred years later Bishop Pontoppidan devoted a chapter of *Natural History of Norway* to various monsters, including the sea serpent, the kraken, and the mermaid. In the case of the sea serpent he obtained a firsthand account by Captain Lorenz von Ferry, who ordered a boat to pursue the creature. Von Ferry was able to describe in some detail the horselike head with a white mane and black eyes and the many coils or folds—he thought there were seven or eight, with about a fathom between each fold.

In an illustration from Mansson, a sea serpent devours a ship.

Legends of the kraken—a vast octopoid monster that sometimes attacked swimmers, ships, and even coastal villages—can be traced back as far as the Roman scholar Pliny the Elder, who in the first century CE described a "polyp" with 30-foot-long arms that climbed ashore to steal fish at Carteia in Spain. In fact just about every seagoing culture in the world has had its equivalent of the legendary kraken.

A giant squid, photographed off Japan in 2006

Mystery Solved!

By the end of the eighteenth century science had dismissed such creatures as mythical. But the large number of sea serpent sightings in the nineteenth century off the coast of North America began to erode the skepticism. Huge sucker marks found on sperm whales, and fragments of enormous tentacles found in their stomachs, made it clear that the giant squid was no fiction either.

In November 1861 crewmen on the French gunboat *Alecton* saw a giant squid near Tenerife and tried to harpoon it. The creature was clearly dying, because they were able to slip a noose around it, but it broke in two as they tried to heave it aboard. The squid was about 24 feet long; the mouth measured 18 inches across. The *Alecton* arrived at Tenerife with enough of the monster to leave no possible doubt of its existence, and an account of it was read before the French Academy of Sciences on December 30, 1861. Yet a zoologist named Arthur Mangin continued to express disbelief and wanted to know why the creature had not simply dived below the surface. It was more likely, he thought, that everybody concerned in the report was a liar.

Fast-forward to autumn 2004. That's when—for the first time in history—a live giant squid was photographed in its natural habitat.

A team of researchers found the beast approximately 10 miles off the coast of Japan's Ogasawara Islands and at a depth of between 2,000 and 3,000 feet. For three years the Japanese research had toiled, searching for a live giant squid. Up until that time, only dead squid (and parts of dead squid) had been found, washed ashore or captured in fishermen's nets. But now, in September 2004, the crew had photographed a 26-foot-long squid tangling with a baited hook set by the researchers. (Except for losing one tentacle, the squid escaped unharmed.)

And so it seems that these enormous predators of the deep were not a figment of a drunken sailor's imagination, but also that Olaus Magnus and Bishop Pontoppidan are owed an apology.

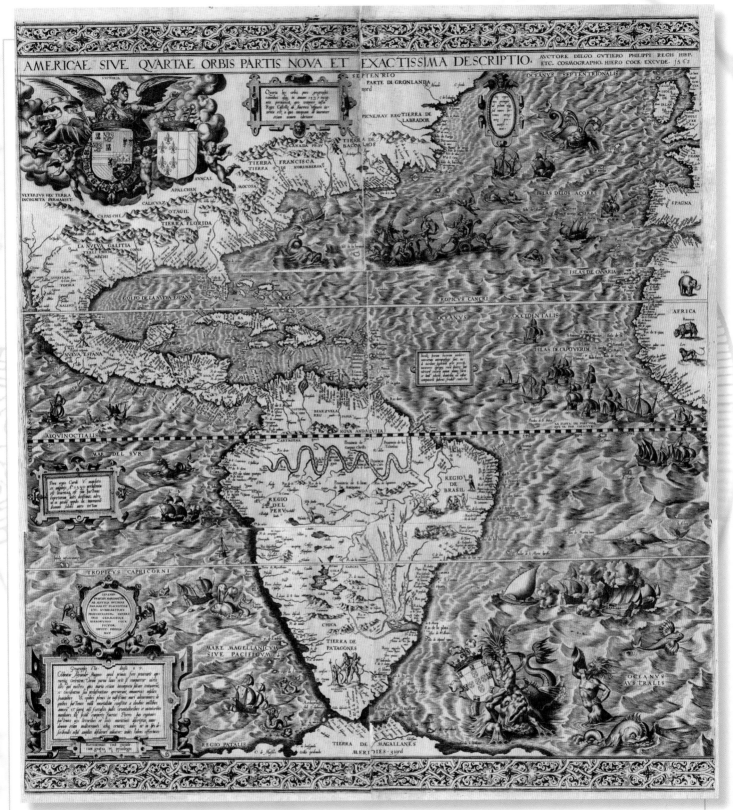

Whether one believed in sea monsters or not, they were familiar images for centuries. For example, mapmaker Hieronymous Cock included them in his 1562 map of the Americas, which includes drawings of imaginary marine animals swimming the Atlantic and Pacific Oceans.

The Legend of the Yeti

(1832 to present)

When British Himalaya mountain climber Eric Shipton was crossing the Menlung Glacier on Mount Everest in 1951, he came upon a line of surprisingly large footprints. Baffled, he photographed one of them, placing an ice axe beside it to provide scale. The print measured a stunning 18 inches long and 13 inches wide. Its shape was curious, with three small toes and a gigantic big toe that appeared almost circular.

Shipton was certain that the footsteps were those of a two-legged creature, not a four-legged wolf or a bear. The only animal with a vaguely similar foot is an orangutan, but they are not found in Tibet.

Mount Everest, or Sagarmatha

First Reports

For as long as European travelers have ventured into Tibet, locals had repeated to them the legends of a huge apelike creature called the *metoh-kangmi,* which translates roughly as "the filthy snowman." The stories cover a huge area, from the Caucasus Mountains to the Himalayas, from the Pamirs through Mongolia to the far eastern tip of Russia. In central Asia the creatures are called *mehteh,* or *yetis,* while tribes of eastern Asia refer to them as *almas.* The earliest reference to them is a report in 1832 by B. H. Hodgson, the British Resident at the Court of Nepal, who mentioned that native hunters were frightened by a "wild man" covered in long, dark hair.

More than half a century later, in 1889, Major Laurence Waddell was climbing the Himalayas when he came across huge footprints in the snow at 17,000 feet; his local guides told him that these were the tracks of a yeti. This, according to the guides, was a ferocious creature that was likely to attack humans and carry them off for food. The best way to escape was to run downhill because the yeti's long hair would fall over its eyes and blind it.

In 1921 an expedition led by Colonel Howard-Bury was making a first attempt on the north face of Everest. The men saw in the distance a number of large dark creatures moving against the snow of the Lhapta-la Pass. The Tibetan porters said these were yetis. In 1925 N. A. Tombazi, a fellow of the Royal Geographical Society, tried to snap a photograph of a naked, upright creature on the Zemu Glacier; it had vanished by the time he focused the camera.

These legends and the sightings continued to leak back to civilization, always with enough doubt that scientists could dismiss them as lies or mistakes. Shipton's photograph of 1951 caused an enormous sensation because it was taken by a member of a scientific expedition who seemed to have no possible motive for stretching the facts. Besides, the photograph spoke for itself.

In 1960, after Everest mountaineer Sir Edmund Hillary claimed to have seen the creature's tracks, *Radar* magazine ran a cover depicting a yeti attack.

Doubts Are Raised

The Natural History Department of the British Museum did not agree that Shipton's prints were those of a yeti. One of its leading authorities, Dr. T. C. S. Morrison-Scott, was soon committing himself to the view that the footprint was made by an ape called the Himalayan langur. His assessment was based on a description of the yeti by sherpa Tenzing Norgay, who had guided Sir Edmund Hillary on his journey up the slope. Norgay said the creature was about 5 feet tall, walked upright, and had a conical skull and reddish brown fur. This, said Dr. Morrison-Scott, sounded quite like a langur.

Objections to the langur theory included the fact that those animals, like most apes, walk on all fours most of the time and have five very long toes, quite unlike the four rounded toes of the photograph. Morrison-Scott's theory was greeted with disdain.

A more imaginative view was taken by the Dutch zoologist Bernard Heuvelmans in a series of articles published in Paris in 1952. He pointed out that in 1934, Dr. Ralph von Koenigwald had discovered some ancient teeth in the shop of a Chinese apothecary in Hong Kong. One of these was a human-type molar that was twice as large as the molar of an adult gorilla. This suggested that the tooth's owner had stood about 12 feet tall. Evidence suggested that this giant—he became known as *Gigantopithecus*—lived around half a million years ago. Heuvelmans suggested that Shipton's footprints were made by a huge biped related to *Gigantopithecus*.

Could this be the yeti? Although the Hanuman langur, native to the Himalayas, usually walks on all fours, it is among the animals that some claim have been mistaken for the Abominable Snowman.

The Abominable Snowman

Just how did the yeti come to be called the Abominable Snowman? It seems that in 1921 a writer mistranslated *metoh*, meaning "filthy" or "dirty," as "abominable." The new name stuck.

Holy Relics

In 1954 the *London Daily Mail* sent an expedition to try to capture (or at least photograph) a yeti. The expedition members spent 15 weeks plodding through the Himalayan snows without so much as a glimpse of the "filthy snowman." But the expedition did gather one exciting piece of information: several monasteries possessed "yeti scalps," which were revered as holy relics. They tracked down several of these scalps. They were fascinating, long and conical, rather like a bishop's mitre, and covered with hair, including a "crest" in the middle, made of erect, bristly hair.

One of the scalps proved to be a fake, sewn together from fragments of animal skin. But others were undoubtedly made of one piece of skin. Hair from the scalps were sent to experts for analysis, who declared that it came from no known animal. It looked as if the existence of the yeti had finally been proved.

The hairy, domed object in this reliquary is allegedly the scalp of a yeti. On view at Khumjung Monastery in Nepal, the scalp is kept under lock and key for safekeeping.

A Yeti that Bleats?

Alas, it was not to be. Sir Edmund Hillary—the first white man to reach Everest's summit—was allowed to borrow one of the scalps; he had Bernard Heuvelmans examine it. The scalp reminded Heuvelmans of a creature called the southern serow, a kind of goat native to Nepal that he had seen in a zoo before the war.

Heuvelmans tracked down a serow in the Royal Institute in Brussels. Comparison with the "yeti" scalp revealed that it came from the same animal. The skin had been stretched and molded with steam. It was not a deliberate fake but was made to be worn in certain religious rituals in Tibet. Over the years its origin had been forgotten, and it had been designated a yeti scalp.

In a pinch, the pate of the mainland serow—a mountain goat native to Nepal—can double for a yeti scalp.

An artist's representation of the yeti. Although most observers who claim to have seen the creatures describe them as dark colored, many illustrations, such as this one, depict yetis as white. The fact that they are thought to live in high snow-covered terrain and are even referred to by locals as "snowmen" may have engendered this common misconception.

The Skeptics and the Believers

The serow hair convinced the skeptics that the yeti was merely a legend. Yet the snowman's tracks were still being observed and photographed in abundance. A Frenchman, the Abbé Bordet, followed three separate sets of tracks in 1955. Squadron Leader Lester Davies filmed oversized footprints in the same year. Climber Don Whillans saw an apelike creature on Annapurna in June 1970, and Lord Hunt photographed more yeti tracks in 1978.

In Russia additional evidence began to emerge. In 1958 Lieutenant Colonel V. Karapetyan saw an article on the yeti—or, as it is known in Russia, the *alma*—in a Moscow newspaper. He sought out leading Soviet professor Boris Porshnev to tell him his own story. Karapetyan's unit had been fighting the Germans in the Caucasus near Buinaksk when he was approached by a unit of partisans and asked to examine a prisoner. The partisans explained that the prisoner was being kept in a barn because as soon as this "man" was taken into a heated room, he stank and dripped sweat; besides, he was covered in lice. The prisoner proved to be more apelike than human: naked and unkempt, he looked dull and vacant and blinked often. He did not attempt to defend himself when Karapetyan pulled hairs from body, and he did not understand speech. Finally Karapetyan left the partisans to make up their own minds about what to do with the creature. He heard a few days later that the wild man had escaped. But a report from the Ministry of the Interior in Daghestean confirmed the truth: the wild man had been court-martialed and executed as a deserter.

It was in January 1958 that Dr. Alexander Pronin, of Leningrad University, reported seeing an *alma*. He was in the Pamir Mountains, a range in central Asia, where he saw a creature outlined against a cliff top. It was humanlike and covered with reddish gray hair. Pronin watched it for more than five minutes. A few days later he saw it again at the same spot.

140

Sangay Wangchuk, Bhutan's National Director of Conservation, claims that these plaster footprint casts are yeti footprints. In many places across the Himalayas, the yeti's existence is taken seriously.

A Mountain of Evidence

For some reason Russians poured scorn on the notion of a "wild man," but the evidence continued to accumulate. Soon Boris Porshnev began to coordinate sightings. The considerable body of evidence is described in some detail in Odette Tchernine's impressive book *The Yeti*. She concludes that the creature could be a Neanderthal man, a species that died out in Europe about 25,000 years ago.

The evidence for the existence of the yeti is strong: hundreds of sightings make it unlikely that it is an invention.

Renewed Interest

Yeti research got a boost in 2004, when Henry Gee, the editor of the well-respected magazine *Nature*, cited the creature as one worth further study. Three years later, in 2007, a U.S. TV crew found footprints while working near Everest. They made casts and sent them to Idaho State University for analysis. Results showed that the prints were very likely real; they were morphologically accurate and showed no trace of having been faked. These kinds of hopeful results have spurred a Japanese team of adventurer to head to Tibet in fall 2008, determined to capture a live yeti on film.

Bigfoot: Monster or Myth?

(1910 to present)

A Bigfoot crossing sign, Washington State

Like the gunfight at the O.K. Corral, the siege of Ape Canyon has become part of American folklore . . . among some people, anyway.

In 1924 a group of miners were working in the Mount St. Helens range in Washington State, 75 miles north of Portland, Oregon, when one of them spotted a large apelike creature peering out from behind a tree. One of the miners fired at it and thought the bullet had hit its head. The creature ran off into the forest. Another miner, Fred Beck—who was to tell the story 34 years later—met another of the "apes" at the canyon rim and shot it in the back three times. It toppled over and fell into the canyon. But the miners found nothing when they went to look for the creature's body.

Attack of the Bigfoots

That night the miners found themselves under siege. From dusk until dawn the next day the creatures hurled rocks and pounded on the doors, walls, and roof of their bunkhouse. The miners braced the heavy door from inside and fired shots through the walls and roof. But the creatures were obviously angry, and the assault ceased only at sunrise. That day the miners decided to abandon the site.

Beck described the "Bigfoot" as apparently humanoid creatures about 8 feet tall and very muscular.

The verdant forests of the Pacific Northwest of the Canada and the United States, such as those of the Mount St. Helens range, above, are said to be home to Bigfoot. This creature, shown in an artist's representation at left, has been described as a hairy, half-human, half-ape creature with gigantic feet—hence its name.

Kidnapped by a Bigfoot

One of the most remarkable Bigfoot stories dates from 1924, although it was not recorded until 1957, when John Green, author of *On the Track of the Sasquatch*, uncovered it. Albert Ostman, a logger and construction worker, was looking for gold at the head of the Toba Inlet in British Columbia. While there, an American Indian told him stories about "big people" living in the mountains. Ostman, undisturbed by the tales, settled down in a campsite opposite Vancouver Island after a hike. When he awoke the next morning, he found that his supplies had been disturbed. He decided to stay awake that night, so when he climbed into his sleeping bag—with his rifle—he removed only his boots. Hours later he reported, "I felt something picking me up. I was asleep and at first I did not know where I was. As I began to get my wits together, I remembered I was in my sleeping bag."

Hours later, his captor dumped him onto the ground. Ostman crawled out of the sleeping bag and found himself in the midst of a "family" of Sasquatches: two adults (one male and one female) and two young (also one male and one female). Ostman described them in considerable detail. The "mother" was more than 7 feet tall, around 70 years of age, and weighed between 500 to 600 pounds. She apparently made no attempt to hurt him but seemed determined to keep him with the group. Possibly she regarded him as a future husband for the younger female, who was small and flat-chested. Ostman spent six days in their company until, choosing his moment, he fired off his rifle. While his captors dived for cover, Ostman escaped. Asked by John Green why he had remained silent for so long, Ostman explained that he figured nobody would believe him.

Toba Inlet in British Columbia. This isolated inlet may be Bigfoot territory.

Two members of the Quinault people of the Pacific Northwest fish from a canoe, 1913. Tales of Bigfoot were common among American Indian tribes decades before the first European reported seeing the hirsute creature.

Bigfoot Legends

Fred Beck's account of the siege, together with other sightings on the West Coast, made Bigfoot something of a national celebrity in the late 1950s. But stories about the creature had been in circulation for centuries. The Salish Indians of British Columbia called it *Sasquatch*, which means "wild man of the woods." The Huppa tribe of northern California calls the creature *Oh-malt-alt*.

The notion that colonies of monsters live quietly in the modern United States and Canada without being detected admittedly sounds absurd. This is partly because few people grasp the sheer size of the North American coniferous forests—thousands of square miles of totally uninhabited woodland, some still unexplored, where it would be possible to hide a herd of dinosaurs, never mind a band of humanoid apes.

In 1910 the *Seattle Times* carried a report about "mountain devils" who attacked the shack of a prospector at Mount St. Lawrence, near Kelso. The attackers were described as half-human and half-monster between 7 and 8 feet tall. According to the legends of the Clallam and Quinault Indians—who call the creatures *Seeahtiks*—"man was created from animals"—*Seeahtiks* were left in a half-finished state.

Carried Away... Literally

On a day in 1928 an American Indian of the Nootka tribe named Muchalat Harry arrived at Nootka, on Vancouver Island. Clad only in torn underwear, Harry was badly shaken. He explained that he had been making his way to the Conuma River to do some hunting and fishing when he, like Ostman, was picked up in his sleeping bag and carried several miles by a Bigfoot. At daybreak he found himself in the midst of a group of about 20 of the creatures and was at first convinced that they intended to eat him.

One of the creatures tugged at his underwear; it was astonished that it was loose, probably assuming it to be skin. Harry sat motionless for hours. By afternoon the beasts seemed to lose interest and wandered away. Harry took the opportunity to escape, and ran a dozen or so miles to where he'd hidden his canoe. He then paddled 45 miles back to Vancouver Island, where he told his story to Father Anthony Terhaar of the Benedictine Mission. According to Terhaar, Harry was in such a state of nervous collapse that his hair turned white, and he needed to be nursed back to health. The experiences shook Harry so much that he never again left the village.

The Hunting Practices of Bigfoot

On an autumn day in 1967, Glenn Thomas, a logger from Estacada, Oregon, was walking along a path at Tarzan Springs near Round Mountain. He came upon three large, hairy figures pulling rocks out of the ground, and then digging down 6 or 7 feet. The male figure removed a nest of rodents and ate them. Investigators looking into his story found 30 to 40 holes, from which rocks weighing as much as 220 pounds had been shifted. Woodchucks and marmots often hibernate under such rocks.

Below, a collection of Bigfoot footprint casts collected over the years. Although the casts show a variety of shapes and sizes, most of the reports of face-to-face encounters with the creatures have described similar-looking creatures. The reports also agree that Bigfoots often behave aggressively toward humans.

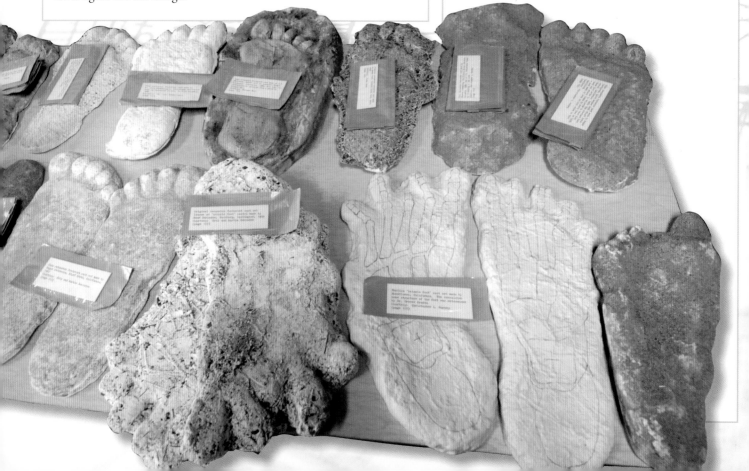

Bigfoot: The Movie

By the late 1960s one of the most convincing pieces of evidence for the existence of Bigfoot had emerged. On October 20, 1967, two young men, Roger Patterson and Bob Gimlin, were horseback riding at Bluff Creek in northern California. They rounded a bend and saw, about 100 feet ahead of them on the other side of the creek, a huge, hairy creature that walked like a human. Roger Patterson grabbed his camera and started filming. The creature—which they had by now decided was female—stopped dead, then looked around at them. "She wasn't scared a bit. The fact is, I don't think she was scared of me, and the only thing I can think of is that the clicking of my camera was new to her."

As Patterson tried to follow, the creature suddenly began to run, and after 3.5 miles they lost her tracks.

The film, which has become famous, shows a creature about 7 feet tall, weighing 350 to 450 pounds, with reddish brown hair and prominent furry breasts and buttocks. As it strides past it turns its head and looks straight into the camera, revealing a fur-covered face. The top of the head is conical. (Both mountain gorillas and Bigfoot's cousin the yeti, or Abominable Snowman, display this feature. According to zoologists, its purpose is to give more anchorage to the jaw muscles to aid in breaking tough plants.)

One of the most famous pieces of evidence in the case for the existence of Bigfoot is a frame from the Patterson-Gimlin film. Although many scientists have dismissed it as a hoax, there has never been any definitive proof for or against it.

Guilt-Free Belief in Bigfoot

Many scientists dismissed the film as a hoax, claiming that the creature was a man dressed in an ape suit. But in his book *More Things*, zoologist Ivan Sanderson quotes three scientists, Dr. Osman Hill, Dr. John Napier, and Dr. Joseph Raight, all of whom seem to agree that there is nothing in the film that leads them, on scientific grounds, to suspect a hoax. Casts taken of the footprints in the mud of the creek indicate a creature roughly 7 feet tall.

This new piece of evidence did not silence the skeptics. But it did allow the rest of us to remain open-minded without feeling guilty.

Since the 1960s reports of the creature have continued to pile up. In fact, since 2000, believers and nonbelievers have gathered annually for a Bigfoot conference. The event, hosted by the Texas Bigfoot Research Center, exhibits casts of footprints and hosts lectures about the latest sightings and other evidence that supports the existence of Bigfoot.

Jeffrey Meldrum, a tenured professor of anatomy at Idaho State University in Pocatello, is one of the world's foremost experts on Bigfoot. He is shown here in his laboratory displaying a casting of a footprint from a Bigfoot creature.

The famous "surgeon's photo" (1934),
later revealed as a hoax

The Loch Ness Monster

(1933 to present)

Loch Ness, the largest of British lakes, is 22 miles long and about 1 mile wide; at its greatest depth, it is 950 feet deep. It is part of the Great Glen, which runs like a deep crack right across Scotland, from one coast to the other. Earthquakes formed the Great Glen between 300 and 400 million years ago, and later glaciers deepened them. At the southern end of the Loch Ness lies the small town of Fort Augustus; at the northern end is Inverness. Until the eighteenth century, the loch was nearly inaccessible. The one road near it was steep and took a long detour: clearly, it did not take the shortest route from Fort Augustus. In the early 1930s a road was finally hacked and blasted out of the northern shore, and vast quantities of rock were dumped down the steep sides of the loch. Thus virtually nobody came to the shores of Loch Ness with regularity until the 1930s.

Early Sightings

Although few ventured near the shores of Loch Ness before the 1930s, reports of observing a lake version of a sea monster are ancient. The first account comes from about 564 CE. According to the *Life of Saint Columba*, the saint encountered a gigantic sea creature after it had killed a fisherman. When Columba made the sign of the cross, the creature retreated.

Sightings picked up in the late nineteenth century, and witnesses as varied as a group of children (who sighted an enormous creature waddling into the water in 1879) to a forester and hotel keeper (who described seeing a "horrible great beastie" in 1895) all reported observing something weird in the water.

Setting Off a Craze

On April 14, 1933, just after the road's completion earlier that month, Mr. and Mrs. John Mackay, proprietors of the Drumnadrochit Hotel to the west of Loch Ness, were returning home from a trip to Inverness. It was about three in the afternoon when Mrs. Mackay exclaimed, "What's that, John?" as she noticed a commotion in the middle of the loch. At first she thought it was two ducks fighting, and then she realized that the area of disturbance was too wide. As her husband pulled up they saw a large animal in the middle of the surging water. The Mackays watched in horrified fascination as the gigantic creature swam toward the other side of the loch. For a moment they glimpsed two black humps, which rose and fell in an undulating manner—then the creature made a half-turn and sank from sight.

The Mackays made no attempt to publicize their story, but gossip about the sighting reached a young water bailiff, Alex Campbell, who happened to be the local correspondent for the *Inverness Courier*. His report went into the *Courier* on May 2, more than two weeks after the sighting occurred. The editor is said to have remarked: "If it's as big as they say, it's not a creature, it's a monster." And so the "Loch Ness Monster" acquired its name.

Notoriety!

By the end of summer 1933, one of the hottest Scottish summers on record, readers all over the British Isles had come to know the Loch Ness monster.

By now there had been recent sightings of the monster on land. On a peaceful summer day, July 22, 1933, Mr. and Mrs. George Spicer were on their way back to London after a holiday in the Highlands. At about four o'clock in the afternoon, they were driving along the southern road from Inverness to Fort William (on the eighteenth-century road). About 200 yards ahead of them, while they were between Dores and Foyers, they saw a trunklike object stretching across the road. Then they saw that it was in motion and that they were looking at a long neck. A gray body, about 5 feet high, soon followed, which moved jerkily across the road (George Spicer later said, "It was horrible—an abomination"). By the time the Spicers' car had reached the spot where the creature had crossed, it had vanished into the undergrowth.

After the Spicers' story hit the papers, others came forward with their own tales. Margaret Munro, a young maidservant, reported observing a long-necked creature with gray, elephantlike skin on the loch's shore. She watched it for nearly 20 minutes before it slipped back into the water, appearing to propel itself with two short front flippers or forelegs. Then in August 1933, a motorcyclist named Arthur Grant not only saw the creature but claimed to nearly run into it on the northeastern shore of the loch. In the early hours of a moonlit night, Grant could make out a small head and an extremely long neck as the creature disappeared back into the loch.

Loch Ness is Scotland's second-largest loch, with a surface area of nearly 22 square miles. With its poor visibility (due to the surrounding soil's high peat content) and its impressive depth (about 620 feet at its deepest), the loch seems an appropriate home for a gigantic, but elusive, sea creature.

The First Photograph

On Sunday, November 12, 1933, Hugh Gray of the British Aluminium Company was carrying a camera as he walked by the loch when he saw the monster rising up out of the water, about 200 yards away. He snapped a picture while it was 2 or 3 feet above the surface of the water. It is not the clearest of photographs, and Gray was so ambivalent about the sighting and afraid of derision that he left the film in his camera for two weeks. His brother finally took it to be developed, and the first picture of Nessie appeared in the *Scottish Daily Record* and the *London Daily Sketch* on December 6, 1933, together with a statement from the Kodak film company confirming that the negative had not been retouched.

Hoax!

The most famous photograph was the celebrated "surgeon's photograph." This showed a dinosaurlike neck and tiny head.

The surgeon, Robert Kenneth Wilson, sold the copyright of the photograph to the *Daily Mail*, where it appeared on April 21, 1934, creating a sensation. But the fact that it had been taken on April 1 (the holiday for practical jokers) aroused much skepticism. This was justified when, in 1979, it was proved to be a hoax, taken by a journalist named Marmaduke Wetherall.

Monster Investigation Bureau

In August 1960 the painter Sir Peter Scott, founder of the Wildfowl Trust, and Richard Fitter of the Fauna Preservation Society approached Member of Parliament David James and asked for his help in getting government assistance for a "flat-out attempt to find what exactly is in Loch Ness." In April 1961 a panel decided that there was "a prima facie case for investigating the loch." The result was the formation of the Bureau for Investigating the Loch Ness Phenomena—a registered charity. In October 1961 two powerful searchlights scanned the loch every night for two weeks, and on one occasion caught an 8-foot "fingerlike object" standing out of the water. In 1962 another team used sonar and picked up several "large objects." One of these sonar recordings preceded an appearance of the monster on the surface.

In November 1972 Robert H. Hines, president of the Academy of Applied Science, released this photo of the fin of the Loch Ness monster, taken that summer. Along with the photo he and his team substantiated the find with sonar readings and other scientific data.

The New Generation

Fascination with the monster, revived in 1957 by the best book on it so far: *More Than a Legend* by Constance Whyte. Whyte interviewed every witness she could find and produced the first comprehensive survey of the evidence since Rupert Gould's *The Loch Ness Monster and Others of 1934*. *More Than a Legend* aroused widespread interest, the author was deluged with correspondence, and once again the Loch Ness monster was front-page news.

The immediate result was a new generation of "monster-hunters." In 1959 an aeronautical engineer named Tim Dinsdale spent most of that winter reading everything he could on the subject of the monster. In the following April he went to Loch Ness to hunt the monster. But after five days he had seen nothing. On the day before he was due to return home he was approaching his hotel in Foyers when he saw something out in the loch; his binoculars showed a hump. He snatched his 16-mm movie camera and began to film as the creature swam away.

In 1966 the Royal Air Force's JARIC (Joint Air Photographic Intelligence Centre) group subjected the Dinsdale film to analysis. It reported that the object filmed was certainly not a boat or a sub-marine. That same year computer-enhancement experts from NASA discovered that two other parts of what appear to an animate body also broke the surface besides the main hump.

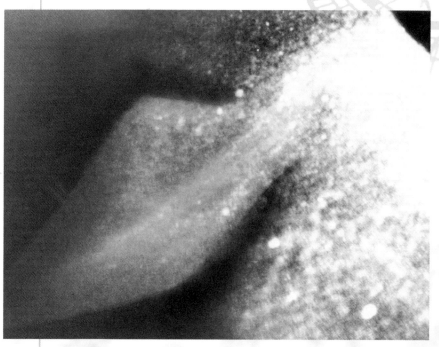

The Nessie Solution?

A 1975 photograph clearly showed a long-necked creature and its front flipper. This was particularly impressive because sonar evidence—waves of sound reflected back from the creature—made it clear that this was not some trick of the light, piece of floating wreckage, or lake weed.

Nicholas Witchell triumphantly concludes his book *The Loch Ness Story* (1975) with a chapter entitled "The Solution," in which he describes his excitement when Robert H. Hines telephoned him from the United States to describe his color photo of the monster. Writes Witchell, "With the official ratification of the discovery of the animals in Loch Ness, the world will lose one of its most popular mysteries." He declares that it would be ignoble now to gloat about the shortsightedness of the scientific establishment for its skeptical attitude towards Loch Ness.

It is now clear that Witchell was premature. Most people still regard the question of the monster's existence as an open question, and the majority of scientists and the general public still regard the whole thing as something of a joke.

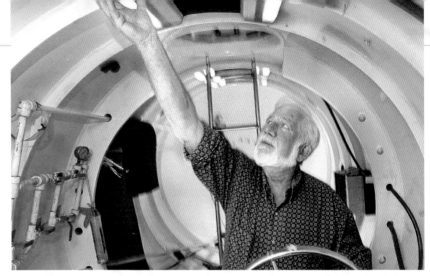

Dan Taylor aboard *Nessa*, a submarine he designed to plummet the depths of Loch Ness

An American Joins the Fray

Dan Taylor, a former Naval submariner who lived in Hilton Head, South Carolina, was among those who were convinced that the Loch Ness monster existed. He was so sure, in fact, that he self-financed and built not one but two small submarines, each designed to plumb the depths of Loch Ness and find the elusive monster. He piloted the first sub, the fiberglass *Viperfish*, through the lake in 1969. It was then that he claimed he first saw the beast in a swirl of muddy water. "It wasn't until I was back on the surface and on dry land," he told a reporter "that it occurred to me that this might have been the monster saying hello."

Taylor funded the construction of his second vessel, the 44-foot submarine *Nessa*, by selling his home and spending his inheritance. His goal, he said, was not to capture the Loch Ness monster, but rather, to obtain a tissue sample from the beast, to determine whether it was a mammal or fish. Sadly, Taylor died in 2005 and never returned to the lake.

The Real Nessie?

In 1976 Roy Mackie, a director of the Loch Ness Investigation Bureau and professor of biochemistry at the University of Chicago, published a balanced and thoroughgoing scientific assessment, *The Monster of Loch Ness*. He turns a critical eye on the evidence, but concludes: "It is now proven that a population of moderate-sized piscivorous aquatic animals is inhabiting Loch Ness."

Nonetheless the most recent explorations of Loch Ness have not been fruitful. In 1987, 19 boats, sending out sonar signals, swept the entire loch. The two-day search turned up nothing.

A second BBC-sponsored sonar sweep of Loch Ness, undertaken in 2003, also found nothing hiding in the depths.

When and if the "monster" is finally identified and classified it will undoubtedly be something of an anticlimax, and Loch Ness will probably lose most of its tourist industry at a blow. Half the fascination of the monster lies in the notion that it is terrifying and dangerous. In fact all the evidence suggests that, like that other legendary marauder the killer whale, it will turn out to be shy, amiable, and quite harmless to humans.

A chupacabra statue

El Chupacabra—The Goat Sucker

(1995 to present)

The killing began during March 1995, in the mountainous inland districts of Morovis and Orocovis on the island of Puerto Rico. Each morning unlucky inhabitants would find their smaller livestock (such as chickens, sheep, and goats) lying dead in their pens, drained of blood from deep puncture wounds to the neck or chest. Within weeks the slaughter had spread across the island, reaching near-epidemic proportions.

Search parties—some of 200 men—made nightly patrols. Animals were rigorously guarded. Yet it was not until six months had passed that anyone saw the *chupacabra* (a Spanish word meaning "goat sucker") in the flesh . . .

A Beastly Death Toll

In September 1995, housewife Madelyne Tolentino spotted the monster near the town of Canovanas in the eastern part of the island. She described a fanged, furry kangaroolike beast with bulging red eyes. The *chupacabra* was then sighted regularly over the next four months. Later reports suggested a pig or human-oid-headed creature with a tail and spikes, or pointed tufts of hair, running down its back. Some even swore that the beast walked erect, stood about 4 feet high, and had clawed hands.

By mid-December 1995 the *chupacabra* had killed more than 1,000 animals, including goats, chickens, turkeys, sheep, rabbits, cats, dogs, and even cows and horses. Fortunately the creature seemed to have no taste for human prey, although in November 1995 a red-eyed, hairy beast was seen breaking open a bedroom window, reaching inside, and ripping a teddy bear to pieces—presumably out of frustration.

The Puerto Rican government could not deny that the attacks were happening—their impact on the rural economy was self-evident on such an impoverished island—but officials insisted that the attacks were the work of wild dogs or feral monkeys. This explanation didn't convince the locals, however, they knew that dogs and monkeys are not known for their vampiric habits.

Traveling Monster

Although the *chupacabra* attacks dwindled on Puerto Rico after their initial frenzy in late 1995, the menace has never completely left the island. The creature also seems to have learned to swim great distances, because it began to appear on the North American mainland.

By late March 1996 locals had blamed the goat sucker for more than 60 animal deaths (including goats, chickens, ducks, and geese) in a Latino neighborhood of South Miami. One woman claimed to have seen "a doglike figure standing up with two short hands in the air." Against these claims, zoologist Ron Magill insisted that the marks on the victims were "classic canine punctures from dogs."

By late April, farmers in 11 Mexican states reported dozens of vampiric attacks, most often on goats. Mexican officials admitted that the animal casualties were genuine, but placed the blame on coyotes and bats driven to desperation by the recent drought. Why such attacks had never happened before in a country particularly prone to droughts was not explained.

Goats make fine meals for *chupacabras*, who have a taste for livestock.

The Texas Carcasses

For well over a decade, the *chupacabra* attacks were reported over a growing region of the world. In the Americas vampiric attacks on animals were also reported in Costa Rica, El Salvador, Guatemala, and as far south as Brazil and Amazonia. In October 1996 the goat sucker managed to cross the Atlantic, attacking a herd of 28 sheep in Idanha-a-Novo, Portugal. A local farmer claimed that each animal had suffered a single deep puncture to the left side of the neck—nine died.

By March 2005 the *Komsomolskaya Pravda* newspaper was reporting the vampiric killing of sheep, turkeys, and chickens in the Saraktash region of central Russia by a dog- or kangaroolike creature with long fangs.

In August 2007 at Cuero, Texas, farmer Phylis Canion started to lose chickens to a creature that did not eat them, but instead drained them of blood. She spotted a strange, smallish, hairless, doglike creature on her property that she believed was the culprit. It had long back legs and very long canine fangs. In speaking with her neighbors, she learned that three animals identical to the creature she had seen had been hit by cars or trucks.

Forensic testing revealed that the Cuero *chupacabra* was a canine, probably a coyote-dog or coyote–Mexican wolf crossbreed.

Phylis Canion of Cuero, Texas, holds a photo of what she calls a *chupacabra*. Canion believes that the strange-looking animal, which she found dead outside her ranch in late summer 2007, is responsible for killing many of her chickens.

Lingering Questions

But even if the *chupacabra* is actually just a type of dog, coyote, wolf, or a hybrid of these closely related species, questions remain. Why are the creatures hairless when skin samples show that they naturally should sport a fur coat? Mange, the most common ailment that causes canines to shed clumps of hair has not, to date, been seen to destroy all the fur on an entire animal, let alone every member of the species, as was found with the Cuero carcasses.

There is also the odd physical shape of the *chupacabras* found in Texas. The back legs are uniformly much longer than the front legs; thus, perhaps, the common comparison by eyewitnesses of the *chupacabra* to a kangaroo. This is not a common feature of dogs, coyotes, or wolves. On the other hand, it may explain why some witnesses claimed that the creature was bipedal. Four-legged animals with longer back legs often perch on them, briefly, to scan the immediate area for danger or prey.

Most troubling is the vampiric diet of the *chupacabra*, which was repeatedly and officially confirmed from attack sites across the globe. Prey animals are not thoroughly mauled or partially eaten, as is typical with a canine attacker. They suffer one or more deep puncture wounds and are drained of blood. Hematophagia, or blood-drinking, is rare outside of the insect world, the sole exception among mammals being the South American vampire bat (*Desmodus rotundus*). In fact, there is some doubt as to whether a creature larger than a small bat could survive on a diet consisting only of fresh blood.

If the *chupacabra* is some newly discovered, or even newly evolved species, it remains outside all previous scientific experience.

Occult Mysteries

Real-Life Vampires?

(1110s-present)

Vlad Dracula, aka Vlad the Impaler

Although the man who lent his name to the world's most famous vampire was not a vampire himself, he was surely just as bloodthirsty. Vlad Dracula, who inspired Bram Stoker to name his infamous character Count Dracula, was a fifteenth-century prince of Wallachia, which is now part of Romania. Vlad made a name for himself as a ruthless warrior who fought with great success against the Turks, who planned to conquer Europe.

Vlad, also known as Vlad Tepes (*tepes* means "impaler" in Romanian), was, as his nickname implies, a man of sadistic temperament whose greatest pleasure derived from impaling his enemies on pointed stakes. Vlad subjected an estimated 100,000 people to impalement during the course of his lifetime.

By the early 1730s, Vlad's enemies, the Turks, had been driven out of Serbia, and the Austrians occupied Belgrade. The Austrians soon became aware of a strange superstition among the peasantry; they dug up corpses and beheaded them, alleging that they were vampires, or *upirs*.

The Undead

Tales of the "living dead" have been told in Eastern Europe since the days of ancient Greece. The Greeks called the bloodthirsty creature a *lamia* or *empusa* and seemed to identify it with a witch. *Lamiae* were not just blood drinkers, though, but also cannibals.

Tales of "undead" creatures—known as *vrykolakas*—persisted in Greece down through the centuries, and on January 1, 1701, a French botanist named Pitton de Tornefort visited the island of Mykonos, where he witnessed a gruesome scene of dissection. An unnamed peasant, of sullen and quarrelsome disposition, was murdered in the fields by persons unknown. Two days after his burial, his ghost was reported wandering around at night, overturning furniture and "playing a thousand roguish tricks." Ten days after his burial, a Mass was said to "drive out the demon" believed to be in the corpse, after which the body was disinterred and the local butcher given the task of tearing out the heart. But even after the villagers burned the heart at the seashore, the ghosts continued to cause problems until they finally burnt the corpse on a pyre.

The ancient Greeks believed that the lamia, shown at right in a painting by John William Waterhouse, was a vampire who stole little children to drink their blood. She was portrayed as a snakelike creature with a female head and breasts.

Do Vampires Really Exist?

The problem of the vampire can be stated simply: any rational person will agree that the notion that vampires actually exist has to be pure superstition. There has to be some simpler, more sensible, explanation.

But this view is contradicted by a number of early accounts written with such an air of sobriety and authority that it is difficult to dismiss them as pure fantasy. For example, an early eighteenth-century report about an undead Serbian, known as *Visum et Repertum* ("Seen and Discovered"), is signed by no fewer than five Austrian officers, three of them doctors:

> *After it had been reported in the village of Medvegia* [near Belgrade] *that so-called vampires had killed some people by sucking their blood, I was, by high decree of a local Honorable Supreme Command, sent there to investigate the matter thoroughly. What I learned was as follows: About five years ago, a local haiduk called Arnod Paole broke his neck in a fall from a hay wagon. In 20 or 30 days after his death, some people complained that they were being bothered by this same Arnold Paole; and in fact, four people were killed by him. In order to end this evil, they dug up Arnold Paole 40 days after his death— this on the advice of their Hadnack* [a bureaucrat], *who had been present at such events before; and they found that he was quite complete and undecayed, and that fresh blood had flowed from his eyes, nose, mouth, and ears; that the shirt, the covering, and the coffin were completely bloody; that the old nails on his hands and feet, along with the skin, had fallen off, and that new ones had grown. And since they saw from this that he was a true vampire, they drove a stake through his heart—according to their custom—whereupon he gave an audible groan and bled copiously. Thereupon they burned the body to ashes the same day and threw these into the grave. . . . these same people also say that all those who have been tormented and killed by vampires must themselves become vampires.*

> *Signed: L.S. Johannes Fluchinger, Regimental Medical Officer of the Foot Regiment of the Honorable B. Furstenbusch.*

> *L.S. J. H. Siegel, Medical Officer of the Honorable Morall Regiment.*

> *L.S. Johann Friedrich Baumgarten, Medical Officer of the Foot Regiment of the Honorable B. Furstenbusch.*

Do the spirits of the dead leave their graves to kill the living? In eighteenth-century Eastern Europe, the answer wold be yes. This era saw a rise in the belief in vampires, not just among superstitious peasants but also highly educated doctors, such as those who examined the corpse of Arnold Paole.

As we study this strange account, an obvious temptation is to dismiss it as peasant superstition. Yet this is no secondhand tale of absurd horrors; the three doctors were officers in the army of Charles VI, Emperor of Austria. Although some critics explain away the details of the case as ignorance about the process of decomposition, these doctors were thoroughly familiar with corpses, having fought the Turks from 1714 to 1718.

A fifteenth-century woodcut, above, depicts Vlad the Impaler enjoying a feast in the midst of a "forest" of impaled bodies. Although Bram Stoker took Vlad's name for his vampire character, he made his character far less brutal. He lived in a crumbling ruin of a castle and slept in a coffin, but Bela Lugosi's Count Dracula in the 1931 film version of Stoker's novel, *Dracula*, at left, was sophisticated—even seductive—a far cry from the monstrous killers of historical accounts of vampires.

Birth of the Count

A brief sketch of the historical background may clarify the emergence of vampires in the first half of the eighteenth century. For more than 400 years, the Turks had dominated Eastern Europe, marching in and out of Transylvania, Wallachia, and Hungary, and even conquering Constantinople in 1453. Don John of Austria defeated them at the great sea battle of Lepanto (1571), but it was their failure to capture Vienna after a siege in 1683 that caused the breakup of the Ottoman Empire. Four hundred and twenty years later, in 1897, Bram Stoker immortalized Vlad the Impaler as the sinister Count Dracula, no longer a sadistic maniac but a drinker of blood.

According to some stories of eighteenth-century Eastern Europe, the vampire's body, thriving even after death, may have remained in a coffin while its spirit or projection stalked its living victims. A fear of premature burial may have exacerbated the fear of vampires.

Realistic Accounts

Twenty years after the Turks left Eastern Europe, gruesome tales of disinterments astonished Western Europe. Still more alarming, many of the accounts were firsthand.

The official account of what happened when respected townspeople of the Serbian village of Kisilova, Serbia, exhumed the body of suspected vampire Peter Plogojowitz dates from 1725. An official reported:

After a subject by the name of Peter Plogojowitz had died, 10 weeks past—he lived in the village of Kisilova, in the Rahm district [of Serbia]—and had been buried according to the Raetzian custom, it was revealed that in this same village of Kisilova, within a week, nine people, both young and old, died also, after suffering a 24-hour illness. And they said publicly, while they were yet alive, but on their deathbed, that the above-mentioned Peter Plogojowitz, who had died 10 weeks earlier, had come to them in their sleep, laid himself on them, and throttled them, so that they would have to give up the ghost.

I went to the village of Kisilova . . . and viewed the body of Peter Plogojowitz, just exhumed, finding that I did not detect the slightest odor that is otherwise characteristic of the dead, and the body—except for the nose, which was somehow sunken—was completely fresh. The hair and the beard—even the nails, of which the old ones had fallen away—had grown

on him; the old skin, which was somewhat whitish, had peeled away, and a new fresh one had emerged under it. The face, hands, and feet, and the whole body, could not have been more complete in his lifetime. Not without astonishment, I saw some fresh blood in his mouth, which according to the common observation, he had sucked from the people killed by him. In short, all the indications were present (as remarked above) as such people are supposed to have. All the people sharpened a stake and pierced the heart, and not only did much blood, completely fresh, flow also through his ears and mouth, Finally, according to their usual practice, they burned the aforementioned body, in hoc casu, to ashes.

Signed: Imperial Provisor, Gradisk District

Here again a respectable official vouches for the fact that the corpse looked remarkably fresh and had fresh blood in the mouth.

So it seems clear that the vampire is not a physical body that clambers out of its grave—as in *Dracula*—but some sort of ghost or spectral "projection." What the villagers allege is that the body has been taken over by a demonic entity, which attacks the living and somehow drains their vitality—not the Dracula-like vampire who sinks his pointed fangs into the victim's flesh. The corpse that is the home of the demonic entity then flourishes in the grave and even continues to grow new skin and nails.

The Shoemaker of Breslau

On September 21, 1591, a well-to-do shoemaker of Breslau, in Silesia—one account gives his name as Weinrichius—cut his throat with a knife and soon after died from the wound. Because suicide was regarded as a mortal sin, his wife tried to conceal it and announced that her husband had died of a stroke. She admitted the truth to one old woman, who washed the body and bound up the throat so skillfully that the wound was invisible. A priest who came to comfort the widow was taken to view the corpse and noticed nothing suspicious. They buried the shoemaker on the following day, September 22.

Perhaps because of this unseemly haste and the refusal of the wife to allow neighbors to view the body, a rumor sprang up that the shoemaker had committed suicide. After this, townspeople began to see his ghost in the town. Soon it was climbing into bed with people and squeezing them so hard that it left the marks of its fingers on their flesh. This finally became such a nuisance that in the year following the burial, on April 18, 1592, the council ordered the grave opened. The body was complete and undamaged by decay but "blown up like a drum." The skin had peeled away from the feet, and another layer had grown, "much purer and stronger than the first." He had a "mole like a rose" on his big toe—which was interpreted as a witch's mark—and there was no smell of decay, except in the shroud itself. Even the wound in the throat was undecayed. The corpse was laid under a gallows, but the ghost continued to appear. By May 7 it had grown "much fuller of flesh." Finally the council ordered that the corpse be beheaded and dismembered. When the body was opened up, the heart was found to be "as good as that of a freshly slaughtered calf." Finally, the city folk burned the body on a huge bonfire of wood and pitch and threw the ashes into the river. After this, the ghost ceased to appear.

The Gateway to Breslau, now part of Poland. It was in the houses here that the revenant shoemaker of Breslau appeared to his sleeping victims.

Dead Man Wandering

There are even earlier accounts of the walking dead. French vampire expert Jean Marigny remarks:

> Well before the eighteenth century, the epoch when the word "vampire" first appeared, people believed in Europe that the dead were able to rise from their graves to suck the blood of the living. The oldest chronicles in Latin mention manifestations of this type, and their authors, instead of employing the word vampire (which did not yet exist) utilized a term just as explicit, the word sanguisugae (Latin for "leech," or "bloodsucker"). The oldest of these chronicles date from the twelfth and thirteenth centuries and, contrary to what one might expect, are not set in remote parts of Europe, but in England and Scotland.

Marigny goes on to cite four cases described by twelfth-century chronicler William of Newburgh, author of *Historic Rerum Anglicarum*. The first, "of the extraordinary happening when a dead man wandered abroad out of his grave," describes a case recounted a local archdeacon described to the chronicler: In Buckinghamshire, a man returned from the grave the night after his burial and attacked his wife. When he attacked again the following night, the wife asked various neighbors to spend the evening with her, and their shouts drove the ghost away. Then the ghost began to create a general disturbance in town, attacking animals and alarming people. That he was a ghost, and not a physical body, is proved by the comment that some people could see him while others could not (although they "perceptibly felt his horrible presence"). The archdeacon consulted the bishop, Hugh of Lincoln, whose learned advisers suggested that the body should be dug up and burned to ashes. Hugh of Lincoln felt this would be "undesirable" and instead wrote out a charter of absolution. When the tomb was opened, the body proved to be "uncorrupt," just as on the day it was buried. The absolution was placed on his chest and the grave closed again; after that, the ghost ceased to wander abroad.

Odoriferous Ghosts

Another of William of Newburgh's accounts sounds slightly more like the traditional vampire in that the ghost—of a wealthy man who had died at Berwick on Tweed—gave off an odor of decomposition that affected the air and caused plague. The body was exhumed (it is not recorded whether it was undecayed) and burned.

Smell also gave up the ghost of Alnwick Castle. In this story a dissolute lord in Northumberland spied on his wife's adultery by lying atop the "roof" that covered her four-poster bed. The sight of his wife and her lover "clipping at clicker" so incensed him that he fell and injured himself, dying a few days later without absolution. He returned as a ghost to haunt the district, his stench causing a plague that killed many people. When the corpse was exhumed, it proved to be "gorged and swollen with a frightful corpulence"; when attacked with a spade, there gushed out such a stream of blood "that they realized that this leech had battened on the blood of many poor folk." The body was cremated and the haunting ceased.

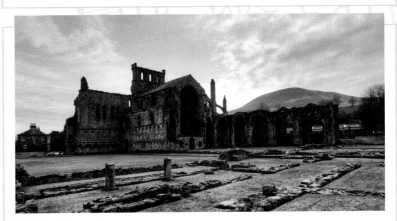

Melrose Abbey, burial place—and haunting grounds—of a thirteenth-century priest

The Haunted Abbey

A priest, chaplain of a lady of rank, at Melrose Abbey, whose life had been far from blameless, is the center of Another tale from William of Newburgh. After his death, his ghost of the chaplain haunted the cloister and appeared in the bedchamber of the lady. Officials finally had the body exhumed and burned.

This and the other cases told by William of Newburgh took place long before Western Europe heard tales of vampires. But the talk of *sanguisugae* creating a disturbance suggests that they have much in common with poltergeists, or noisy ghosts, which have been widely chronicled down the ages. And the poltergeist is basically a type of earthbound spirit, a dead person who is not aware that he is dead.

The Monstrous Man-Wolf

(1520–1630)

The bloodthirsty lycanthrope

Do werewolves exist? Here, as in the case of its celebrated cousin the vampire, we have many impressive accounts that attest to their existence.

In the 110 years between 1520 and 1630, there are no fewer than 30,000 reports of lycanthropy (*lycos* means "wolf," *anthropos* means "man") in central France alone, where they were called *loups-garous*. There are also reports from Belgium, Denmark, Germany, Great Britain, Holland, Hungary, Iceland, Finland, Norway, Russia, Spain, and Sweden, so it is difficult to dismiss the belief in werewolves, as Rossell Hope Robbins does in his *Encyclopedia of Witchcraft and Demonology,* as a sign of superstition or madness.

Pierre Gandillon

A typical case is that of Benoit Bidel who lived at Naizan in the Jura region of France In 1598 the 16-year-old Bidel was found dying from a stab wound. He claimed that he had climbed a tree to pick fruit when a wolf attacked his sister, who was down below. Bidel tried to fight off the wolf with a knife, but he claimed that the wolf snatched the knife from him—with human hands—and stabbed him. The boy then died. A search was made of the area and a girl named Pernette Gandillon was found. Deciding that she might be the werewolf, the townspeople killed her. Then someone remembered that her brother Pierre was scarred with scratches; he was arrested, together with his other sister, Antoinette, and his son, Georges. All three confessed to being werewolves. Judge Henri Boguet, author of *Discourse on Sorcerers,* visited the Gandillons in jail and said that they ran around on all fours. They confessed that they had turned themselves into wolves with the aid of a witch's salve, and that they had attended "sabbats." All three were sentenced to death and burned.

The forest primeval of Jura, France, where young Benoit Bidel and his sister were attacked by a werewolf

Witches' Salves?

Could devil's weed (*Datura stramonium*)—which has strong narcotic and potentially fatal effects—be the source of lycanthropic madness?

Rossell Hope Robbins takes the commonsense view that all three Gandillons were insane. But Nevill Drury and Stephen Skinner suggest an interesting possibility in *The Search for Abraxas* (1971). Discussing Carlos Castaneda and his Don Juan books, they note that Castaneda described how the "sorcerer" Don Juan had taught him to make a paste of the root of the datura plant, also called devil's weed, and how, when he rubbed it on his body, he felt he was flying at great speed through the air. Is it possible, ask the authors, that the witches' salves of past centuries were made of a similar substance that produced a similar hallucination? (In fact, Lord Lytton had already made such a suggestion in his occult novel *A Strange Story*.) Of course much of Castaneda's work has been discredited after astute critics noticed that his books were full of factual contradictions, especially regarding dates; yet this particular suggestion remains plausible.

The Witchcraft Connection

In studying the reports of werewolves, one thing becomes clear: the beast was very closely bound up with witchcraft. The Gandillon family, whether they were insane or not, believed that they had attended witches' sabbaths and that they could turn themselves into wolves by means of a salve. They believed that their powers came ultimately from the Devil. It is interesting to note that Pierre Gandillon fell into a trance on Maundy Thursday (a Christian holy day celebrating the Last Supper). When he had recovered, Gandillon claimed he had attended a sabbath of werewolves. He believed, then, that he attended these sabbaths in the spirit, rather than in the flesh, a belief that ties in with theories of astral bodies. Indeed, according to the nineteenth-century French magician Eliphas Levi, a werewolf is simply the astral body of the sorcerer projected into the shape of a wolf.

This 1508 German woodcut depicts a witches' sabbath, or sabbat. During the nocturnal gathering, the attendants allegedly rode goats and consumed a stew of human flesh.

The Role of Delusions?

It is undoubtedly true that many so-called werewolves were people who suffered from delusions. In 1603 a teenage boy named Jean Grenier claimed to some girls that he was a werewolf; when he was arrested, he implicated his father and a neighbor. In fact children *had* been attacked in the area. But the parliament of Bordeaux accepted the father's explanation that his son was an imbecile; Jean was placed in custody in a monastery, where he died a few years later.

Peter Stubbe: The Werewolf of Cologne

In other cases the explanation may be less simple. In the late sixteenth century the case of a werewolf named Peter Stubbe caused a great stir all over Europe. There had been many wolf attacks in the Cologne area. After a wolf attacked a group of children, nearly tearing the throat out of one of them, a hunt was organized. The wolf vanished, but the hunters found a man—Peter Stubbe—walking toward Cologne in the area where the wolf had apparently vanished. Under torture Stubbe confessed. He claimed that he was a witch and that the Devil had given him a magic belt (which was never found) that enabled him to transform into a werewolf. He admitted to incest with his sister and daughter, with whom he had had a child. He claimed that he had killed many children, as well as large numbers of sheep, lambs, and goats, over a period of 25 years. After his confession, authorities tortured and decapitated him.

Even by the violent standards of his day, Stubbe's execution was excessively brutal. His condemners tied him to a wheel, and then, wielding red-hot pincers, they tore flesh from 10 places on his body. Next they tore flesh from his arms and legs. They then hammered him with the blunt side of an axe head until his limbs broke—this would prevent him from returning from the grave. Stubbe was finally beheaded and his body burned on a pyre. His severed head was then displayed as part of a grotesque tableau. Authorities ordered a pole be erected with Stubbe's head placed upon a wolf figure, which stood on the torture wheel.

Executioners also strangled and burned Stubbe's daughter and sister.

A contemporary woodcut shows the execution of Peter Stubbe in 1589 near Cologne. It shows the sequence of punishment from the tearing of flesh, to the placing of his severed head atop a pole.

Actual Transformation?

Could an obsession with shape-shifting and wolves cause actual physical changes? William Seabrook has a remarkable description of how a Russian émigré woman meditated on hexagram 49 from the I Ching, whose meaning is associated with an animal's fur and with molting. She imagined herself to be a wolf in the snow, then began to make baying noises and slaver at the mouth. When one of the witnesses attempted to wake her up, she leapt at his throat and tried to bite it.

A Confession of Witchcraft

Sex often lies at the heart of stories of witchcraft. In 1662 a Scottish farmer's wife, Isobel Gowdie, startled and shocked the elders of the neighboring church in Auldearne (near Inverness) when she suddenly confessed that for 16 years she had been a witch, attended sabbaths, and had sexual intercourse with the Devil. A pretty, redheaded girl at the time of her marriage, she had obviously become increasingly disillusioned with her husband, who is said to have been stupid and boorish. Gowdie said that she left a broomstick in bed beside him when she attended covens (she was the first to use the word). Witches, she said, had the power to change themselves into animals or birds—a cat, a hare, a crow—or a wolf.

The Gray Devil

According to Gowdie—who made four confessions between April and her trial—she encountered the Devil, a man dressed in gray, when she was traveling between two farms. She promised herself to him and agreed to meet him at the church in Auldearne. There a woman called Margaret Brodie held her while the Devil sucked blood from her shoulder, making a Devil's mark, and baptized her. She described the Devil as a big, black, hairy man, who came to her a few days later and copulated with her. He would copulate freely with all the female witches of the coven, who thoroughly enjoyed it.

Sometimes the Devil changed himself into an animal, such as a deer or bull or goat, before he copulated. His sperm, she said, was freezing cold.

The odd thing about the Gowdie case is that no one had accused her of witchcraft; she had no reason to come forward and confess. Even stranger, women she mentioned often confirmed what she said in detail.

A fifteenth-century illustration of a witches' sabbath shows several practitioners of witchcraft paying homage to a horned goat. The goat is often associated with satanic rituals. The reason may come directly from Matthew 25:33, which describes the judgment: "And before him shall be gathered all nations; and he shall separate them one from another, as a shepherd divideth his sheep from the goats: And he shall set the sheep on his right hand, but the goats on the left."

Some people accused as werewolves were reported to assume the posture—but not always the physical characteristics—of wolves when they committed their grisly deeds.

Gilles Garnier

Gilles Garnier, executed as a werewolf in 1574, seems to have attacked children while assuming either the shape of a man or a wolf. The charge, drawn up at Dole, alleged that he had seized a 12-year-old girl and killed her in a vineyard with his hands and teeth, and then, with his teeth, dragged her along the ground into the wood at La Serre, where he ate most of her. He so enjoyed it that he took pieces of the girl's body home to his wife.

Garnier also killed a 12-year-old boy in a wood and was about to eat the flesh ("although it was a Friday") when some men interrupted him. They testified that he was in human form—a fact that Garnier did not dispute. But he insisted that he was in the shape of a wolf when he strangled the boy and, with his fangs, tore off the child's leg.

Garnier also attacked a 10-year-old girl—again wearing his wolf shape—but was forced to flee when interrupted; she died of her wounds. On this occasion, the peasants who interrupted Garnier saw him as a wolf, but nevertheless thought that they recognized Garnier's face. He was sentenced to be burned alive.

The Witch Trials

One possible explanation for Stubbe and Garnier is that they confessed to a great deal of nonsense under torture. But it is surely more significant that the great majority of werewolf reports date from the same period as the witch-craft trials in Europe and that many "werewolves," like the Gandillons, confessed to being witches. A study of witch-craft trials leaves little doubt that the majority of cases were miscarriages of justice.

In cases of vampirism, it seems a reasonable assumption that the vampire is a so-called "hungry ghost" or earthbound spirit; in cases of lycanthropy, it seems clear that individuals with a taste for sorcery or witchcraft attempted to invoke spirits in order to change into a wolf. In effect, such individuals were inviting the spirits to possess them.

And, as in the case of vampirism, there seem to be powerful sexual undertones in many werewolf legends. Many modern sex killers—for example, the child murderer Albert Fish and the necrophile Ed Gein—have behaved very much like the traditional idea of the werewolf.

But could invocations cause actual physical changes? In the Gandillon case, the 16-year-old victim, Benoit Bidel, said that the wolf had human hands; in the Garnier case, Garnier confessed to strangling a young boy. And peasants who interrupted Garnier as he was attacking a 10-year-old girl said they thought they recognized his face. It certainly sounds as if the "wolf" remained in many respects human—rather like the upright beast into which Lon Chaney is transformed in the film *The Wolf Man*.

Transforming Possession

In his classic work *Man into Wolf*, the Jungian psychologist Robert Eisler suggests that early humans had to transform from herbivorous apes into carnivores struggling for supremacy with other carnivores, and that in the course of this battle, humans deliberately acquired something of the ferocity of wild animals. Some serial killers, such as the Yorkshire Ripper, have believed themselves possessed by the Devil. Isn't it possible that lycanthropy, like vampirism, should be understood as a special case of ferocious demonic possession?

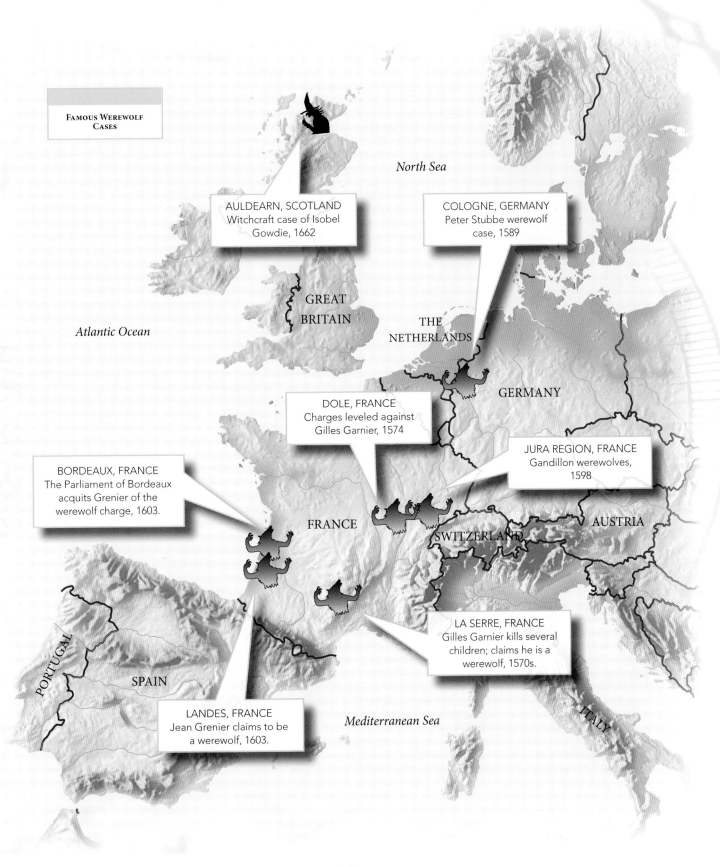

FAMOUS WEREWOLF
CASES

North Sea

AULDEARN, SCOTLAND
Witchcraft case of Isobel
Gowdie, 1662

COLOGNE, GERMANY
Peter Stubbe werewolf
case, 1589

GREAT
BRITAIN

THE
NETHERLANDS

Atlantic Ocean

GERMANY

DOLE, FRANCE
Charges leveled against
Gilles Garnier, 1574

JURA REGION, FRANCE
Gandillon werewolves,
1598

BORDEAUX, FRANCE
The Parliament of Bordeaux
acquits Grenier of the
werewolf charge, 1603.

FRANCE

AUSTRIA

SWITZERLAND

LA SERRE, FRANCE
Gilles Garnier kills several
children; claims he is a
werewolf, 1570s.

PORTUGAL

SPAIN

ITALY

LANDES, FRANCE
Jean Grenier claims to be
a werewolf, 1603.

Mediterranean Sea

Poltergeists and Possession by the Dead

(1660–present)

The poltergeist, or "noisy ghost," is one of the most baffling phenomena in the realm of the paranormal. Poltergeists cause objects to fly through the air, doors to open and close, pools of water to appear from nowhere, and more. And they are by no means a rarity; at this very moment some case of poltergeist activity is probably going on within a dozen miles of you.

One of the earliest known cases was recorded in a chronicle called the *Annales Fuldenses* and dates to 858 CE. The disturbance took place in a farmhouse at Bingen, on the Rhine River; the chronicle describes an "evil spirit" that threw stones and made the walls shake as if men were striking them with hammers. Stone throwing is one of the most typical of poltergeist activities. The poltergeist also caused fires—another favorite activity.

A spirit keeps a watchful eye.

The Adolescent Link

It was only after the formation of the Society for Psychical Research in 1882 that the poltergeist was carefully studied. Researchers observed that in the majority of cases there were adolescent children present in the houses where such occurrences took place; it seemed a reasonable assumption that the children were somehow the "cause" of the outbreak. And in the age of Sigmund Freud (1856–1939), the famous psychoanalyst, the most widely held theory was that the poltergeist is some kind of "unconscious" manifestation of adolescent sexual energies; but no one has offered a theory as to how this occurs.

A researcher observes a subject during an experiment with levitation at the Society for Psychical Research near the turn of the twentieth century. The society is still a thriving organization.

The Phantom Drummer

In England one of the most spectacular cases is also one of the earliest to be thoroughly recorded: the so-called phantom drummer of Tedworth. It took place in the home of a magistrate named John Mompesson in March 1661. Trouble started when the whole household was kept awake all night by loud drumming noises.

Soon before this, Mompesson arrested a vagrant named William Drury, who attracted attention in the street by beating a drum. Mompesson confiscated the drum, despite Drury's appeals. Drury escaped from custody—he was being held for possessing forged papers—without his drum. It was after this that the disturbances in Mompesson's household began. They continued for two years. The "spirit" also slammed doors, made panting noises like a dog, scratching noises like huge rats, and purring noises like a cat. It also developed a voice and shouted, "A witch, a witch!" It emptied ashes and chamber pots into the children's beds, and caused various objects to fly through the air. In 1663 Drury, imprisoned again for stealing a pig, admitted to a visitor that he was responsible for the disturbances, and said they would continue until Mompesson gave him satisfaction for taking away his drum. But the phenomena finally faded away.

In 1668 Joseph Glanvill published *Saducismus Triumphatus, or, Full and Plain Evidence Concerning Witches and Apparitions*. The right-hand page illustrates the tale of the phantom drummer. This book introduced the story of a Wiltshire landowner plagued by a noisy, drum-banging ghost. It is one of the earliest accounts of the mischievous spirits known as poltergeists.

Cock Lane, London, 1760

The Cock Lane Ghost

The famous poltergeist case known as the Cock Lane ghost ended with an innocent man going to prison for two years. The focus of the Cock Lane disturbances was 10-year-old Elizabeth Parsons, daughter of a clerk named Richard Parsons. The Parsons family had two lodgers: William Kent, a retired innkeeper, and his common-law wife, Fanny Lynes, whose sister Elizabeth had been Kent's previous wife.

One night when Kent was away Fanny asked Elizabeth to sleep with her to keep her company. During the night scratching and rapping noises from behind the wainscot kept the woman and child awake. Soon after this Fanny died of smallpox, and Kent moved elsewhere. But the strange rappings continued, and a clergyman named Moore tried to communicate with the spirit using a code of one rap for "yes," two for "no." By this means the spirit identified itself as Fanny Lynes and accused her ex-husband of poisoning her with arsenic.

"Thou Art a Lying Spirit"

Dr. Johnson—editor, essayist, and lexicographer, among other things—took time out of his schedule to weigh in on the credibility of the Cock Lane ghost.

Parsons was unfortunately unaware that poltergeists tell lies more often than not. Nor was he displeased to hear that Kent was a murderer, for he was nursing a grudge against him. Kent had lent Parsons money, which Parsons had failed to repay, and was now suing him. So Parsons overlooked the fact that the knockings began *before* the death of Fanny Lynes and made no attempt to keep the revelations secret.

When Kent heard that he was being accused of murder by a spirit, he went back to the house in Cock Lane to hear it for himself. When the raps again accused him of murder, he shouted angrily, "Thou art a lying spirit!"

A committee, which included famed author Dr. Samuel Johnson, came to investigate. The spirit preferred to remain silent, convincing Johnson that it was a fraud. Kent then decided to prosecute for libel. The burden of proof lay with Elizabeth's father, who was for legal purposes the accuser. Elizabeth was told that if the ghost did not manifest itself her mother and father would be thrown into prison, and so, naturally, she made sure something happened. But servants peering through a crack saw her making the raps with a wooden board. She was denounced as a trickster, and after a trial, Parsons was sentenced to two years in prison. The populace proved distinctly sympathetic, even taking up a collection for him while he suffered in the pillory.

LONDON, ENGLAND
The Cock Lane ghost incident sends a man to prison for two years, 1762.

North Sea

TEDWORTH, ENGLAND
So-called Phantom Drummer is revealed to be a hoax, 1663.

GREAT BRITAIN

WINDSOR, ENGLAND
Queen Victoria participates in séances, mid-1800s.

Atlantic Ocean

THE NETHERLANDS

BELGIUM

GERMANY

FAMOUS POLTERGEIST CASES

BINGEN, GERMANY
Poltergeist throws stones and sets fires, 858 CE.

FRANCE

SWITZERLAND

PORTUGAL

SPAIN

PARIS, FRANCE
Allan Kardec posits that poltergeists were "earth-bound spirits," 1860.

ITALY

Mediterranean Sea

A Unique Haunting

America's most famous poltergeist case occurred on the farm of John Bell, a Tennessee pioneer who had built a fine log house for himself and his growing family in Robertson County, settling in the Red River community, which is today called Adams, Tennessee. By 1817, the year the haunting began, John and his wife, Lucy, had nine children. For three years, the Bell family lived in torment and fear, haunted by a malevolent spirit. The case of the Bell Witch, as the story came to be known, is unusual—in fact, unique—in that the poltergeist caused the death of its victim.

Although the Bells razed the original log house in which the Bell Witch hauntings occurred, one of the plantation's original log structures still stands in Adams, Tennessee. It was used as an outbuilding.

The Bell Witch

The disturbances began in 1817, when John encountered a strange-looking animal in his cornfield. The creature, which had the head of a rabbit and the body of a dog, disappeared after John took a few shots at it. But that evening Bell and his family began hearing beating noises on the outside walls of their log house. Although no source could be found, the beating and thumping noises grew more frequent and increased their intensity. Then they were joined by knocks coming from the walls.

Soon invisible hands began pulling bedclothes off the beds; choking noises came from a human throat. Stones were thrown. The spirit frequently targeted Betsy, the younger of the two Bell daughters, slapping her and pulling her hair. After about a year the ghost developed a voice—a strange asthmatic croak. (Poltergeists sound like humans talking mechanically—it is as if the entity has to use an unfamiliar medium.) After such manifestations Betsy was usually exhausted—she seemed to be the source of the poltergeist's energy.

A sign in Robertson County introduces visitors to the Bell Witch.

BELL WITCH
To the north was the farm of John Bell, an early, prominent settler from North Carolina. According to legend, his family was harried during the early 19th century by the famous Bell Witch. She kept the household in turmoil, assaulted Bell, and drove off Betsy Bell's suitor. Even Andrew Jackson who came to investigate, retreated to Nashville after his coach wheels stopped mysteriously. Many visitors to the house saw the furniture crash about them and heard her shriek, sing, and curse.

Killer Kate

Although almost every member of the Bell family suffered from the sinister spirit's visitation, John Bell came under particular attack. The same year that the hauntings began, he developed a strange ailment; his jaw stiffened and his tongue swelled. The poltergeist, which had now developed a normal voice, identified itself first as an Indian and then as a witch named Old Kate Batts. Kate, as the Bell Witch is most often known, declared that she would torment John until he died, which she then proceeded to do. She pulled off his shoes, hit him in the face, and caused violent physical convulsions. All this continued until one day he was found in his bed in a deep stupor.

The death of John Bell

The witch claimed that she had given him a dose of a medicine that would kill him. And when Bell did in fact die, on December 20, 1820, the witch filled the house with shrieks of triumph.

After John's funeral, the disturbances all but ceased. But Kate made another appearance in April 1821, to visit John's widow, Lucy, and promised that she would visit again in seven years. In 1828 Kate was back for a three-week visit. Before she left she made an oath to visit Lucy's descendants in 107 years time. Although Dr. Charles Bailey Bell of Nashville, the closest living direct descendant of John Bell in the year 1935, had published a book about the Bell Witch the year before the promised visitation, Kate was never heard from again.

The Dawn of Spiritualism

A series of poltergeist disturbances started the extraordinary nineteenth-century craze known as Spiritualism. The first began with typical knocking noises in the home of the Fox family in Hydesville, New York, in 1848. Two daughters—Margaret, 15, and Kate, 12—were obviously the focus. A neighbor who questioned the spirit (using the usual code: one knock for "yes," two for "no") was told that the spirit was a peddler who had been murdered in the house. (Many years later, human bones and a peddler's box were found buried in the cellar.) The notoriety of the case caused many Americans to take up Spiritualism. Participants in séances would sit around a table in the dark with clasped hands and ask for spirits to manifest themselves. The Hydesville spirit finally delivered a message and sparked a new era in spirit communication. Spiritualism swept across the United States, then across Europe. Even Queen Victoria took it up.

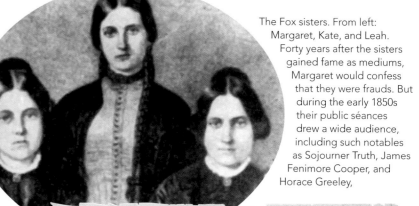

The Fox sisters. From left: Margaret, Kate, and Leah. Forty years after the sisters gained fame as mediums, Margaret would confess that they were frauds. But during the early 1850s their public séances drew a wide audience, including such notables as Sojourner Truth, James Fenimore Cooper, and Horace Greeley,

Queen Victoria and Prince Albert, shown above with five of their nine children in 1846, found Spiritualism fascinating. They are said to have even participated in séances.

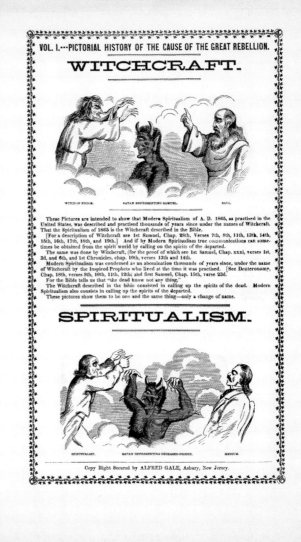

In the mid-1800s many religious leaders equated Spiritualism with witchcraft.

170

Automatic Writing

In the early 1850s a French educator named Hippolyte Léon Denizard Rivail became caught up in the new Spiritualist craze, particularly spirit rapping. As it turned out, two daughters of a friend of his proved to be proficient in another method of spirit communication, automatic writing. With this method a person "automatically" writes messages that are supposedly coming directly from a spirit. Rivail asked the spirits all kinds of questions and received unusually constructive and serious answers. In due course Rivail published these as *The Spirits' Book,* under the pseudonym Allan Kardec, which became for a while a kind of bible of Spiritualism, although there was later a split within the movement. Eventually many influential Spiritualists came to reject Kardec's belief in reincarnation.

Hippolyte Léon Denizard Rivail, better known as Allan Kardec

Allan Kardec

In 1860 a series of violent disturbances—the usual window smashing and furniture throwing of poltergeist hauntings—occurred in a house in the Rue des Noyers, Paris. When Kardec visited the house to investigate the event, he asked to speak to the spirit responsible, and an entity that claimed to be a junk dealer declared that it had used the "electrical energy" of a servant girl in the house to cause the disturbances. The girl, it said, was quite unaware of this—in fact, she was the most terrified of them all. The spirit had been doing these things merely to amuse itself.

Kardec was convinced that poltergeists were "earthbound spirits," dead people who for various reasons have been unable to advance beyond the purely material plane. Kardec insisted that most human beings can be unconsciously influenced by spirits, because they can wander freely in and out of our bodies and minds. Psychical investigator Carl Wickland, whose *Thirty Years Among the Dead* is a classic, declared that "these earthbound spirits are the supposed devils of all ages; devils of human origin. The influence of these discarnate entities is the cause of many of the inexplicable and obscure events of Earth life and of a large part of the world's misery." Wickland states that these entities are attracted to the magnetic light emanating from mortals; they attach themselves to these auras, finding an avenue of expression through influencing, obsessing, or possessing their victims.

Allan Kardec's grave in Paris draws Spiritualists from all around the world.

Making Contact

Many people believe that poltergeist and earthbound spirits can easily be contacted by means of a Ouija board, a smooth tabletop with letters arranged in a semicircle. Participants place their fingers on an upturned glass, which moves of its own accord from letter to letter, spelling words. But beware—anyone who has ever tried it will have noticed that the spirits seldom tell the truth.

Borley Rectory

(1863–1939)

The Rev. Harry Bull

Borley Rectory in Suffolk, has become known as "The Most Haunted House in England." Constructed in 1862 by the Rev. Henry D. E. Bull, the rambling Victorian-era brick rectory replaced a Georgian built by Bull's predecessor, which itself stood on the grounds of an earlier structure (although the legend that a Benedictine abbey occupied the site proved to be groundless). The house was a quiet one, except for the taps of a few unexplained footsteps a year after it was built, until 1900. That summer the four daughters of the current rector saw what they thought was the ghost of a nun about 40 yards from the house. It was the first sighting in what became nearly 40 years of hauntings.

Ghostly Tenants

After the Rev. Henry Bull's death in 1892, his son, the Reverend Harry Bull, had taken over his father's duties. The younger Bull was interested in psychical research and claimed that he saw many ghosts in the building. His daughter claimed that Bull had seen a phantom coach and that one day in the garden, the family dog had howled with terror while looking toward a pair of legs visible under a fruit tree. Bull assumed that the person was a poacher and followed the legs as they walked toward a postern gate. At that point Bull realized that the "poacher" was incomplete: the legs—which were attached to no body—disappeared through the gate without opening it.

Rev. Harry Bull and his daughters on the rectory lawn

Smith Moves In

Harry Bull died in 1927, and the rectory was empty until 1928, when the Rev. Guy Smith and his wife moved in.

One stormy night, Smith was disturbed by the furious ringing of his doorbell; when he got to the door, no one was there. Later the bell rang again—a peal so prolonged that Smith reached the door before it stopped—again, there was no one. Then the Smiths began hearing slippered footsteps and the sound of small pebbles being thrown. Lights switched on. One day Mrs. Smith saw a horse-drawn coach in the drive. Mr. Smith heard a voice whisper, "Don't, Carlos, don't," as he walked into the chapel. The Smiths decided to contact the *Daily Mirror* newspaper, which asked famed British ghost hunter Harry Price to investigate. The Smiths told Price their story and gave him every facility. But within nine months, they had had enough of the place—perhaps because its plumbing left much to be desired—and moved to Norfolk.

At right, the *Daily Mirror* from July 10, 1929. Above, Rev. Smith and reporter V. C. Wall inspect the summerhouse after Smith reported the "ghost" to the newspaper.

GHOST VISITS TO A RECTORY

Tales of Headless Coachmen and a Lonely Nun

THE ELOPERS

Mysterious Happenings on 'Si of Old Monastery

FROM OUR SPECIAL CORRESPONDEN

LONG MELFORD, Sunday.

Ghostly figures of headless coachme and a nun, an old-time coach, drawn two bay horses, which appear and vanish mysteriously, and dragging footsteps empty rooms.

All these ingredients of a first-cla ghost story are awaiting investigation psychic experts near Long Melford, Su folk.

The scene of the ghostly visitations is t rectory at Borley, a few miles from Long Me ford.

It is a building erected on the part of the si of a great monastery which, in the Middle Age was the scene of a gruesome tragedy.

The present rector, the Rev. G. E. Smith, his wife, made the rectory their residence the face of warnings by previous occupiers.

Since their arrival they have been puzzl and startled by a series of peculiar happenin which cannot be explained and which confi the rumours they heard before moving in.

The first untoward happening was the sou of slow, dragging footsteps across the floor of unoccupied room.

Then one night Mr. Smith, armed with hockey stick, sat in the room and waited f the noise.

Once again it came—the sound of feet some kind of slippers treading on the ba boards.

Mr. Smith lashed out with his stick at t spot where the footsteps seemed to be, but t stick whistled through the empty air, and t steps continued across the room.

Then a servant girl, brought from Londo suddenly gave notice after two days' work, claring emphatically that she had seen a m walking in the wood at the back of the house.

Finally comes the remarkable story of old-fashioned coach, seen twice on the la by a servant, which remained in sight lor enough for the girl to distinguish the bro colour of the horses.

HEADLESS COACHMEN

New Tenants, New Specters

Marianne Foyster

In October 1930 the Reverend L. A. Foyster, and his much younger wife, Marianne, took over the rectory. The Foyster incumbency saw the most spectacular exhibitions of the Borley poltergeist. Foyster kept a diary of the disturbances. Bells were rung, bricks thrown, footsteps heard, and water poured onto the couple when they were in bed. Foyster was even awakened by a violent blow on the head from his own hairbrush. The two saw a number of apparitions, including a nun and a clergyman, who was identified as the Rev. Henry Bull, the builder of the rectory. Writing appeared on the walls, asking for a mass to be said, and asking for "light."

There is much independent confirmation of all these events. Guy L'Estrange, a justice of the peace visited Borley at the invitation of the Foysters and wrote a lengthy account of his stay. The Foysters were telling L'Estrange about mysterious fires that kept breaking out in locked rooms when there was a loud crash in the hall. When the three went to investigate, they found it littered with broken crockery. Then bottles began flying about. L'Estrange notes that they seemed to appear suddenly in midair, although they had to come from a locked storage shed outside. All the bells began to ring, making a deafening clamor—yet all of the bell wires had been cut. L'Estrange shouted: "If some invisible person is present, please stop ringing for a moment." Instantly the bells stopped—stopped dead, as if each clapper had been grabbed by an unseen hand.

In bed L'Estrange felt the room's temperature drop to icy cold and saw a shape materializing from a patch of luminosity. He walked toward it, and thought he fe.lt something trying to push him back. He spoke to it, and it slowly vanished. In 1935, the Foysters decided they had had enough, and moved from the rectory.

The stairway in the main hall of the rectory, where more than one mysterious manifestation took place

The Haunted Rectory Burns

Harry Price rented the rectory in 1937 and arranged for a team of investigators to visit the house. But the major phenomena had ceased. Even so the chief investigator, Sidney Glanville, a retired engineer, became completely convinced of the reality of the haunting.

In March 1938 the team was experimenting with a planchette—a small heart-shaped or triangular board on castors that, when touched lightly with the fingers, produces messages. The board produced a message that fire would destroy Borley. And it did just that, reducing the rectory to ruins in February 1939. Yet the phenomena continued. A Cambridge team investigating the ruins heard footsteps, saw patches of light, and recorded sudden sharp drops in temperature.

In August 1943, Price decided to try digging in the cellars at Borley—which a planchette message had advised. He found a cream jug, which had also been referred to by the planchette, and some fragments of a human skull. The jawbone showed signs of a deep-seated abscess—investigator Peter Underwood speculates that this is why the phantom nun always looked miserable.

Borley, falling into ruins after the disastrous fire

Pearl Curran

Patience Worth: The Ghost Who Wrote Novels

(1913–1939)

On August 1, 1912, Emily Grant Hutchings and Pearl Lenore Curran, both of whom were married to successful businessmen, spent the afternoon at another friend's home in Saint Louis, Missouri. Hutchings had just bought a ouija board and expressed her interest in trying to "contact the spirits." Curran thought it was all a waste of time. And on that first August afternoon she was right: the ouija board planchette, or pointer, spelled a few recognizable words, but it was mostly nonsense.

But Emily and Pearl tried again—and again. And finally, on June 22, 1913, the planchette guided them to spell out the word "pat" several times and then wrote not just words, but a poem.

A Quaker Poet

The ouija board spelled out the following message from the unknown spirit:

> Oh, why let sorrow steel thy heart?
> Thy bosom is but its foster-mother,
> The world its cradle and the loving home its grave.

Six days later, the board revealed the spirit's identity: "Many moons ago I lived. Again I come, Patience Worth my name."

Eventually Patience explained that she was a Quaker girl, born in 1649 or 1694 (the board had dictated both) in Dorset, England. She had worked hard—apparently on a farm—until her family emigrated to the Americas. Shortly afterward, she was killed by Indians.

Placing the fingertips lightly on a planchette allows spirits to spell out messages on a ouija board.

Foretelling the Future

Just before Christmas, Patience displayed an interesting ability to predict the future. Emily asked her what Pearl intended to give her for Christmas and Patience replied "Fifteen pieces, and one cracked." In fact Curran had ordered a set of kitchen jars for her friend, and when they were delivered the next day, one of the 15 was cracked.

During the next couple of years, Curran, who had gone from a skeptic to a believer, seemed to forge a strong bond with Patience. She claimed to visualize the long-dead woman, who seemed to be about 30 years old. Curran could see her in almost picture-book images, saying, "her hair was dark red, mahogany, her eyes brown, and large and deep, her mouth firm and set, as though repressing strong feelings."

Fame

In 1915 Patience became something of a celebrity when Caspar Yost, editor of the Sunday supplement of the *St. Louis Globe-Democrat*, wrote a series of articles about her. Those pieces caused a sensation, and Yost later wrote a book.

By now Pearl, through channeling the spirit of Patience, had embarked upon writing *Red Wing*, a six-act medieval play, and a 60,000-word medieval novel, *Telka*. But "Patience" was a disappointing writer, so long-winded as to be almost unreadable.

In June 1917 Henry Holt published Patience's vast pseudo-Biblical epic *The Sorry Tale*. Again, many papers were ecstatic, which is curious, as the writing is atrocious and often illiterate, with phrases such as "The temples stood whited and the market place skewed emptied."

THE SORRY TALE
A STORY OF THE TIME OF CHRIST

BY
PATIENCE WORTH

COMMUNICATED THROUGH
MRS. JOHN H. CURRAN

EDITED BY
CASPER S. YOST

NEW YORK
HENRY HOLT AND COMPANY
1917

Patience's book

The classic ouija board

Enough Is Enough

By 1918 there were signs that the Patience fad had run its course. In the *Atlantic Monthly* that August a writer, Agnes Repplier, expressed dismay that Patience—who was already dead—could be on the literary scene forever. Of Patience's books, Miss Repplier said tartly, "they were as silly as they were dull." Most people now agreed.

John Curran, whose health had begun to fail, died in June 1922. Pearl, who was now 39 years old, was pregnant with their first child; a girl was born six months later. Pearl now had a family to support on a dwindling income. It was at this point that a New York admirer, Herman Behr, came to the rescue: he not only made her an allowance of $400 a month but also paid for the publication of Patience's poems, which appeared under the title *Light From Beyond*.

But in the age of James Joyce, Ernest Hemingway, Gertrude Stein, and John Dos Passos, the ramblings of Patience Worth now seemed irrelevant.

Curran would marry twice more. In November 1937 she announced to her old friend Dotsie Smith that "Patience has just shown me the end of the road, and you will have to carry on as best you can." Pearl seemed to be in excellent health; but on Thanksgiving Day she caught a cold, and on December 3, 1937, she died of pneumonia in a Los Angeles hospital. Patience Wee, who by the age of 27 had been twice married, also died suddenly, in 1943, after the diagnosis of a mild heart ailment.

Patience Worth Wee

One of the most bizarre episodes in the entire story of Patience Worth began in August 1916. The Currans were told "ye shall seek a one, a wee bit, one who hath not;" and then, "Aye, this be close, close."

Soon it became clear what Patience meant: the Currans, who did not have children, should adopt a baby and that this baby would be, in some sense, Patience's own daughter.

A pregnant widow was located; her husband had been killed in a mill accident, and she agreed to relinquish her unborn child to the Currans. Patience seemed quite certain it would be a daughter, and so it was. And on Patience's instructions the child was named Patience Worth Wee Curran.

Who Was Patience?

For those who are willing to accept the possibility of life after death, the most convincing explanation is certainly that Patience was a "spirit." But if Patience was a spirit, then it was probably of a frustrated would-be writer with a strong tendency to mythomania.

Fairies: Are the "Little People" Just a Fairy Tale?

(1917)

Life of a fairy

In the summer of 1897 the poet W. B. Yeats traveled to Coole Park, in Galway, with Lady Augusta Gregory, who was to become his close friend and patroness. The two of them began collecting fairy stories from the local peasantry. Yeats had already compiled two collections of Irish myths and fairy tales based on interviews of peasants in his home county of Sligo. But during this visit he came to realize that the majority of Irish country folk accepted the existence of fairies, not as some kind of half-believed superstition, but as a concrete fact of life.

The Fairy Faith

Yeats's father was a skeptic, and yet Yeats himself had been inclined to toy with a belief in fairies as a kind of reaction to the materialism of the modern world. His collaboration with Lady Gregory made him aware that belief in fairies could hardly be dismissed as wishful thinking.

A few years later Yeats encouraged Orientalist W. Y. Evans Wentz to study the folklore of the fairies; the result was Wentz's first book, *The Fairy Faith in Celtic Countries* (1911), a bulky and scholarly volume based upon his own extensive fieldwork. In it Wentz concluded that the factual and scientific evidence for the existence of fairies is overwhelming and that "there are hundreds of proven cases of phenomena."

William Butler Yeats, right, had an abiding interest in Irish folktales and the occult. In his early life, encouraged by his patroness, Lady Augusta Gregory, he expressed a belief in the existence of fairies.

Case in Point

In 1920 the front cover of the Christmas issue of the *Strand Magazine* announced "Fairies Photographed—An Epoch Making Event Described by A. Conan Doyle." Facing the opening page of the article was a photograph of two teenaged girls, sitting in a grassy field gazing at a group of four cavorting fairies, complete with gossamer wings.

It was not a seasonal joke. Doyle and his fellow investigators were convinced that the photographs virtually proved the existence of "the little people." The resulting controversy was to remain unsettled for the next 60 years.

The two girls, Elsie Wright and Francis Griffiths, lived in the village of Cottingley, in Yorkshire. They had taken the photographs three and a half years earlier, in the summer of 1917, and had consistently claimed that the photographs were of real fairies.

Frances Griffiths and Elsie Wright took a series of photos of each other posing with local "fairies." They produced five images: Frances with dancing fairies (at right), Elsie shaking hands with a gnome, two show each girl with a single fairy, and the last shows two fairies dancing.

A Fairy Haunt

In 1917, Cottingley, near Bradford, was surrounded by green English countryside. In April of that year 10-year-old Frances Griffiths had moved to the village with her mother, Annie, who was from South Africa. Frances later claimed that she soon realized that there were fairies in the fields around her home, especially near the local beck (stream) that ran down a steep-sided dell at the bottom of her garden:

> *One evening after school I went down to the beck to a favourite place—the willow overhanging the stream . . . then a willow leaf started shaking violently—just one. I'd seen it happen before—there was no wind, and it was odd that one leaf should shake . . . as I watched, a small man, all dressed in green, stood on the branch with the stem of the leaf in his hand, which he seemed to be shaking at something he was looking at. I daren't move for fear of frightening him. He looked straight at me and disappeared.*

Frances decided not to tell anyone for fear of being laughed at. After she'd fallen into the stream several times, her mother and aunt pressed hard for an explanation. It was then that Frances admitted, "I go to see the fairies!"

At this point her cousin, 15-year-old Elsie Wright, came to her defense insisting that she too had seen fairies. No amount of questioning could shake the girls' story.

An obliging "fairy" perches long enough to pose with Elsie.

The Cottingley fairies dance on a bird's nest

The Camera Never Lies

On a Saturday afternoon in July 1917, Elsie asked her father, Arthur Wright, if she could borrow his plate camera. The girls hurried off to the stream and returned within half an hour. As the plate started to develop, Wright realized that it was a picture of Frances leaning on a bank. Near her were tiny human forms with wings growing from their backs; they were apparently four dancing fairies.

The whole affair might have been forgotten if it had not been for the local Theosophical Society. At a meeting after the war, Polly Wright approached the speaker and told him about the photographs. Copies were soon circulating among the Bradford Theosophists. Edward L. Gardner, head of the Theosophist Lodge in London, was excited about the photographs and asked to see the original prints and negatives.

Gardner took them to a professional photographer, Harold Snelling. Snelling examined the four dancing fairies negatives and told Gardner that he believed they were genuine.

Gardner was delighted. In the summer of 1920 he was flattered to receive a letter from the creator of Sherlock Holmes. The 60-year-old Arthur Conan Doyle was not a Theosophist, but in recent years he had become convinced of the truth of Spiritualism. He had already been commissioned by the *Strand* to write an article on fairies, and the news of the Cottingley photographs must have sounded like a gift from beyond.

Toward the end of July 1920 Edward Gardner visited the Wrights. And although Elsie's father expressed his opinion that the photographs were fakes, Gardner told Doyle that he was convinced that the girls were genuine.

Sensation!

When the magazine was published that Christmas it caused a sensation. The Cottingley fairies were the talk of every London dinner table. But skeptics were outraged at what they regarded as the public's infantile gullibility.

In due course the debate ran out of steam and for the next 40 years Elsie and Frances were forgotten.

In 1965 Peter Chambers, a *Daily Express* reporter, tracked down Elsie, then in her 60s, in the Midlands. He believed that the pictures were faked, and Elsie's comment that people should be left to make up their own minds on the subject only deepened his skepticism.

In 1976 the Yorkshire psychical investigator Joe Cooper organized a television program about the case. Elsie and Frances returned to Cottingley. In the intervening years, Elsie had lived in India with her husband, Frank Hill, a Scottish engineer; Frances had married a soldier, Frank Way, and had spent much time with him abroad.

On camera, Elsie and Frances identified the place where Frances had seen a gnome and flatly denied that they had fabricated the photos.

By the late nineteenth century, the image of fairies as minuscule, winged females was well-established in Anglophone iconography (this is an example from *Harper's Weekly* in 1898). Their very familiarity may have helped the girls perpetuate their fairy hoax.

Cottingley's verdant landscape looks like a likely home for fairies.

New Evidence

The year 1977 brought an interesting development. A researcher named Fred Gettings, who was working on nineteenth-century fairy illustrations, came upon *Princess Mary's Gift Book.* The book had been published during World War I to make money for the Work for Women fund. It contained a poem entitled "A Spell for a Fairy" by Alfred Noyes, illustrated by Claude Shepperson. Two of the fairies in the illustration were virtually identical to the fairies in the first Cottingley photograph.

In September 1981 Frances asked Joe Cooper to visit her, telling him that there were "some things he should know." As they sat in a coffee shop, she dropped her bombshell:

"From where I was, I could see the hat pins holding up the figures. I've always marveled that anybody ever took it seriously."

"Why are you telling me?" asked the flabbergasted investigator. "Because Elsie has already told Glenn [Elsie's son]," she answered. "What about the other four? Are they fakes?" asked Cooper.

Her answer was, in its way, as astonishing as the original admission: "Three of them. The last one's genuine."

Cooper and Elsie then discussed writing a book together, but his publisher felt there would be no interest.

Late in 1982 a magazine called *The Unexplained* published Cooper's article "Cottingley: At Last the Truth," in which he revealed that the fairies in the first four photographs were cut-outs stuck to branches with hat pins. This upset both Frances and Elsie. When Frances called Joe Cooper's wife on New Year's Day,

James Randi, stage magician and professional scientific paranormal debunker is one of a long line of skeptics to question the Cottingley fairies. He has pointed out the impossible crispness of the fairies' wings in comparison to other moving creatures.

1983, and Joe answered the phone, she called him a traitor and hung up. Frances died in 1986. Elsie died in 1988, maintaining that she had never seen the fairies.

Zombies: Evidence for the Walking Dead

(1932 to present)

Night of the Living Dead, 1968

Ever since Bela Lugosi starred in *White Zombie* in 1932, zombies have been horror-movie staples, challenging the vampire, mummy, and Frankenstein monster in popularity. These monsters may be popular in film and folklore, but what are they really, and do they actually exist?

Zombies, according to Alfred Metraux's book, *Voodoo* (1959), are "people whose decease has been duly recorded and whose burial has been witnessed, but who are found a few years later . . . in a state verging on idiocy." In Port-au-Prince, Haiti, says Metraux, "there are few, even among the educated, who do not give some credence to these macabre stories."

Understandably, such tales have met with skepticism outside Haiti.

Zombified!

One of the first non-Haitians to record an actual incident of zombiism was the writer and ethnographer Zora Neale Hurston, who trained in the United States under famed anthropologist Franz Boas. In October 1936 a woman was found naked and wandering in Haiti's Artibonite Valley. Her name was Felicia Felix-Mentor, and she had died and been buried at the age of 29. Hurston visited the woman in the hospital at Gonaives and described her as having "a blank face with dead eyes" and eyelids "white as if they had been burned with acid."

According to Hurston, people were "zombified" if they betrayed the secrets of the Haitian secret societies. No one believed her; Metraux wrote patronizingly of "Zora Houston [sic], who is very superstitious." Nevertheless he relays a story about two members of "high society." After the car of one of them broke down, he was invited to the home of a little white-bearded man—a *houngan,* or vodoun, or voodoo, priest.

Piqued by his guest's skepticism about a *wanga* (magical charm), the old man asked him if he had known a certain Monsieur Celestin—who had, in fact, been one of the visitor's closest friends. Summoned by a whip crack, a man shambled into the room. The visitor, much to his horror, recognized his old friend Celestin, who had died six months earlier. When the zombie reached for the visitor's glass—obviously thirsty—the houngan stopped him, saying that nothing could be more dangerous than giving or taking something from the hand of a dead man. The houngan told his visitor that Celestin had died from a spell and that the magician who had killed him had sold him to the *houngan* for $12.

Other stories recounted by Metraux make it clear that he considers zombies to be people who have literally died and then been raised from the dead. Understandably, he rejects this as superstition. In fact, Zora Neale Hurston was correct and Metraux was wrong.

Zora Neale Hurston.

Vestige of the Slave Trade

Columbus discovered Haiti in the West Indies in 1492, but it was not until two centuries later that it became a base for pirates and buccaneers. French colonists developed Haiti's rich sugar trade, using black slaves from Africa. The Spanish ceded Haiti (or Saint-Domingue, as it was called) to the French in 1697.

The slaves were treated with unbelievable cruelty—for example, hanged from trees with nails driven through their ears or smeared with molasses and left to be eaten alive by ants. In spite of the risks of terrible punishments if they were caught, slaves often ran away and hid in the mountains.

In the 1740s a slave named Macandal, who had lost his arm in a sugar press, escaped to the mountains and taught the Maroons (as the runaway slaves were known) to use poison against the slave owners, as well as some colonists and cattle. Macandal was eventually betrayed and sentenced to be burned alive (although, according to legend, he used his magical powers to escape). From then on, secret societies spread revolt among the black slaves. After the great revolts of the 1790s, French authority virtually collapsed, and although it was savagely restored under Napoleon, the emperor was never able to conquer the interior of the island. A series of black emperors ruled until 1859, but the island has alternated between a state of virtual anarchy and harsh authoritarian rule ever since, both of which have nurtured the secret societies.

Zora Neale Hurston asserted that "zombification" was effected by means of a "quick-acting poison." Her assertion was given further credence in the early 1980s, when a young American anthropologist, Wade Davis, heard rumors that poison from the pufferfish was used to zombify people.

The Haitian Revolution

Jimsonweed or "zombie's cucumber" in bloom

Brother Zombie

Wade Davis heard about two cases from New York psychiatrist Nathan Kline that seemed to demonstrate that zombification was not a fantasy. In 1962 a Haitian peasant in his 40s, Clairvius Narcisse, was admitted to the Albert Schweitzer Hospital in the Artibonite Valley suffering from fever. He died two days later and was buried the next day. Eighteen years later, in 1980, a man approached Narcisse's sister Angelina and identified himself as her brother, Clairvius. He said that he'd been "zombified" by order of his brother, with whom he had had a land dispute. Clairvius said that he'd been removed from his grave and taken to work with other zombies. After two years their master was killed and he escaped to wander the country for the next 16 years. It was not until he heard of his brother's death that he dared to make himself known.

Narcisse's identity was confirmed, and the British Broadcasting Corporation (BBC) made a short film about the case. In the same year, a group of "zombies" was found wandering in northern Haiti, exactly where Narcisse had been forced to work, confirming his story of the escape.

When Davis went to Haiti to investigate, his attention focused on *Datura stramonium,* known in America as jimsonweed or devil' trumpet and in Haiti as zombie's cucumber. He visited Max Beauvoir, an expert on voodoo. He interviewed Clairvius Narcisse and confirmed his story.

A film depiction of a zombie rising from the grave

Poison

Davis's research led him to a highly poisonous toad, the *Bufo marinus,* and to two varieties of pufferfish, so called because they inflate themselves with water when threatened. Both are full of deadly neurotoxin called tetrodotoxin, a fatal dose of which would just cover the head of a pin.

Captain James Cook suffered severely after eating the cooked liver and roe of a pufferfish in 1774. Today pufferfish sashimi is a delicacy in Japan. Chefs there discard the poisonous parts of the fish, but the deadly liver is also eaten after being cleaned and boiled.

It was clear to Davis that the poison of the pufferfish was not the sole secret of "zombification." In his book *The Serpent and the Rainbow* (1985), he describes his search for samples of zombie poison. His aim was to obtain samples and have them tested in a laboratory. He met a number of houngans and witnessed some remarkable ceremonies. In some, he saw people who were "possessed" by spirits—one woman was able to place a lighted cigarette on her tongue without being burned.

Deadly pufferfish

Real Zombies

Davis's quest came to a premature end when one of his major backers died and another suffered a debilitating stroke. His book leaves little doubt, however, that the secret of "zombification" is a poison that can produce all the signs of death. Once the body is dug up and an antidote is administered, the victim is often stupefied by further drugs that reduce him or her to a level of virtual idiocy.

A 1984 British television program produced by the BBC confirmed that "zombification" results from a poison that affects certain brain centers, reducing consciousness to the level of dreaming. Wade Davis was left with little doubt about the reality of "zombification." But his investigation into the voodoo religion also seems to have convinced him that not all the phenomena of voodoo can be explained in such naturalistic terms.

The Work of a Jealous Husband

In 1976 a 30-year-old woman named Francina Illeus, known as *Ti Femme*, was pronounced dead. Three years later she was found alive by her mother, who recognized a scar on her temple. When Illeus's coffin was inspected, it was found to be full of rocks. She believed that she was poisoned on the orders of a jealous husband.

Hundreds of followers of the voodoo religion line up as they prepare to take part in a ceremony to show their devotion to the spirits in Souvenance, Haiti, in 2008. Voodoo, which came to the islands with the West African slaves, is one of the state religions of Haiti.

Further Reading

Adushkin, Vitaly, and Ivan Nemchinov. *Catastrophic Events Caused by Cosmic Objects*. Dordrecht: Springer, 2007.

Anderson, Mark. *Shakespeare by Another Name: The Life of Edward de Vere, Earl of Oxford, the Man Who Was Shakespeare*. New York: Penguin Group, 2006.

Auderhub, Werner, and Hans Peter Roth. *Crop Circles: Exploring the Designs and Mysteries*. New York: Lark Books, 2002.

Bales, Richard F., and Thomas F. Schwartz. *The Great Chicago Fire and the Myth of Mrs. O'Leary's Cow*. North Carolina: McFarland & Co Inc. Pub., 2005.

Barber, Richard W. *Myths & Legends of the British Isles*. UK: Boydell & Brewer, 1999.

Begg, Paul. *Mary Celeste: The Greatest Mystery of the Sea*. New Jersey: Pearson Longman, 2007.

Berlitz, Charles. *The Bermuda Triangle*. New York: Doubleday, 1974.

Binns, Ronald. *The Loch Ness Mystery Solved*. New York: Prometheus Books, 1985.

Burnett, Thomas. *Conspiracy Encyclopedia: The Encyclopedia of Conspiracy Theories*. Stuttgart: Franz Steiner Verlag, 2005.

Carroll, Robert Todd. *The Skeptic's Dictionary: A Collection of Strange Beliefs, Amusing Deceptions, and Dangerous Delusions*. Hoboken, NJ: John Wiley and Sons, 2003.

Castleden, Rodney. *Atlantis Destroyed*. New York: Routledge, 1998.

Chalker, Bill. *Hair of the Alien: DNA and Other Forensic Evidence of Alien Abductions*. New York: Simon and Schuster, 2005.

Clancy, Dr. Susan. *Abducted: How People Come to Believe They Were Kidnapped by Aliens*. Cambridge: Harvard University Press, 2005.

Clark, John. *Unnatural Phenomena: A Guide to the Bizarre Wonders of North America*. Santa Barbara, CA: ABC-CLIO, 2005.

Clarkson, Michael. *Poltergeists: Examining Mysteries of the Paranormal*. Ontario: Firefly Books, 2006.

Click, Patricia Catherine. *Time Full of Trail: The Roanoke Island Freedmen's Colony, 1862–1867*. Chapel Hill: University of North Carolina Press, 2001.

Cohen, David. *The Encyclopedia of Ghosts*. New York: Dodd, Mead, 1984.

Cooper, Joe. *The Case of the Cottingley Fairies*. London: Hale, 1990.

Cremin, Aedeen. *Archaeologica: The World's Significant Sites and Cultural Treasures*. London: Frances Lincoln, 2007.

Cromie, Robert. *The Great Chicago Fire*. Nashville, TN: Thomas Nelson Inc., 1994.

Daegling, David J. *Bigfoot Exposed: An Anthropologist Examines America's Enduring Legend*. Lanham, MD: Rowman Altamira, 2004.

Daniken, Erich von. *Chariots of the Gods?* New York; Bantam Books, 1971.

Davies, Rodney. *Supernatural Vanishings: Otherworldly Disappearances*. New York: Sterling Publishing, 1996.

Davis, Wade. *The Serpent and the Rainbow*. New York: Simon & Schuster, 1985.

Dinsdale, Tim. *Loch Ness Monster*. London: Taylor & Francis, 1976.

Donnelly, Ignatius. *Atlantis, the Antediluvian World*. New York: Harper, 1882.

———. *Ragnarok, Or the Age of Fire and Gravel*. New York: D. Appleton and Company, 1883.

———. *The Great Cryptogram*. London: Sampson Low, Marston, Searle & Rivington, 1888.

Drake, Walter Raymond. *Gods and Spacemen in the Ancient East*. New York, Signet, 1973.

———. *Gods and Spacemen in the Ancient West*. New York, Signet, 1973.

Drury, Nevill, and Stephen Skinner. *The Search for Abraxas*. Spearman, TX, Spearman Publishing, 1971.

Dyall, Valentine. *Unsolved Mysteries*. London: Hutchinson, 1954.

Eisler, Robert. *Man into Wolf*. New York: Greenwood Press, 1969.

Ellis, Richard. *Monsters of the Sea*. New York: Lyons Press, 2000.

———. *The Search for the Giant Squid*. New York: Penguin Books, 1998.

———. *Singing Whales and Flying Squid*. Guilford, CT; Lyons Press, 2006.

Evans, Stewart P., and Keith Skinner. *The Ultimate Jack the Ripper Companion: The Illustrated Encyclopedia*. New York: Carroll & Graf Publishers, 2000.

Fanthorpe, Lionel. *The World's Greatest Unsolved Mysteries*. Canada: Dundum Press Ltd., 1997.

Fanthorpe, Lionel, and Patricia Fanthorpe. *Unsolved Mysteries of the Sea*. Canada: Dundum Press Ltd., 2004.

Feuerbach, Johann Anselm and Jeffery Moussaieff Masson. *Lost Prince: The Unsolved Mystery of Kasper Hauser*. New York: Free Press, 1996.

Floyd, E. Randall. *100 of the World's Greatest Mysteries*. Boyne City, MI: Harbor House, 2000

Fort, Charles. *The Book of the Damned*. New York: H. Liveright, 1919.

Fuller, John G. *The Interrupted Journey*. Dial Press, 1966.

Furneaux, Rupert. *The Money Pit*. New York: HarperCollins, 1977.

Gaddis, Vincent. *Invisible Horizon*. New York: Chilton, 1965.

Galanopoulos, Angelos Geórgiou, and Edward Bacon. *Atlantis: The Truth Behind the Legend*. Indiana: Bobbs-Merrill, 1969.

Goldstone, Lawrence, and Nancy Goldstone. *The Friar and the Cipher: Roger Bacon and the Unsolved Mystery of the Most Unusual Manuscript in the World*. New York: Broadway Books, 2006.

Gould, Rupert Thomas. *Oddities: A Book of Unexplained Facts: A Book of Unexplained Facts*. Charlottesville: University of Virginia Press, 1965.

Green, John. *On the Track of the Sasquatch*. Surrey, BC: Hancock House Publishers, 1995.

Griffiths, Major Arthur. *Mysteries of Police and Crime*. London: Cassell, 1898.

Group, David. *The Evidence for the Bermuda Triangle*. Kent, UK: Aquarian Press, 1984.

Hapgood, Charles H. *Maps of the Ancient Sea Kings: Evidence of Advanced Civilization in the Ice Age*. Stelle, IL: Adventures Unlimited Press, 1996.

Hardaker, Christopher, and Charles Naeser. *The First American: The Suppressed Story of the People Who Discovered the New World*. Franklin Lakes, NJ: Career Press, 2007.

Haugton, Brian. *Hidden History: Lost Civilizations, Secret Knowledge, and Ancient Mysteries*. Franklin Lakes, NJ: Career Press, 2007

Hein, Simeon, Ira Liss, and Ron Russell. *Opening Minds: A Journey of Extraordinary Encounters, Crop Circles, and Resonance*. Boulder, CO: Mount Baldy Press, 2002.

Heuvelmans, Bernard. *In the Wake of the Sea Serpents*. N.p.: Hart-Davis, 1968.

Hicks, Brian. *Ghost Ship: The Mysterious True Story of the Mary Celeste and Her Missing Crew*. New York: Ballantine Books, 2004.

Hoffmann, Calvin. *The Murder of the Man Who Was Shakespeare*. New York: J. Messner, 1955

Holiday, F. W. *The Great Orm of Loch Ness: A Practical Inquiry Into the Nature and Habits of Water-Monsters*. New York: Norton, 1969.

Hynek, Joseph Allen. *The UFO Experience*. Chicago: H. Regnery, 1972.

Joshi, S. T. *Icons of Horror and the Supernatural*. Westport, CT: Greenwood Publishing, 2006.

Kitchen, Martin. *Kasper Hauser: Europe's Child.* Hampshire, UK: Palgrave, 2001.

Knight, David C. *Poltergeists: Hauntings and the Haunted.* Philadelphia: J. B. Lippincott & Co., 1972.

Knight, Stephen Thomas. *Robin Hood: A Mythic Biography.* Ithaca, New York: Cornell University Press, 2003.

Kupperman, Karen Ordahl. *Roanoke: The Abandoned Colony.* Maryland: Rowman & Littlefield, 2007.

Lamb, Lee. *Oak Island Obsession: The Restall Story.* Canada: Dundurn Press Ltd., 2006.

Lincoln, Henry. *Key to the Sacred Pattern: The Untold Story of Rennes-le-Chateau.* New York: Palgrave Macmillian, 1998.

Lockhart, J. *A Great Sea Mystery: The True Story of the Mary Celeste.* Alcester, UK: Read Country Books, 2006.

Lockhart, John Gilbert. *Here Are Mysteries.* Los Angeles: P. Allen & Co., 1927.

Mack, John E. *Abduction: Human Encounters with Aliens.* New York: Ballantine Books, 1995.

Mackal, Roy P. *The Monster of Loch Ness.* Edinburgh: Macdonald and Jane's, 1976.

Mansson, Olaf. *A History of the Goths, Swedes, and Vandals.* Sweden: N.p. 1555.

Matters, Leonard. *The Mystery of Jack the Ripper.* London: Hutchinson & Co., Ltd, 1929.

McIntosh, Gregory C. *The Piri Reis Map of 1513.* Atlanta: University of Georgia Press, 2000.

Melton, J. Gordon. *The Vampire Book: The Encyclopedia of the Undead.* Detroit, MI : Omnigraphics Incorporated, 1999.

Messner, Reinhold. *My Quests for the Yeti: Confronting the Himalayas' Deepest Mystery.* New York Macmillian, 1998.

Metraux, Alfred. *Voodoo in Haiti.* London: Oxford University Press, 1959.

Michell, John. *The Flying Saucer Vision.* Hazard, KY: Sphere, 1969.

Michell, John, and Bob Rickard. *Unexplained Phenomena: A Rough Guide Special.* London: Rough Guides, 2000.

Miller, Lee. *Roanoke: Solving the Mystery of the Lost Colony.* New York: Arcade Publishing, 2001.

Muck, Otto Heinrich, and Otto Muck. *The Secret of Atlantis.* New York: Times Books, 1978.

Newbold, William Romaine, and Roland Grubb Kent. *The Cipher of Roger Bacon.* Philadelphia: University of Pennsylvania Press, 1928.

Nickell, Joe. *Adventures in Paranormal Investigation.* Lexington: The University Press of Kentucky, 2007.

———. *Real-life X-files: Investigating the Paranormal.* Lexington: The University Press of Kentucky, 2001.

———. *The Mystery Chronicles.* Lexington: The University Press of Kentucky, 2004.

Noone, John. *The Man Behind the Iron Mask.* Hampshire, England: St. Martin's Press, 1988.

O'Connor, D'Arcy. *The Money Pit: The Story of Oak Island and the World's Greatest Treasure Hunt.* New York: Coward, McCann & Geoghegan, 1978.

———. *The Secret Treasure of Oak Island: The Amazing True Story of a Centuries-Old Treasure Hunt.* Guilford, CT: Globe Pequot Press, 2004.

Odell, Robin. *Ripperology: A Study of the World's First Serial Killer and a Literary Phenomenon.* Kent, Ohio: Kent State University Press, 2006.

Ogburn, Charlton, *The Mysterious William Shakespeare.* New York: Dodd, Mead, 1984.

Pauwels, Louis, and Jacques Bergier. *The Morning of the Magicians.* New York: Stein and Day, 1960.

Pontoppidan, Erich. *A Natural History of Norway.* N.p.: H. Linde, 1755.

Price, Harry. *The Most Haunted House in England: Ten Years' Investigation of Borley Rectory.* New York: Time-Life Books, 1990.

Pyle, Robert Michael. *Where Bigfoot Walks: Crossing the Dark Divide.* New York: Houghton Mifflin Harcourt, 1997.

Quasar, Gian J. *Into the Bermuda Triangle: Pursing the Truth Behind the World's Mystery.* New York: McGraw-Hill, 2005.

Radford, Benjamin, and Nickell, Joe. Lake *Monster Mysteries: Investigating the World's Most Elusive Creatures.* Lexington: The University Press of Kentucky, 2006.

Randles, Jenny, and Hough, Peter. *Spontaneous Human Combustion.* London: Robert Hale, 2007.

Ridgeway, John M. *A Fighting Chance.* London: Hamlyn, 1967.

Ridpath, Ian. *Message from the Stars: Communication and Contact with Extraterrestrial Life.* New York: Harper & Row, 1978.

Robbins, Rossell Hope. *Encyclopedia of Witchcraft and Demonology.* New York: Crown Publishers, 1959.

Robyns, Gwen. *The Mystery of Agatha Christie.* New York: Doubleday, 1978.

Rosenberg, Aaron. *The Bermuda Triangle.* New York: Rosen Publishing, 2002.

Sanderson, Ivan. *Things and More Things: Myths, Mysteries and Marvels!* N.P: N. p.: Adventures Unlimited Press, 2008.

Shuttlewood, Arthur. *The Warminster Mystery.* Spearman, TX: Spearman Publishing, 1967.

Silva, Freddy. *Secrets in the Fields: The Science and Mysticism of Crop Circles.* Virginia: Hampton Roads Publications, 2002.

Story, Ronald, and J. Richard Greenwell. *The Encyclopedia of UFOs.* Castine, ME: Dolphin Books, 1980.

Strieber, Whitley. *Communion.* New York: HarperCollins, 1987.

Sugden, Philip. *The Complete History of Jack the Ripper.* New York: Carroll & Graf Publishers, 2002.

Temple, Robert. *The Sirius Mystery.* New York: Random House, 1998.

Thompson, Harry. *The Man in the Iron Mask: A Historical Detective Investigation.* London: Weidenfeld and Nicolson, 1987.

Twyman, Tracy R. *The Merovingian Mythos and the Mystery of Rennes-le-Château.* Dragon Key Press, 2004.

Vallee, Jacques. *The Invisible College.* New York: Dutton, 1975.

Vandenberg, Phillipp, and Klaus Dieter Hartel. *The Curse of the Pharaohs.* New York: Lippincott, 1975.

Ventura, Varla. *The Book of the Bizarre: Freak Facts and Strange Stories.* San Francisco: Weiser, 2008.

Verma, Surendra. *The Tunguska Fireball: Solving One Of the Great Mysteries of the Twentieth Century.* London: Icon Books, 2005.

———. *The Mystery of the Tunguska Fireball.* London: Icon, 2006.

Wentz, W. Y. *The Fairy Faith in Celtic Countries.* London: Oxford University Press 1911.

Whalen, Richard F. *Shakespeare—Who Was He? The Oxford Challenge to the Bard of Avon.* Westport, CT: Greenwood Publishing, 1994.

Wickland, Carl. *Thirty Years Among the Dead.* Pomeroy, WA: Health Research Books, 1996.

Wilkins, Harold. *Captain Kidd and His Skeleton Island.* New York: Liveright Pub. Corp., 1937.

Williamson, Dr. George Hunt. *Secret Places of the Lion.* Rochester, VT: Destiny Books, 1996.

Index

U

U.S. Air Force, 116–117
UFO Museum, 117
Underwood, Peter, 173
Unidentified Flying Object
(UFO), 14
Universal Studios, 55
University of Chicago, 47
University of Minnesota, 125
University of New England, 11
University of Paris, 31, 47
University of Pennsylvania, 47
upirs, 154
USS *Cyclops*, 91
USS *Rosalie*, 90

V

Vallee, Jacques, 116, 119
Valley of the Kings, 18–20
Valley of the Queens, 19
"Vampire, The," 54
Vampyr, The, 54
Vancoleurs, 30
Vancouver Island, 144
Variety (magazine), 117
Vaughan, Anthony, 80
Velasco, Jean-Jacques, 119
Venus, 16
Vere, Edward de, earl of Oxford,
34–35
Victoria, queen of England, 65
Villa Diodati, 54
Viperfish, 149
Visum et Repertum, 155
Vlad Tepes. *See* Vlad Dracula
Vlad the Impaler. *See* Vlad
Dracula
vodoun. *See* voodoo
Volkonsky, Prince [Pyotr
Mikhailovich], 40
Voltaire, 50
Von Daniken, Erich, 117
Von Ferry, Captain Lorenz, 136
Von Koenigwald, Dr. Ralph,
139
von Scheer, Admiral, 69

voodoo, 180–183
Voynich, Ethel, 47
Voynich, Wilfred, 46
Voynich manuscript, 46–47
vrykolakas, 154

W

Wakely, Chuck, 92
Wall, V. C., 172
Walter, Elizabeth, 73
Wangchuk, Sangay, 141
Warenne, John de, 26
Way, Frank, 178
Weeks, W. H., 57
Weigel, Arthur, 19
Weigel, Hortense, 19
Wentz, W. Y. Evans, 176
Wessenig, Captain, 60
Western Gazette, 57
West Country, 58
Wetherall, Marmaduke, 147
Whale, James, 55
Whillans, Don, 140
White, John, 79
Whitechapel, 64
White Zombie (1932), 180
Whyte, Constance, 148
Wickland, Carl, 171, 184
Wilkins, Harold, 83, 184
Williamson, Dr. George
Hunt, 117
William III, king of England,
83
William of Newburgh, 159
Wilmot, James, 32
Wilson, Robert Kenneth, 147
witchcraft, 161, 163
witch trials 162
Witchell, Nicholas, 149
Wolf Man, The (1941), 164
Wool, Joel, 21
World War I, 20, 69. 70, 179
Worth, Patience, 174–175
Wright, Elsie, 177
Wright, John, 42
Wright, Polly, 178

X

X (book), 126

Y

Y (book), 126
Yale University, 47
Yardley, Herbert Osborne, 47
Yeats, W.B., 176
yeoman, 26
yeti, 138–141
scalps, 139–140
Yorkshire Ripper, 164

Z

Z (book), 126
Zemu Glacier, 138
Zeus, 77
zombie's cucumber. *See Datura
stramonium*
zombies, 180–183

Credits

6 *top row, from left:* SS/Csaba Peterdi; WI/Ferdinand Teus; WI/PD; WI/New York Times; *second row, from left:* SS/fotoar; WI/PD; FL/Greg75; FL/LePetitPoulailler; *third row, from left:* WI/PD; FL/Thomas Roche; WI/PD; SS/Mwaits; *bottom row, from left:* JI; WI/PD; SS/Dariusz Urbanczyk; WI/PD **7** *from left:* FDLHS; pablorpalenzuela.files; LOC; SS/photoBeard **10***tl* pablorpalenzuela.files. **10***bl* WI/Ryan Somma **11** WI/Avandergeer **12***tl* SS/Brian Brockman **12***mr* WI/Jose-Manuel Benito **14***tl* WI/Ferdinand Teus **14***mr* SS **15***bl* NASA/G. Bacon **15***tr* NASA/G. Bacon **16***tr* NASA **16***bl* SS/Kirsz Mardin **17***bl* FL/mharrsch **17***m* PD/Frederic Leighton **18***tl* SS/Rachelle Burnside **18***bm* WI/Gerbil **19** WI/Nikater **20***tl* WI/*New York Times* **20***bl* LOC **21***bl* LOC **21***m* LOC **21***tr* LOC **21***br* LOC **24***tl* WI/PD **24***br* NASA **25** WI/PD **26***tl* WI/Olaf1541 **26***br* WI/PD **27** SS/Ingvar Tjostheirm **29***tl* JI **29***m* WI **30***tl* WI/PD **30***bl* LOC **31***br* WI/PD **31***tr* PD/Eugene Thirion **32***tl* WI/PD **32***br* SS/gary718 **33***tm* WI/PD **33***br* PD/Johann Heinrich Fussli **34***tl* WI/PD **34***bmr* WI/PD **35***bl* SS/Lance Bellers **35***br* WI/PD **36***tl* WI/PD **36***br* WI/Maximaximax **37***tl* WI/PD **37***tr* WI/PD **38***tl* PD/Franz Krüge **38***br* PD/Nicolas Gosse **39***tr* PD/ Jean-Laurent Mosnier **39***br* SS/Pavelk **40***bl* WI/PD **40***tr* LOC **41***tr* WI/PD **41***br* SS/Irina Korshunova **42***tl* PD **42***ml* WI/PD **42***bm* PD/Jacques Nicolas Bellin **42***mr* WI/PD **43** WI/PD **44***tl* iS/Stanislav Pobytov **44***mbr* WI/*Boston Post* **45** LOC **46***tl* WI/PD/Melesse **46***mr* WI/PD/Melesse **47***tr* LOC **47***br* WI/PD/Melesse **50***tl* PF **50***tml* WI/PD **51***mr* FR/Bella Baita B&B View **51***tr* JI **52***tl* PD/Charles-Antoine Coypel **52***br* PD/

Hyacinthe Rigaud **53***bl* WI/H. Goudemetz **53***tr* LOC **54***tl* WI/PD **54***bl* WI **55***tr* PD/Theodore Von Holst **55***br* PF **56***tr* WI/Pascal Rehfeldt **56***br* PD **57***bl* WI/Achim Hering **57***br* SS **57***tr* WI/Erbe, Pooley: USDA **58** WI/Harriet Moore **59** AP/Robert F. Bukaty **60***tl* PD **60***bl* LOC **60***br* PD **61***tl* WI/PD **61***mb* PD **62***bl* WI/PD/Michael Zaschka **62***mr* LOC **63***tr* PD **63***mr* WI/PD **64***tl* PF **64***mb* WI/PD **66***ml* FL/Greg75 **66***br* WI/Seekthetruth29 **67***tl* AP/Tim Ireland **67***tr* WI/*The Graphic* **67***mb* WI/PD **68***tl* JI **68***mb* LOC **68***br* WI/PD **69** WI/PD **70***tl* LOC **70***mb* LOC **71***tr* LOC **71***mb* LOC **72***tr* PD **72***br* WI/Dragon tomato **73***tl* PD **73***tr* LOC **73***bl* LOC **76***tl* JI **76***bl* SS/Dariusz Urbanczyk **77***tr* PR/David Hardy **77***br* NASA **78***tl* LOC **78***bl* WI/PD **79***tr* LOC **79***br* SS/Zack Frank **80** FL/Kris Griffon **81** Neil Dvorak **82** NASA **83** LOC **84***tl* PD **84***mr* Gus Yoo **85***bl* Gerry Viazey **85***tr* Gerry Viazey **86***tl* WI **86***bm* WI/Hawobo **87***tr* PD/Nicolas Poussin **87***br* WI/PD **88***tl* Peter Standing **88***br* WI **89** WI/Andreas Trepte **90***tl* WI **90***br* LOC **91***tr* LOC **91***bl* LOC **92** FL/unloveablesteve **93** iS/ABDESIGN **96***tl* SS/Suzanne Tucker **96***br* PD **97** PD **98***tl* FL/Frank Da Silva **98***br* FL/LePetitPoulailler **99***tr* WI/PD **99***br* PR/David Parker **100** FL/Frank Da Silva **101** FL/Bertrand Monney **102***tl* JI **102***br* WI/PD/Roger Griffith **103***tr* WI/PD **103***br* PD **104***tl* LOC **104***bl* LOC **105** WI/PD **106** WI/Rklawton **107** PD **108***ml* WI/Royalbroil **108***mr* WI/Royalbroil **109***t* WI/Royalbroil **109***b* WI/Royalbroil **110** WI/Evil Monkey **111** WI/PD/E. Weiß **112***tl* WI **112***br* WI **113***tr* WI/Idalia Skalska **113***br* WI/Demeulenaer & Van Ginderdeuren **114***tl* WI/PD **114***bl* WI **115** SS/Sebastian Kaulitzki **116***tl* WI/PD **116***ml* U.S. Air Force **117** SS/Mwaits **118***tr* U.S. Air Force **118***bl* SS/ragsac **119** SS/photoBeard **120***tl* SS/Lepro **120***br* AP/Susan Walsh **121** AP **122** iS/jallfree **123** AP/Steven Senne **124** SS/Andrey Arkusha **125** AP **126***tl* SS/WizData, inc. **126***br* SS/modestlife **127** PD/Jacques-Louis David **128** SS/Roman Krochuk **129***tr* WI/Женя **129***br* NOAA **132***tl* SS/fotoar **133***bl* WI/PD **133***tl* JI **133***br* WI **134***tr* WI **134***bl* SS/Larsek **135** WI **136***tr* WI/ **136***ml* AP/Tsunemi Kubodera of the National Science Museum of Japan **137**

LOC **138***tl* WI/r hyland **138***mb* PR/Mary Evans **139***bl* WI/Nuno Nogueira **139***tr* SS/Larsek **140***bl* SS/Andreas Meyer **140***tr* WI/Melanochromis **141** AP/Saurabh Das **142***tl* SS/Angie Chauvin **142***bl* SS/Andreas Meyer **143** LOC **143** FL/Dru! **144** AP/The Idaho State Journal, Bill Schaefer **145***bl* AP/Jesse Harlan Alderman **145***tr* FL/Thomas Roche **146** iS/Matt84 **147** SS/Jeff Banke **148** AP/Norm Goldstein **149** AP/*The Gazette*, Megan Lovett **150***tl* FL/daedrius **150***br* SS/Dennis Donohue **151** AP/Eric Gay **154***tl* WI/PD **154***br* PD/John William Waterhouse **155** SS/Csaba Peterdi **156***l* PF **156***tr* PD **157** SS/ChipPix **158** SS/WojciechKozlowski **159** SS/Chad Bontrager **160***tl* SS/Linda Bucklin **160***br* WI/Brian **161***tl* SS/Richard Thornton **161***br* WI/PD **162** WI/PD/Lucas Mayer **163** WI/PD **164** WI/Siristru **166***tl* WI/PD **166***br* Society for Psychical Research **167***bl* PD **167***tr* PD **168** WI/PD **169***bl* FL/theparadigmshifter **169***mr* WI/PD **169***tr* FL/Shades of Gray **170***mt* WI/PD **170***br* WI/PD **170***bl* WI/PD **171***tr* PD **171***mr* WI/Duimdog **172***tl* FDLHS **172***bl* FDLHS **172***m* FDLHS **172***br* PD **173***bl* FDLHS **173***tm* WI/Pafmax **173***br* FDLHS **174***tr* WI/PD **174***bm* PD **175***tl* Project Guttenberg **175***tr* SS/R. Formidable **176***tl* WI/PD/Richard Doyle **176***m* WI/PD **176***br* LOC **177***tr* WI/PD **177***br* WI/PD **178***tl* WI/PD **178***br* LOC **179***t* WI/MGSpiller **179***br* WI/Terabyte **180***tl* PF **180***br* LOC/Carl Van Vechten Collection **181***bl* WI/PD/January Suchodolski **181***tr* SS/LianeM **182***t* PF/The Jerry Gross Organization **182***br* SS/Clarence Holmes **183** AP/Ramon Espinosa